The Way of the Sacred

Francis Huxley

The Way of the Sacred

Doubleday and Company, Inc.
Garden City, New York

©1974 Aldus Books Limited, London
First published in the United States of America in 1974 by
Doubleday and Company, Inc., New York
ISBN 0-385-04618-9
Library of Congress Catalog No. 73-19368
Printed and bound in Spain by
Novograph S.L. and Roner S.A., Crta. de Irun Km. 12,450, Madrid 34.
Dep. Legal: M- 22319- 1974

Contents

1 The Sacred

The man who goes beyond appearances is a searcher after truth. We see him here, crouched upon all fours, thrusting his head through the adamantine vault of heaven in order to see backstage into the secret machinery of the universe. It is a prodigious sight, full of immense cogs and wheels. And yet, although he is looking beyond appearances, all that he sees are other appearances equally acceptable to the technological spirit in man. He is merely confirming his belief that God is an intelligence like his own, susceptible of a mechanical explanation.

But God, as William Blake remarked, is not a mathematical diagram. No clockwork can do justice to the immensity of His workings. If a man is to thrust his head through the appearances of this world—through the customary scenery of his own habits and the conventions of his society—he must for a time abandon any simple ideas of machinery. What is beyond conceptualizing may then present itself to his naked mind, perhaps as a void full of unmannerly energies, a darkness without bottom, or a light that cannot be withstood; perhaps as an enormous and disreputable joke perpetrated upon mankind; or perhaps as an exquisite harmony of contradictions—like the burning bush seen by Moses, that burned with fire and yet was not consumed.

The story of Moses is an excellent paradigm for our purpose. It demonstrates not only the manner in which the sacred can reveal itself to men, but also the mingled fear and strength that such a revelation imparts, and the obedience it exacts. A revelation is a challenge to accept something as yet unknown, and only if that acceptance is offered does the unknown make itself apparent. Thus, Moses said: "I will now turn aside, and see this great sight, why the bush is not burnt.

"And when the Lord saw that he turned aside to see, God called unto him out of the midst of the bush, and said, Moses, Moses."

But there is danger in seeing too much, even to such a man as Moses, who had the courage to face the sublime and the strength not to be destroyed by

The astronomer's search after truth—a 16th-century German woodcut.

it. When, after much prophetic intercourse with the presence that hid itself under an appearance, Moses asked to see that presence in its full glory, the Lord replied: "Thou canst not see my face: for there shall no man see me, and live." Instead, the Lord promised to place Moses in a cleft of rock and cover him with His hand until He had passed. Then: "I will take away mine hand, and thou shalt see my back parts: but my face shall not be seen."

"Unorganised innocence," said Blake again: "an impossibility." It is impossible as much because innocence depends upon order as because, where no order is seen, there is chaos and the mind is overwhelmed. The sacred can be just such a chaos of energy in the face of which the unprepared spirit can be lost. What image of the sacred could Moses have received when the Lord revealed to him those back parts that were the reflections rather than the full flood of His glory? The Pentateuch gives no answer to this question. It is almost an impertinence. We may, without offence, suppose that he was dazzled by light, since after his revelations the skin of his face shone; and that, as the later prophets suggest, he also saw images of power and terror, appearances that were both a warning and a promise.

The feeling of terror that can accompany a total revelation of what is beyond appearances cannot be confined to one religion. It is to be found with variations the world over. In the story of the warrior Arjuna, told in the Indian sacred poem the *Bhagavad-Gita,* there is a close parallel to the Mosaic experience. Arjuna is faced on the battlefield by an army composed of his kindred and his friends. He cannot accept the fate imposed on him of either killing those he loves or being killed by them. He is recalled to his duty by his charioteer Krishna, who eventually reveals himself to be the Lord of the Universe. Like Moses, Arjuna begs for a sight of the divine form. When Krishna does reveal himself, full of revelations, resplendent, boundless, of ubiquitous regard, Arjuna cries out:

> Ah, my God, I see all gods within your body;
> Each in his degree, the multitudes of creatures;
> See Lord Brahma throned upon the Lotus,
> See all the sages, and the holy serpents . . . .
> At the sight of this, your Shape stupendous,
> Full of mouths and eyes, feet, thighs and bellies,
> Terrible with fangs, O mighty master,
> All the worlds are fear-struck, even as I am . . . .
> Now with frightful tusks your mouths are gnashing,
> Flaring like the fires of Doomsday morning—
> North, south, east and west seem all confounded—
> Lord of all devas, world's abode, have mercy!

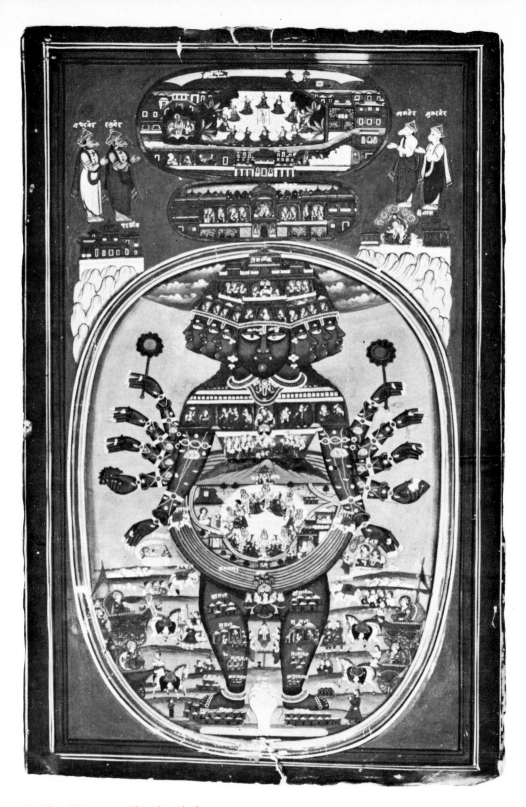

In this 18th-century Tantric painting,
Krishna is shown in his cosmic form as
Universal Man. At his navel is the
world mountain, encircled by the sevenfold stream of Ocean.

And Krishna, who had shown himself as Time, the waster of the people, in mercy resumes his human form.

It is indeed a dreadful thing to fall into the hands of the Living God—an awesome phrase that describes the irruption of the sacred into the heart of man. How can we avoid it? The simple answer is: by sanctifying it. We sanctify that which is both a terror and a fascination, because to sanctify is also to veil. This is clear from the biblical account of the Lord's manifestation on Mount Sinai, when he told Moses:

"Go down, charge the people, lest they break through unto the Lord to gaze, and many of them perish.

"And let the priests also, which come near to the Lord, sanctify themselves, lest the Lord break forth upon them.

"And Moses said unto the Lord, The people cannot come up to mount Sinai: for thou chargedst us, saying, Set bounds about the mount, and sanctify it."

In other words between the world of appearances and that of numinous divinity a barrier has to be erected, to act as a prohibition against going farther. It is, if you will, a tabu. This barrier is the very sign and expression of the sacred. Like the danger sign erected at the entrance of a powerhouse, it shows the presence of a creative energy that is normally set out of limits but which it is the business of religious forms to turn into human matter.

To set bounds around a place, a person, or a state of mind is to set it apart, which is one of the customary definitions of the sacred. At the same time, people who go beyond all normal bounds set themselves apart by their own behavior and, as a result, may be treated as sacred, their utterances being taken as oracles. In some societies madmen are treated in this way. Certain kinds of extravagant behavior, carried out with panache and resolution and in full consciousness of their nature, have something of the same flavor. Sarah Bernhardt, who for 35 years lived with theatrical brilliance a life of scandal and publicity, was called a *monstre sacré*. Her breaking of the rules gave such a sense of pleasurable outrage to the world that she was allowed to get away with it. Indeed, she could scarcely have been stopped, and it was this unsuppressible force that came to be celebrated by her epithet. There is no point in declaring that someone is untouchable if they persist in touching you and the touch is itself enlivening.

But the sacred has very definite rules about how and when it can be touched, and these bring its promises and its menaces within the category of human status. Prohibitions always go with power, being laid either upon the holders of power or upon those who are subject to it, and they are obeyed as a matter of honor. But anyone who looks behind the scenes of

Above, one of a pair of gate-keepers (10th-13th century) that guard the entrance to China's Mai-chi-san caves. His threatening attitude and visage keep evil at bay.

Left, a 14th-century Turkish illumination shows the new-born Mohammed in his mother's arms. Both are veiled; it would be idolatrous to look upon their faces.

power, and examines the motives that inform them, may well think that hypocrisy has more to do with the matter than any sense of the sacred. This is especially so when secular power becomes more important than religious, and men dress themselves up in the trappings of the past. As Jonathan Swift remarked, men are constantly dressing up to make an impression, and they may come to the view, held in some traditional systems of thought, that the universe itself is a large suit of clothes covering, and therefore concealing, something. As for the acquirements of a man's mind, Swift asked: "Is not religion a *cloak*; honesty a pair of *shoes*, worn out in the dirt; self-love a *surtout*; vanity a *shirt*; and conscience a pair of *breeches*, which, though a cover for lewdness as well as nastiness, is easily slipt down for the service of both?"

We can see this to be true. Shame sets things apart, as does the sacred, by hiding them under clothes, so there is an unavoidable alliance between shame, the obscene, and the sacred. Man's scatological interest is made use of for religious purposes in many traditional societies. It is reported, for instance, that in the past the dried and powdered excrement of the Dalai Lama was sold to the faithful as a salve for the eyes or as an elixir. As for clothes, everything suggests that they emphasized the sexual parts rather than diminished interest in their invitations. The Dogon of West Africa say, "To be naked is to be speechless," meaning that a woman without clothes or ornaments is not seductive. But a woman's clothes and ornaments are more than seductions, they are symbols investing all matters of generation with divine force. That clothes eventually come to hide what they were once meant to show off tells us not only how prurience can develop at the expense of a lusty aesthetic of the sacred, but how shame and a sense of the sacred both find their origin in self-consciousness.

Covens of witches in modern England still take off their clothes during ceremonies, an act which may or may not herald orgiastic rites but which always indicates the shedding of the social persona in front of a religious mystery. Ritual nakedness has a long history. It was perhaps for orgiastic purposes that Aaron made the people naked while they danced around the Golden Calf, at a time when Moses was still upon the Mount. But to take off one's clothes in public may be done for quite other reasons. In Amsterdam during the 16th century, for instance, the Anabaptists were driven to such frenzy and despair by persecution that they stripped themselves naked and ran through the streets crying "Woe! Woe! Woe! The wrath of God! The wrath of God!" When they were brought before the magistrates they refused to dress. "We are," they said, "the naked truth."

When the constraints of society become too much for man, it is then that he attempts to go into the nakedness either of the body or the spirit. But the naked truth can be a disconcerting sight, if only because it is a judgment upon one's preconceptions and the blindness of habit. That is why it arouses all the forces of self-righteousness. Simone Weil understood this when she wrote: "They killed the Christ, out of anger, because he was nothing but God." She did not mean to deny the humanity of Jesus; in the context of her writings it is plain that she was describing man's reaction to the force of a naked mind, or to that steely barb of the infinite that Baudelaire remarked on, which is indeed hard to bear. To be confronted by that force is a sacred experience, and the way in which one reacts to it can lead either to a blessing or to a curse.

The sacred is both, as French usage implies. The word *sacré* can be either a title of holiness or an execration. In either sense, it is a pronouncement of doom, for good or bad, and its service is an imposition laid upon men. The view that Sir James Frazer did so much to popularize in *The Golden Bough*, that religion is the practice of superstition imposed on the people by priestly cunning for priestly advantage, has something to be said for it. One look at the intellectual and physical structures erected by religions the world over, and at the extravagant rites invented to celebrate their gods, may well make one gasp at the energy with which men enslave themselves in the service of an idea and at the monuments they create to celebrate this bondage. The

An 18th-century engraving of Adamites running naked through the streets of 16th-century Amsterdam in protest against religious and political persecution. Their name refers to their disregard for the outward trappings of religion. "We are," they said, "the naked truth."

Jews tell a story against themselves about just this state of affairs, to explain how they became the people peculiar to God and why they have to obey the Law. In the beginning God offered the Torah in turn to all the other nations of the world, but all thought it too troublesome to accept. In the end only the Jews were left. Plucking Mount Sinai up by the roots, God poised it over their heads, saying: "Either accept the Torah or I will let the mountain crush you."

On a superficial view, the Jews would seem to have had good reason to have abandoned their faith long ago. That there was an advantage in not doing so can be read in their extraordinary history. They were persecuted precisely because they marked themselves off from the rest of the world by using the interlocking devices of prescription and prohibition in their devotion to that which is single, invisible, and all-powerful—a devotion that even in times of utmost misery brought them strength. The automatic following of a ritual path, however, leads easily to the two sins constantly belabored in the New Testament—self-righteousness and hypocrisy. We then have the ironic situation that the Invisible, so carefully set apart from whatever can be imagined and given shape, is once again being worshiped by the putting on of appearances, both moral and physical, whose sacred character has become a formality. This is as paradoxical in its way as the use of nakedness to signify either the state of the sacred or its negation.

In the face of such paradoxes, it might seem futile to try to define the sacred. How can we define something whose form can turn into its opposite? Perhaps we should simply accept that there is a catch in the matter—a catch that accounts in part both for the fascination the sacred exerts and the fear it can inspire. The catch appears on a simple level in the life of the Irish hero, Cuchulainn, whose supernatural strength and magical virtues went hand in hand with a whole series of *geasa*, or absolute prohibitions, that he had to obey. One of his many extraordinary exploits was the killing of Calatin the Brave and his 27 sons. Calatin's widow, Queen Medb, bore posthumous sextuplets, three sons and three daughters, who vowed revenge upon Cuchulainn. Medb then assembled the four provinces of Ireland and invaded the country of Cuchulainn. The Great Carnage of Mag Muirthemne began. Undeterred by evil omens, the hero rushed into battle. On the way he met Medb's three daughters roasting a dog on a rowan branch. Here he was caught between two of his *geasa*, one that forbade him to pass a hearth without tasting the food that was being cooked upon it, the other that forbade him to eat the flesh of a dog, because of his name, which meant "The Hound of Chulainn." Caught in this fatal dilemma, he accepted the dog's shoulder. At once half his virtue withered away, and he was slain.

"Open everything, go anywhere," said Bluebeard to his bride, "but the little room this key opens, I forbid you to enter."

Here the catch is that supernatural strength is a gift based upon the observance of a tabu. Once the tabu is broken, the strength disappears. But tabus of this nature conceal another catch within them. The only things worth tabuing are those that a man has a natural desire to enjoy. It was thus that Freud explained the nature of the incest tabu, against all those who wished to see in it a prohibition that is universal because it is instinctual. On the contrary, said Freud, it is the incest, not the tabu, that is instinctual. The tabu is something "unnatural" that counters the instinct and sublimates it into an activity of greater force but on a different level.

One consequence of imposing such a tabu is that it makes you realize things you might otherwise never have thought of. A child may never have dreamed of sticking peas up its nose, but forbid it to do so and it will promptly experiment to discover why it shouldn't. Psyche would perhaps have been content never to have seen Cupid by lamplight had he not forbidden her to light a lamp when he was in her bed. There would have been no fairy tale about Bluebeard had there not been a forbidden room in his castle. In his book on fairy tales, Tolkien has remarked upon this lively power of a prohibition: "Thou shalt not—or else thou shalt depart beggared into endless regret. Even Peter Rabbit was forbidden a garden, lost his blue coat, and took sick. The Locked Door stands as an eternal Temptation."

To be fascinated by what one is forbidden to enjoy is something of a sick joke, on a par with Arthur Guirdham's remark that doctors often die from the diseases they have specialized in. Freud pushed the sickness of the joke as far as he could, dismissing religion as no more than the product of an oedipal situation, a caricature of a large-scale neurosis. He thus reduced all religion to a matter of incestuous wishes gone astray. There is something to be said for this analysis, and indeed religion would be of little value to man if it ignored neurosis. We can also turn the idea on its head and see neurosis as the caricature of religion, or as a consequence of a man's failure to concern himself with the sacred. But whichever way we view the matter, we can agree with Freud that both culture and religion originated in a primal act of prohibition that divided the world into the permissible and the forbidden, the one made common and the other set apart.

If at this point we are to trace the process by which the sacred has its effects, we have two alternatives. We may, like Rudolf Otto in his luminous book, *The Idea of the Holy*, pursue the sacred through the emotions (or, as I. A. Richards has it when talking of poetry, the commotions) it arouses. Here we must deal with awe, fascination, and terror, with ignorance shot through by the lightning of certainty, and with feelings of exuberance, love, and bliss. Or we may look at the sacred objectively: examining the methods used to circumscribe it and to make it useful to man. Each alternative has its advantages, and in the end each is but the opposite side of the same coin. Indeed, we can have no proper understanding of what the sacred means unless we hold this two-sidedness firmly in mind. The sacred is by no means a single or simple emotion. It is better understood as what grammarians call an oxymoron—a figure of speech that combines contradictory terms, such as *cruel kindness*, or *falsely true*. Oxymorons are useful to straddle the effects caused by the sacred in the mind, to describe which we can use such paradoxical phrases as "joyful fear," or "fascinating terror." And when we look at the monuments of behavior erected in the name of the sacred and at the hypocrisy it has been responsible for, the oxymoron *falsely true* is a particularly applicable one, describing neatly the combination of pretence with the desire to do away with pretence. But paradoxes such as these, useful though they are to illuminate both sides of a question, are in the end inadequate. They show the negative and positive terms in the sacred equation, but they do not show how these terms can change sign. For the sacred is a process as well as a state—a process which, if it divides, must also unite, but which can unite only if it has previously divided.

The alchemists' axiom for this state of affairs was *Solve et coagulo*, "Dissolve and coagulate." Julian of Norwich put this into religious terms when she

*The Angel of the Lord appears to
Moses as a vision of the burning bush
in Ernst Fuchs' painting.*

wrote that in heaven "the token of sin is turned to worship," a particularly Christian conclusion that T. F. Powys also adhered to in one of his novels, "*Mr. Weston's Good Wine*": "'Tis a good loving act to be a sinner, for a sinner is the true saviour of mankind." The Buddhists worked out this axiom historically—having at first stated that the source of all suffering was to be found in ignorant desire, they eventually formulated the triumphant paradox that the Buddha *was* desire.

As Sterne said in *Tristram Shandy*:

"I enter now directly upon the point.

"—Here stands *wit*—and there stands *judgment*, close beside it, just like the two knobs I'm speaking of, upon the back of this self-same chair on which I am sitting.

"—You see, they are the highest and most ornamental parts of its *frame*—as wit and judgment are of *ours*—and like them too, indubitably both made and fitted to go together, in order, as we say in all such cases of duplicated embellishments—to *answer one another*.

"Now for the sake of an experiment, and for the clearer illustrating this matter—let us for a moment take off one of these two curious ornaments (I care not which) from the point or pinnacle of the chair it now stands on—nay, don't laugh at it,—but did you ever see, in the whole course of your lives, such a ridiculous business as this has made of it?—Why, 'tis as miserable a sight as a sow with one ear; and there is just as much sense and symmetry in the one as in the other: . . . nay, lay your hands upon your hearts, and answer this plain question, Whether this one single knob, which now stands here like a blockhead by itself, can serve any purpose upon earth, but to put one in mind of the want of the other?"

To use only one knob in talking of the sacred would be as ridiculous as Sterne's example. But to think that we can contain the sacred between our two knobs would also be ridiculous—as ridiculous as believing that a series of points on a graph constitute a philosophy of motion. We have to come to a more relativistic way of looking at our mutually defining pairs of concepts. We have to use oxymorons and related devices to reunite the division made in man by his experience of the sacred.

It is possible, for example, to classify religions as those of stillness (called Apollonian) and those of movement (called Dionysiac). But in all such religions stillness and movement are partners in a dialogue. They answer one another within a scenario and create an awareness in which the distinctions between them exist but are no longer troublesome. And this in turn means that the sacred, although its revelation may take but an instant, can unfold all its implications only in time and as a drama.

Above, the Japanese deity Aizen-Myoo, who represents sexual love blossoming as the Lotus flower of enlightenment.

Left, Jupiter and Semele, *by the 19th-century French painter Gustave Moreau. Jupiter made Semele pregnant with Dionysus. He consumed her with thunder and lightning for denying him her bed when he refused to show himself to her. (Moreau has given him the appurtenances of Apollo.)*

Above and below, illustrations from a 14th-century Hebrew prayer book depicting the week of creation, from the division of light from darkness to the Lord enjoying the Sabbath day.

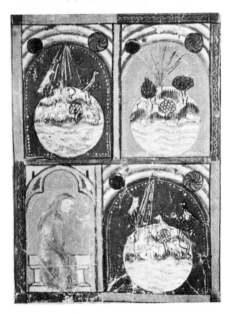

In the theatre, a drama always begins with a formal or even an arbitrary act, such as the raising of a curtain upon the stage. Sacred rites do the same. In the Polynesian island of Tikopia, for instance, annual festivals celebrate the Works of the Gods. During the festivals there must be no noise, no games, and no dancing, and other profane activities are also prohibited. The sign that the time has come for men to cease these activities and to enter the world of the sacred is the cutting in two of a piece of wood, an action that says, clearly enough, the sacred on this side, the profane on that.

To cut something in two is, in fact, the mark of a ritual passage from one state to another. The Balinese employ the device at funerals, when the relatives of the dead, in walking away from the grave, break a string tied between two poles. Among the Bantu tribes of Africa, an incestuous couple are separated and purified of their misdeed by walking between the halves of a sundered animal. The ancient Greeks imagined a man's life as a thread spun by one of the Three Fates and cut off by another. The image was still very much alive in Shakespeare's day; he put it, with tender bombast, into *A Midsummer Night's Dream*:

> O fates! come, come;
> Cut thread and thrum;
> Quail, crush, conclude, and quell!

Symbolic acts can always have many constructions put upon them. The symbolic act of division is of particular interest, however, because it is so fateful; it marks a decision. Moreover, when we look into those two words, *mark* and *decision*, we find that they both meant originally "to divide," "to cut in two." There are many other words that referred originally to the same action, but whose development has provided them with other meanings: such are *vision, wisdom, history,* and *idea,* all of which belong to the same etymological family that produces the word *divide. Science* and *scissors* similarly go together, and are, perhaps, distantly related to another cousinly pair, *shining* and *shadow*. It has even been suggested that the word *sacred* itself can be brought into this family—which would be fitting, although etymologically unlikely. So we cannot help noticing the regularity with which words for cutting, division, seeing, and knowledge spring from the same roots. The history of the word *temple* shows succinctly the process by which the acts of cutting or division become ways by which the world is made sacred. The word originally denoted the space *cut off* or marked by an augur either in the sky or on the earth, in which he noted omens and determined their meaning according to their orientation and their appearance. Thence it came to refer to the space consecrated to the gods, and afterward to the act of contemplation.

To see clearly is thus to discriminate ("to separate the chaff from the grain"). But to discriminate is to know, and the highest form of knowledge is traditionally that of sacred matters. So it is that the Sanskrit word *Veda*, meaning "I know" or "I see," signifies the Hindu scriptures, and *Vedanta* the system of philosophy contained in them.

The primal nature of the act of division can be seen in many accounts of the creation of the world. In the book of Genesis, division is used systematically as the principle tool of creation. God created the heavens and the earth, but in the beginning they were shrouded in chaos—everything was present, but in a state of indistinguishable confusion. Then, by creating light, God divided the light from the darkness; by making a firmament He divided the waters above from those below; by dividing the seas from the earth He created dry land; by creating the sun and the moon He divided the day from the night. He made Eve by dividing Adam from his rib. He prohibited Adam from eating the fruit of the Tree of Good and Evil, which would give him a divisive understanding of the world. And the prohibition itself had divisive consequences, for, after the Fall, Death entered the world and the garden of Eden was set apart by "a flaming sword which turned every way, to keep the way of the tree of life." The Upanishads talk of a similar act of division effected by Prajapati, their Adam, who divided from himself a type of every living thing, including woman, and then coupled with them all. Such stories refer to a primal sacrifice, in which the prototype of the universe is figured as a divine Man. In the Vedas, the prototype is a horse, who is dismembered, his bones turning into mountains, his hair into vegetation, his urine into waters, his eyes into sun and moon. The religious thought of the Dogon of West Africa follows the same pattern today. Their major rite is a commemoration of the original sacrificial dismemberment of a divine being through which the ideas and energies of God were transformed into flesh. Other rites celebrating the founding of a house, the tilling of the fields, birth, marriage, and death, all refer ultimately to the same drama in a system of quite dazzling complexity.

Looking at this drama in psychological terms, C. G. Jung noted the many parallels between dreams, mythologies, ritual actions, and even the practice of alchemy, and saw within it a process he called individuation. For him, individuation was the way by which an Ego could be transformed into a Self, which for the moment we can describe as unity in multiplicity. The process was like a voyage into forbidden but fascinating territory, peopled by aggressive monsters, seductive phantoms of desire, and knowledgeable shadows, all of which eventually found their place in a pattern whose formal appearance hid its energetic activity. This pattern he called a mandala.

An 18th-century Tantric painting of the waters of non-entity, from which—according to the cosmogony of the Jaina—the atoms of individuality become separated.

Masked devil dancers from Bolivia, impersonating horned demons in the form of animals.

Jung himself was not interested in the social forces that give symbols their traditional values, supposing rather (and with some reason) that they were archetypes of human nature, but in fact the process of individuation is as apparent socially as it is psychologically. In Europe, the traditional way of picturing this archetype is to personify society, as Shakespeare did in *Coriolanus*, where he equated head with king, heart with counsellor, arm with soldier, tongue with trumpeter, and great toe with all that is lowest, basest, and poorest in the corporate body of society. Hobbes used the same idea in his *Leviathan*. Its effect is to represent man and the world he lives in, both social and natural, by the same system or representation.

When children play at being what they are not, they have to pretend. All representations make use of pretence, as is made plain in rites that call for the wearing of masks. It is much the same with that kind of definition known as symbolism, which represents a force, an idea, or a relationship by means of an image, and then uses that image as though it were what it stands for. Here lies one of the great dividing lines between rational and religious man, between science and art: the first treats a representation as a sign pointing away from itself to a reality, the second as a symbol in which reality is enclosed by that which reveals it.

One product of this symbolic or magical way of thinking was the doctrine of signatures, which was the basis of so much medieval thought. It can be found full-fledged in Paracelsus, who used it to divine the properties of men and of nature by making a correspondence between their appearances and the ideas those appearances gave rise to. "Behold the *Satyrion* root, is it not formed like the male privy parts? No one can deny this. Accordingly magic discovered it and revealed that it can restore a man's virility and passion. And then we have the thistle; do not its leaves prickle like needles? Thanks to this sign, the art of magic discovered that there is no better herb against internal prickling. The *Siegwurz* root is wrapped in an envelope like armour; and this is a magic sign showing that like armour it gives protection against weapons . . . . The chicory stands under a special influence of the sun; this is seen in its leaves, which always bend toward the sun as though they wanted to show it gratitude. Hence it is most effective while the sun is shining, while the sun is in the sky. As soon as the sun sets, the power of chicory dwindles. Why, do you think, does the root assume the shape of a bird after seven years? What has the art of magic to say about this? If you know the answer, keep silent and say nothing to the scoffers; if you do not know it, try to find out; investigate, and do not be ashamed to ask questions."

Much the same logic is to be found today in what we call "totemic" societies. The dramatic elements of these systems, and their emphasis upon sacred origins and commemorations, long obscured the now obvious fact that they are based on a system of classification by correspondence.

Such a classification seems to be a direct consequence of tabus, particularly the incest tabu, and of the metaphorical nature of language. Both tabu and language use differences in order to see similarities. The incest tabu, for instance, prohibits intermarriage between people related in a particular manner, and thus makes it imperative for them to marry outside that group. In totemic societies this is arranged through the clan system, the members of one clan finding their marriage partners in another with which it is traditionally paired. It is when we look at the names and activities of the clans that we begin to see what totemism is all about. For their names are those of birds, animals, or plants, whose natural characteristics serve to define the difference between the clans. Often the totemic beasts or plants are edible, so that clans come to have ownership of them by eating them, usually only on sacred occasions. But inedible totems also have meaning. They characterize different realms of nature—birds, fish, and animals denoting respectively sky, water, and earth. These distinctions are then brought over into human society in order to separate one clan from another while still holding them within a single frame of reference. It is by means of this logic that a man can say he is an animal, or that an animal is his totem and his totem his ancestor. Such pronouncements of identity are the result of using differences to form correspondences, and correspondences to maintain difference. It shows the process of individuation which, in society as well as the psyche, pivots upon the sacred nature of tabu and of representations, and requires a constant interplay between the opposing forces of setting apart and bringing together.

These two forces are well seen in another pair of concepts, the pure and the polluted. We have already noted that the sacred can mean either to bless or to execrate, since both imply the setting apart of certain things from the common run of life—the one transcending the law, the other cast out from it. Those who occupy either of these positions can be said to be untouchable, to be encircled by tabu—in the first case because they are pure, in the second because they are polluted.

But although purity and pollution are opposed to each other, they share a hidden similarity: both indicate the presence of something extreme that is felt to be dangerous by those occupying the intermediate position. Frazer has collected many examples in which this extremity is seen at work. For the polluted, we might look at the dangers menstruous women are thought to bring if they are not kept firmly in seclusion: their blood can blight the land, frighten away game, make men impotent, and draw down disease. For the pure, we can study the powers traditionally associated with chiefs or kings, which are equally harmful unless these personages are veiled from any secular activities by various prohibitions or by seclusion—their naked feet upon the earth can cause crops to shrivel, and the left-overs from their meals will bring death to those who unwisely or unwittingly eat them. Such parallels between purity and pollution, and the tabus that hedge them about, show that both are in close contact with the sacred—purity tending to be celebrated by the community, pollution tending to be execrated.

Hindu society sets great store upon the concept of purity, as the exigencies of the caste system show. Caste, like so much else in Hindu religion, is a direct product of the primal sacrifice that divided the world of gods from that of men and at the same time divided society into three great groups of Brahmins, Kshatriyas or warriors, and Vaisyas or farmers and traders. This triad is an old Indo-European feature that can also be seen, for instance, in the traditions of Ireland. In India these three sacrificial castes were subserved by a fourth, the Sudras or menials, and at a later date by a fifth, the aboriginal inhabitants of the subcontinent, who were beyond the pale altogether. Between all these castes barriers are set up in the shape of prescriptions dealing with what causes pollution if you touch it, and rites by which you cleanse yourself from

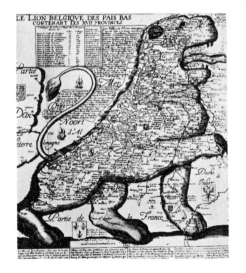

On a 17th-century allegorical map, Belgium is personified, in an almost totemic way, as the heraldic lion that supports the country's coat-of-arms.

pollution in order to carry out your proper offices. Whether a man be a Brahmin or an Untouchable, the concept of purity points to a sacred fact beyond society. That fact is, in Otto's terms, a Wholly Other and by its paradoxical fascination it gives to society the bias that we call value.

The justification for this state of affairs is to be found not only in the application of *force majeure,* although this is necessary to maintain the balance between the sacred and the profane. Common to all social systems is the concept of legality, or the need to have a precedent for one's behavior if it is to be accepted as representative. Traditionally, such a precedent is found in appealing to sacred origins and to the canon of activities that surround them. The origin of the Mosaic law is an obvious example: indeed, such a cataract of prohibitions would hardly commend obedience were they not held to be the commandments of the Lord Himself and not of a human individual. The same tendency to impute law to a source outside society can be seen in South America, for example, where it is widely held that the benefits of culture and the rites pertaining to the sacred were given by a hero whose origin lay outside society—sometimes he is an orphan, sometimes he comes simply from overseas, as did Viracocha to the ancient Peruvians.

The effect of this is to make custom and law something beyond society. It is the same with sacred images. How many Spanish statues of the Virgin, for instance, have been discovered in a miraculous way, usually by shepherds alone in the hills? How many places, the world over, are held sacred because a vision or apparition occurred there? Even the building of temples obeys this pattern. When Yahweh revealed to Moses the plan of the tabernacle, he commanded: "And let them make me a sanctuary; that I may dwell among them. According to all that I shew thee, after the pattern of the tabernacle, and the pattern of all the instruments thereof, even so shall ye make it." Plainly, we are dealing here with something akin to a Platonic Ideal, something insubstantial and yet powerful that exists outside time: a representation of a perfect truth. That it is only to be known by revelation shows that it is sacred, or set apart in eternity.

To appeal to the origins of things is thus one way of gaining a title to the activities developed from them, and is a constant device used to maintain authority. To turn to what is apparently quite a different matter, we must even say that it is only by representing the origins of a disease that a cure can be effected. Psychoanalysis constantly makes use of this process, the analyst teaching his patient to represent his complaint in terms of its history, in the hope that if he can objectify it in this way he can also detach himself from its consequences. The parallel between psychoanalysis and traditional methods of cure has often been pointed out, usually with a sneer. But the sneer is out of place. Ritual cures the world over take advantage of a central psychological process, by which we use the commerce of experience to take things into ourselves at one moment, and to put ourselves into the world at the next—a process that distinguishes subject from object, but that can easily become confused if we lose our way between these distinctions.

When this process becomes confused, we have to objectify it by tracing its history to a source that lies beyond our responsibility. The ritual cures of the Na-Khi, a Tibeto-Burman people of southwest China, exemplify this custom well. Treatment consists of reciting the myths of the creation of the world and of the origin of diseases, which came into being through the anger of the primeval snakes; then comes the history of the first shaman-healer who brought with him the medicines used to cure these diseases. Only after this can medicines be used. The Na-Khi say openly: "Unless its origin is related, one should not speak of it." And their practice shows that until this is done, a cure cannot even be attempted.

We must conclude that sacred matters are also objective ones. We are not here concerned with the objective materialism of science, although that is a development of this process of objectification, and certainly not with the sentimentalities of religion that look to subjective feelings as their hallmark. The sacred is objective in the sense that it is what men traditionally strive

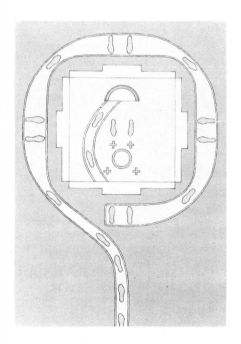

Navaho Indians use sand paintings in healing rites. The plan above shows the way by which a patient must approach the painting. Right, a patient seated on a sand painting of a deity.

toward, besides being the home of that perplexing object known as the Wholly Other. It allows one to introduce an absolute into human affairs— the absolute being, in the wise definition offered by Chambers's dictionary, that which lies outside ordinary syntactic relation. It can be thought of as an operational term that stops us from entering into an endless regress of cause and effect, and instead presents us with a plain fact of experience. There are in mathematics similar absolutes that are called constants—the speed of light, for example, which is what it is for no reason we have yet discovered. Origin myths, however simple or fanciful, in the same way provide constants for those questions about life to which no solution can be found that would allow them to be different.

One consequence of introducing a sacred origin into therapy is that it enables a man to distinguish those matters for which he is truly responsible from those he can do nothing about. It is all too easy to complain about the inescapable facts of life, but a complaint is a burden that a man can well do without and in the end the only thing left for him is to see the matter clearly. Thus Job, seated among the ashes and scraping with a potsherd at the boils that covered him, turned away from his resentment and his wife's impatient advice to curse God and die, and instead recovered his manhood by cele- brating his misfortune as part of the unmitigatable nature of things.

In this way, too, what appears as a total distinction between good and evil, purity and pollution, or any other such moral opposition, can be overcome. It has often been noted that the doctrine of the Atonement bears a striking resemblance to the ancient practice of driving a scapegoat into the wilderness, loaded with curses and execrations, so as to deliver the burden of men's misdeeds back to Azazel, the evil spirit. But the Atonement does more than make this possible, it implies that the scapegoat is God Himself, who thus forgives men their use of the gift of choice He has given them. This astringent paradox is proclaimed on Holy Saturday, when the Paschal candle is lit: "O truly necessary sin of Adam, which the death of Christ has blotted out. O happy fault, which merited such and so great a Redeemer." Here bondage and freedom are seen as belonging together, the passage from the one to the other being possible only if one acknowledges the fact that something other than oneself has bound one: an objectifying of one's subjectivity that it is the business of the sacred to actualize.

Whenever black becomes white in this manner, we may conclude that we are in the presence either of a mystery to be taken with all seriousness or of a mystification that should be exposed. Mystifications are like conjuring tricks, which are nothing but the ability to misdirect the attention, by presenting it with an appearance that seems to be real, while performing the necessary sleight of hand under cover of this illusion. But this is no more than a partial use of the logic of the sacred, which is nothing less than identifying oneself with an ideal state of affairs and by a sleight of mind transforming one's confusions into something serviceable.

To be objectified, the sacred must be acted out according to a canon in which the use of words, images, and acts is spelled out often down to the smallest detail, and in which errors are inadmissible. Wherever such a canon exists, there is no disputing or escaping it: it is the one thing that offers man a proper orientation in the world and that allows private and public knowledge to cohere. This is one reason why the points of the compass have always been treated with the respect due to an infallible disclosure of objective and sacred truth, for upon them the whole plan of the creation of the world depends. East, where the sun rises, West where it sets, and South and North, can be made to carry a wealth of sacred meaning as well as to separate the human world into four social groups, like the four main castes of the Hindus.

This doubled division of the world leads to the formation of a mandala, Jung's sign of individuation. In such a figure it is possible to see how objective matters such as day and night, sun and moon, dry season and wet season, planting and harvest, all have their assigned positions, and how these in turn are interpreted according to the psychological necessities of man. All these matters can be the occasions for appropriate rites, which serve to orient men both in time and space, to separate activities, and to divide the sacred from the profane.

As the sacred divides one thing from the other, then, we can see that it also collects them back into itself—a process that is also known as anamnesis. The value placed upon the proper classification of things allows one to understand how sacred ceremonies are also theatres in which knowledge is revived and actualized—what in later ages came to be known as memory theatres, ways of placing facts according to their association so that they can be recalled without difficulty. In sacred ceremonies, the actors orient themselves within such a system of thought and action that also does justice to their feelings through the medium of a sacrament, an act of communion basic to individuation.

It is disunity that makes acts of communion necessary, because disunity can be overcome only by means of a sacrifice or the undergoing of an ordeal. When sacrifice is part of an initiation it is represented by an ordeal undergone by the young who are to be educated into the meaning of the mystery. Many kinds of scenario have been created to commemorate this process, from tribal initiations to the mysteries of Eleusis and of Christianity. They may have different ends—some attempt no more than to turn young boys into men, some bestow merit or status, others visions or illumination. Ordeals impose strict conditions upon the novice, who is secluded or set apart in some way from the world while he is passing through them. A certain rhythm of the imagination is then imposed upon him by a symbolic drama, which often uses pain to seal the impression on his mind and shock him out of habit into a proper awareness of his responsibilities. He is taught the traditions that govern the usages of the particular rite, and is finally returned to a society in which he must now occupy a different position. The rite may be collective, as in many puberty initiations, or individual, as in the Vision Quest of the Plains Indians, but, however it is practiced, its effect is that of a conversion, by which what lies beyond appearances can be understood.

The simplest method of achieving this is to personate a spirit or god by dressing up in a disguise, often horrifying, to make mysterious noises said to be the voice of the spirit, and to inflict upon the novice various curious torments. When these have had their proper effect, the actors unmask their ordinary and well-known faces, demonstrate how the disguise is worn, and show how the noises can be made with the aid of flutes, trumpets, bull-roarers, or whatever. What is shown is the use of a pretence pointing to something insubstantial and yet necessary. A man who dresses up as Father Christmas for his children is playing out the first half of this game, and, although he will rarely unmask in front of his children, the fact that they are expected to see through the fraud at a certain age shows the same willingness to drop the pretence when it is no longer necessary.

It is a curious fact that religious mysteries so frequently use fear to achieve their effects. In Haiti, the fear of spooks, witches, and monsters is instilled very early into children, to teach them good behavior. Fairy tales that tell how fearless young children learn "to shiver" show that the custom was once as prevalent in Europe. It seems that the experience and overcoming of fear is one of the ways by which a child's imagination is stimulated: it awakens him to the perception of things that can objectify his emotions, and in so doing gives him an awareness of his soul.

Ideas about the nature of the soul must gain enormously from dreams and visions, where one's own double and those of others act out all manner of adventures. The soul is as much an inhabitant of that other world as it is of this, and its dreams are sometimes taken so literally that they are believed to refer to waking events. The convincing nature of dreams can also be ritualized. This has been done by the Australian Aborigines, for whom all rites and myths refer to the Dreamtime, and whose dreams may eventually come to be part of their celebration of the sacred. This Dreamtime is a state

A *19th-century design for a Masonic tracing board, showing the instruments of the Craft. The doorway into the mysteries is guarded by a death's head.*

Christ as the Self carrying the tree of the old Adam, whose skeleton is in the tomb—a sculpture in Strasbourg cathedral.

outside time. In it animals can be men and men may turn into animals. In it the distinctions made by society have not become final but can still be created, and in it the sense of identity that metaphors have at their heart roams among the images of the world, trying them on for size and becoming momentarily swallowed and transformed by them.

The soul, like the sacred, is something given to man and, being given, it can also be taken away. But what we translate as *soul* from the languages of other peoples does not always indicate quite what we are used to. There may be a head and a body soul, each with its own sex. Souls may exist for fingers and toes, which tremble to impart divinatory knowledge. The soul may be one's breath or one's shadow, or its essence may be found in the spinal marrow, the seminal fluid, or blood, not to mention hair, nails, and excrementitious matters. At bottom the soul appears to be a possessive phantom of bodily experience around which one can construct the logic of the sacred and the profane, of the individual and the community.

It is by no means a universal belief that every man's soul is immortal. Sometimes, the only people to possess souls at all are chiefs or kings. We see this plainly enough in the history of mummification in Egypt, where at first only the pharaoh's corpse was mummified and his spirit translated to rule in the kingdom of the gods. Only much later did the practice become democratic, and everyone who could afford it was mummified at his death and subjected to the full course of funeral rites.

The king, in fact, is a Self. Hindu scriptures talk of the Self as "the thread by which this world and the other world and all things are tied together," which is also a succinct description of how a sacred king should be regarded. But no Self is born without having first lived in the world and without an enactment of that life in a particular ritual form. The king becomes the Self of his society through rites of installation, which are as much a way of creating a term between the sacred and the profane as of bringing together under a superordinate figure the various groups and factions over which he must rule. These installation rites create not only a king; they create also a cosmic metaphor that marries social and natural distinctions together by means of a personification which, because it attempts totality, is an image of the sacred.

It is no wonder then that at the death of a Self the principle of continuity that holds together this world, the other world, all things, and all people is held to be destroyed. On the high plane of Hinayana Buddhism this dissolution of the web of appearance, or the attainment of nirvana, is welcomed: the Self that has freed itself thus is not compelled to re-enter the cycle of birth, suffering, and death. But on the everyday plane the death of the Self is regarded as a catastrophe. That is why dramatic forms are used, to ease the passing of one unifying force out of the world and to install a new one. Such an installation can also be regularly celebrated in New Year rites of many kinds which, by putting the past to death, make the present all new.

These then, are some of the matters in which the sacred can be seen at work. The sacred itself is plainly a mystery of consciousness, using the word *mystery* to signify not a problem that can be intellectually solved, but a process of awakening and transformation that must be acted out in order to be experienced, and experienced if one is to make it one's own. Its taste is at once sweet and bitter, for it deals continually with both sides of a question in order to arrive at a position that can contain them both. One of these sides may be fixed in an honored place at the expense of the other, but when the process has worked itself out it can then be seen that it is as necessary to have a mischievous devil as to have an orderly and benign God. It may be that for one man the experience of the sacred comes as an earthquake of the soul, while to another it is a gentle infusion of grace; it may give visions of hell or of heaven, and it may decide one to be an atheist rather than a saint. In some cases it leads to a marvelous elaboration of art and knowledge, in others to a negation of images and a life of poverty. But always these two sides of the question are like the two knobs on Sterne's chair and all such duplicated embellishments—they answer one another, and the answer is always surprising.

A 15th-century French illumination of a dying man commending his spirit to the Lord. An angelic host battles with a devil for the man's soul, while the Lord, bearing the sword of justice, looks on.

2 The Soul

The poet W. B. Yeats wrote, in one of his letters: "We are happy when for everything inside us there is an equivalent something outside us. I think it was Goethe said this. One should add the converse. It is terrible to desire and not possess, and terrible to possess and not desire. Because of this we long for an age which has the unity which Plato somewhere defined as sorrowing and rejoicing over the same things."

Yeats did not have the sacred in mind when he wrote this, but the terribleness that he spoke of is, ultimately, that part of the sacred called Fate—the name by which we recognize a kind of angular obstinacy in the world that prevents the inside and outside of things from corresponding.

But between the inside and the outside of an organism there is a skin, which acts as an intermediary. In man, the skin is alive but carries an outer layer of dead cells to protect it from abrasions; it repairs itself with rapidity; it contains numerous kinds of sense receptors; embryologically it is the layer that by involution forms the brain. It was Freud's opinion that the skin, which gives warning of pain and senses invitations to pleasure, was the original organ of the Ego—of one's consciousness of being an I in the world. There is something to be said for this notion, for skin is one of the models on which ideas of the soul are based.

Any portraitist or painter of nudes will tell you that skin—especially European skin, which is very lightly pigmented—is one of the most difficult things to render faithfully on canvas. This is because it has only an indeterminate color of its own and is semi-opaque—through it can be seen the blues and reds of venous and arterial blood, which combine into subtle hues of pink and even green that are continually and rapidly varying in response to emotional changes. By the constriction of the capillaries in fear the skin is blanched, by their dilation in anger, shame, or desire it is reddened. The skin is thus a mirror of psychological states.

It reacts also to physiological changes. There is a disease called white leprosy, in which the skin becomes covered with smooth white spots. In

An Egyptian painting, of about the 11th century B.C., from the tomb of Sen Nedjen in Western Thebes. In the top register the solar boat is saluted by two baboons—the animal form of Thoth. Underneath, Sen Nedjen and his wife honor the gods, while harvesters ensure their food in the hereafter.

Above and below, old English watermarks of the man in the moon. He bears his lantern slung from a staff over his shoulder. Rightly, he should also have a thorn bush; in the mark below, this has been turned into a cross.

many parts of the world white leprosy is traditionally associated with the breaking of tabus, of the incest tabu in particular. Because of its whiteness the disease is also associated with the moon, so that even where we can observe no direct link between leprosy and incest we can deduce the connection from myths about the origin of the moon. The Urubu Indians of Brazil, for instance, tell the story of a man who lay nightly with his sister, not knowing who she was. One night, she mischievously painted his face black. The brother fled from the village and climbed into the sky, where he turned into the moon, the black paint becoming the spots on its face. His sister climbed after him and became the evening star. At the appearance of the moon, all the women of the tribe menstruated, crying, "Ah, we have seen a bad thing."

The myths of the Urubu contain other remarkable insights into the significance of the skin. One story has it that at the beginning of the world there was a tree called *wira pirok*, the peeling tree. One night the tree began to moan, with a loud and ululating "woooo." The snake, the spider, the scorpion, and the cicada—all animals that shed their skins—heard the cry and approached the tree. They were rewarded with immortality. But the first man was too lazy to get up, which is why man is now subject to death. Since then, a man can become immortal only by undertaking a long and perilous journey to the place where his demigod or hero lives and receiving from him a "shirt," a close-fitting covering proof against weapons.

A skin is a shirt. The image can be seen in the New Testament, where the souls of the righteous are arrayed in robes of white to mark their spiritual natures. These robes are given only to transformed souls—in Freudian terms, those whose Egos have become glorified in the skin. The robes are self-luminous, like the sun; their whiteness is not a leprous one, shining, like the moon, with a borrowed light. So we can see that whiteness may be an index of contact with either purity or pollution.

The skin is not the soul. It is certainly like the soul in being an intermediary between inside and outside, but it lacks the soul's apparent ability to leave the body during sleep, to journey in dreams and visions, and to project itself into the outside world. Man's experiential belief that the soul can do these things explains why a common term for the soul is "the shadow"—something that exists only where there is light and that projects the shape of the human body as does the skin itself.

This simple association of ideas has some complicated results. In Haiti, as well as in many parts of Africa, it is thought that the most dangerous time during the whole 24 hours is midday, when the sun stands overhead and a man's shadow disappears under his feet. Haitians distinguish between two

Right, Cupid and Psyche by the 17th-century French artist Simon Vouet. Cupid lay nightly with Psyche, but refused to be seen. Egged on by her sisters, who said that her lover was a monster, Psyche lit a lamp while he slept. The hot lamp oil dripping onto his nakedness put an end to his nightly visitations.

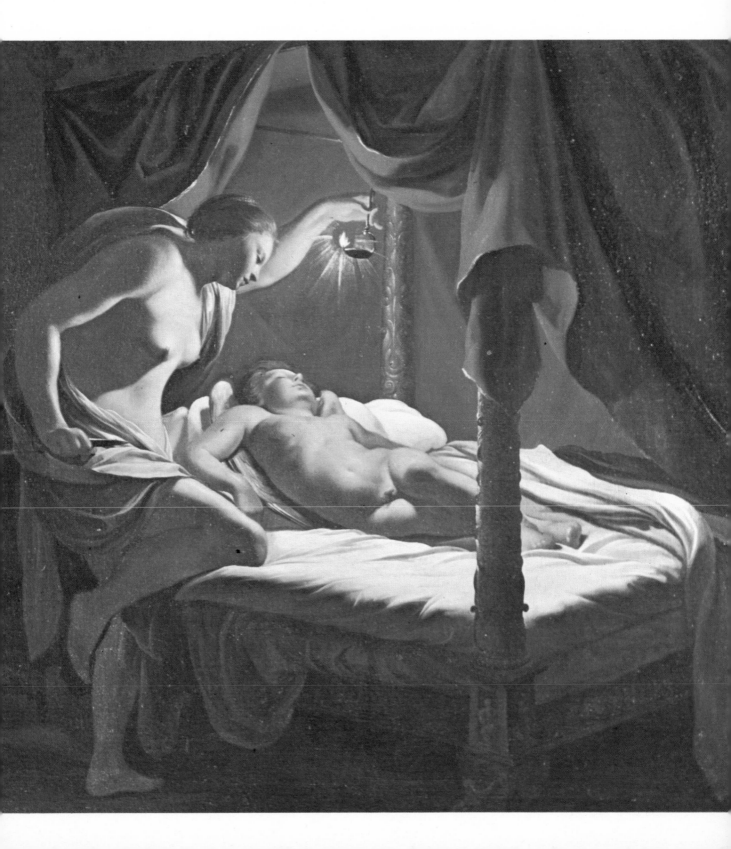

LXXXIII

kinds of psychological entity—the little good angel, which is akin to our ideas about the spirit, and the big good angel, which approximates to our idea of the soul. They are visualized respectively in terms of the shadow and its penumbra, which in turn are equated with the zombi and the breath. (The zombi should be thought of as the automatism of bodily functions, and the breath as the controllable functions of the psyche.) Noon is thus the time when you lose your shadow, which is your soul, and also the time when the air is thought to be filled with a great variety of free-flying souls and spirits that may occupy your body when the sun starts to decline and to produce shadows again. A different kind of danger is incurred by children who hold their hands in front of a candle to make shadows on a wall; they are playing with their souls, a form of spiritual incest to be avoided at all costs.

It is thus easy enough for the mind to accommodate two different models for the soul within one practice, and this particular combination of light, shadow, and breath is a common one. In India, and in Christian and Gnostic traditions, the soul is often described as being a luminous and pneumatic principle—that is, a consciousness whose light is animated. The Latin word *animus*, meaning "mind" or "spirit," parallels the word *anima*, "soul," and both originally meant "breath." It is because animals breathe that we call them *animals*. (The same connection can be found between the Greek words *therion*, "wild animal," and *theos*, "breath" and "god.") And so the image that these associations bring to mind is of a candle whose flame is fed by the wax of the body and fanned by the wind of the spirit—itself another word meaning "breath." There is one logical outcome for any religion that bases itself upon these associations: the light of the sun, which is half-ignorantly worshiped as the light of God, must be seen also as a reflection of the light within the breathing self. When this light shines from a man he can see no shadows, because they all fall behind the objects he sees. Hence heaven is always said to have no shadows.

The soul must be a powerful force to give rise to such grandiose developments of thought from such shadowy and airy beginnings. But what exactly is this soul nesting within the human imagination? It is in one sense an appearance. We can comprehend what this means if we see what is revealed by one pattern of closely related words. The starting point is the Old English word *lich* or *lych*, meaning "a corpse." This word is related to the adjective *like*, the nouns *likeness* and *likelihood*, the verb *to like*, and the verbal noun *liking*. We can understand from this relationship how a likeness is an appearance; how there is nothing left of a dead man but his corpse, the appearance he had in life; how one likes that which is like oneself; and how a liking may imply the likelihood of its being satisfied. This procession of

Above, an Aztec stone mask of Xipe Totec, the flayed god or supreme penitent. Priests of Xipe Totec dressed themselves in the skins of sacrificial victims, in token of regeneration.

Left, an Indian illumination showing a scene from the Mahabharata. *The Brahmin Drona repented of his martial past and laid aside his arms. Captured by his enemy Dhrsta-dyumma, and about to be put to death, he gathered his vital forces so that they might escape as a flame from his head.*

37

dictionary meanings articulates the premises that underlie the logic of funeral practices. For what do people believe occurs at death? Old English is only one of several languages in which the same word is used both for the corpse and the imagined presence of the dead man. These words are usually translated as "soul," which can bring about various misconceptions, because they can also refer to one's reflected image, and they have a penumbra of meaning that can be perceived only by examining *how* they were used.

Let us start with the proposition that the shadow is the soul because it is an appearance of the body. When a man dies his appearance remains, although that which caused it to appear has gone. Funeral practices continually have to negotiate some form of reassuring dialogue between a form and its content, and the word *soul* is invoked to make this possible. For if the likeness of a dead man is there, where are his likings? It is customary to refer to these as his "ghost," which may or may not have the ordinary likeness of the dead man, but the important part of a funeral from the ghost's point of view is to give it a resting place where it can become once more embodied. If this is not done, the likings of the dead are out of control, and may injure, or even kill, the survivors. This problem is usually solved by burying with the corpse-likeness all the objects the living man

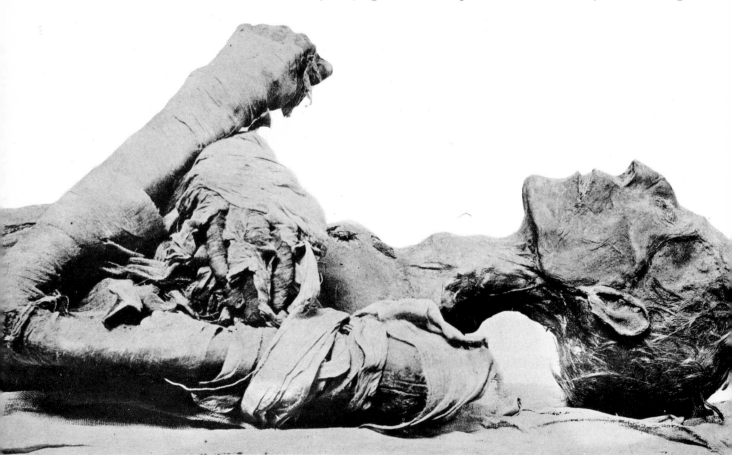

liked during his life. The Urubu Indians, for instance, bury with him his hammock, his bows and arrows, his feather ornaments, and his dog. They light a small fire and place small portions of food in the grave, in order to give the ghost a feeling of substantiality, and they build a small hut over the grave to make the ghost feel at home. In some societies houses of the dead are built of stone and form villages meant to last for eternity. In some the bones of the corpse are carefully cleaned of their flesh and honored as the likeness of the dead man, offerings being made to them so that he will remain changeless. In some—those of Melanesia and Egypt, for example— the corpse was mummified to preserve the outer likeness, and portrait figures were carved to give the dead access to a likeness transformed by the social imagination—access that, in Egypt, was possible only after the figure's eyes had been painted in, so that the ghost could look out.

And what does such a ghost see when he looks out of his image? Not only the wealth he enjoyed during his life, and the tools and weapons that he used and must still use when he is dead, but also pictures of earthly pleasures, divine judgment, and heavenly felicity. From such pictures we can conclude that the interior of a tomb faithfully reproduces the conditions of life in the other world in which the dead enjoy an imperishable existence. But it may

Left, the body of the Egyptian pharaoh Rameses II when the wrappings were removed 3200 years after it had been mummified.

Right, a 17th-century European illustration of a Tupinamba funeral, showing the dead man being buried in his hammock. At left, a shaman waves his rattle and administers the last rites.

be difficult to realize that what we understand as a metaphor was once understood literally. The tomb is not just a picture of heaven, it *is* heaven. A German missionary among the Berg Damaras of Africa was once told that the dead inhabit little huts in the sky and that these huts were also the mounds in which their bodies were buried. He asked how this could possibly be so. "You are separating the two ideas in your mind too much," he was told by an old Damara. "With us, it all coincides."

It is in this way that we should understand the curious ambiguities we encounter when examining the nature of the soul, in our own terms or in those of other peoples. The soul is that which makes an appearance coincide with its nature, or a form with its content. Certainly, when a Brazilian tribesman says that a man's soul is both "waiting by its bones" and also on a journey to the island of souls somewhere off the Atlantic coast, the inefficiency of the coincidence is enough to provoke such questions as, "Do you then have two souls?" The answer is both yes and no, and it depends on one's earnestness in formulating propositions of this nature whether or not one tries to satisfy the inherent contradiction. The young men of another African tribe, the Xhosa, often asked the old men who were the repositories of tradition what it meant for an ancestor to be a snake. "The snake is an ancestor," the old men said, "and that is that." The young men could understand this figure of speech only by supposing that the ancestor was inside the snake, the ancestor being an ancestor and the snake a snake. But this was not the proper theological formulation, although in time the formulation might have been changed to accord with such rationalist doubts. Yet it must have been in such a way that a metaphor about appearances, originally taken *au pied de la lettre*, was eventually separated into its literal and referential meanings, and a theological apparatus constructed to account for the difference between them while still trying to remember the similarities.

We are back then with the contradictory logic of an appearance that makes two distinct realms of experience coincide. There is no doubt that the peculiar attraction of primitive thought to civilized man is in seeing how far a metaphor can be taken literally before it comes to a dead end—which is reached where the intellect sees an impassable difference between a likeness and a liking and begins to systematize its knowledge of these things into aesthetics on the one hand and psychology on the other. And yet the puzzle remains of how such different conceptual systems originated from an impulse strong enough to bind such differences together into a living experience.

The metaphor of the soul forces a particular exchange to take place between the nature of the subject and the appearance of an object. We have

In ancient Greece, dead heroes were worshiped in the form of bearded snakes. The gods, too, could be so figured. The inscription on this relief, of the fourth century B.C., is to Zeus.

here what Elsdon Best, in his book *The Maori*, called the confusion arising from the same term being used to denote both the material representations of immaterial qualities, and the immaterial representations of material objects. The triumph of scientific rationalism in separating these definitions from each other leads to what is now known as *alienation*, the feeling that man does not belong to the world of nature and that the something inside us can only by chance find the something outside us, the two being finally irreconcilable. However necessary a stage in human development this feeling may be, it still cuts us off from some very necessary satisfactions, and perhaps blinds us to one of the basic problems involved.

It is, as we all know, immensely difficult to describe what it means to be self-conscious. To say that a man is self-conscious seems to imply that there is some radical distinction between consciousness and the self—that there is indeed a mind-body problem, and that the machine does have a ghost in it. But an eye can see itself only in a mirror, and a finger cannot touch itself at all, a truism which is the basis for a number of the puzzling replies Zen Buddhists give to questions about ultimate truth—replies that are not answers but invitations to find out the answer for yourself by, for example, listening to the sound of one hand clapping. We can for the moment afford to ignore such invitations, and consider that primitive kind of self-consciousness that is found in a belly-ache. It is notoriously difficult to determine the exact location of any pain within the body, because inner pain is usually referred psychologically to some part of the skeletal musculature that, being under conscious control, allows one to localize sensation. The pain of a heart attack, for instance, agonizes the left arm. The connections between inner organs and outer musculature are more or less constant and are known as Head's zones, after the neurologist who discovered them.

But the inside of a man remains perceptually a murky place, the feelings arising there being difficult to pin down and having no objective representation. What is more, the vegetative life of the body can function without conscious control. It takes a yogi, for instance, to reverse the normal peristaltic movement of the bowels and to suck water into his rectum, to reduce his breathing until it dies away, or his heartbeat until it seems to stop. Such feats of mind over matter are achieved only through long and pertinacious training by a particular method. We can see something of how such a method works by studying the ways of hypnosis. Hypnotists have discovered that they cannot effect changes in a subject's vegetative system, such as altering the pulse rate, by direct suggestion. The subject has to be made to imagine a situation that arouses his emotions, and so causes his heart to beat faster. To produce bodily changes a mental image is needed.

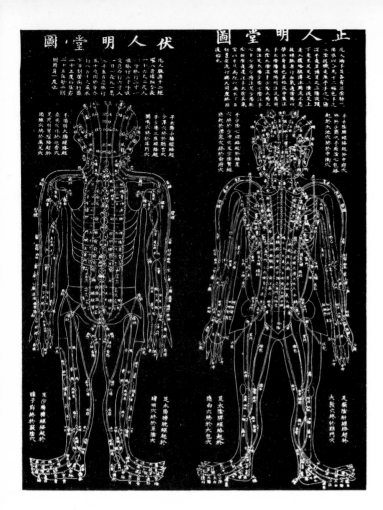

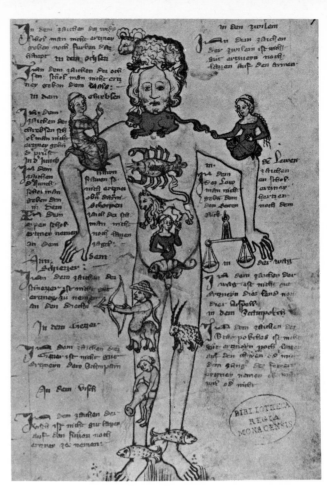

Above, an ancient Chinese chart showing acupuncture points, each associated with an inner organ of the body. The points are arranged on 12 lines or "meridians," through which the energy of the body is held to be in continuous flow.

Above right, a 14th-century German manuscript illumination showing the association of the parts of the human body with the 12 signs of the zodiac.

And the mental image need not be an internal one of the imagination. You can learn to control the movements of the duodenum, for instance, if you can watch its movements through a fluoroscope. A short practice in associating the vague sensations in this part of the body with the image on the screen enables you to control what would otherwise be an unconscious process. For those of us who do not have access to such apparatus, an image of some object in the outside world can be used to achieve similar effects. The disgust aroused in many people by "creepy-crawlies" undoubtedly has to do with the fact that their movements recall certain creepy-crawly sensations inside the body; the peristaltic motion of grubs is thus a metaphor for the motion of the intestines. Were it not that certain objects in the outside world act out in this way movements occurring within our bodies, we should often be hard put to it to make sense of the ill-defined sensations these movements cause. In what is rightly called "primitive" thought inner sensations are regularly attributed to the actions of living things outside the body. A toothache, for instance, may be caused by a small worm biting its way through the dentine—a belief that does not cure the bodily pain but that at least allows the mind to grasp the experience objectively. But "primitives" are not fools. A district commissioner in Fiji was once told that an epidemic from which a tribe was suffering was caused by a neighboring tribe, whose familiar animal was a little black snake with the power of the evil eye. It was these little snakes that were infesting the sick and eating up their stomachs. "And now sir," said one of the villagers, "when the next death occurs you will send, I suppose, for the District Medical Officer to cut the corpse up and look for the snakes. But he won't find any; they are not real snakes, only spiritual ones."

It is not always easy to know the difference between a real and a spiritual object. Consider an extreme example from the pathology of schizophrenia. A schizophrenic was in great distress whenever he stood up because, he said, he felt his substance being sucked out of his backside by the chair he had just vacated. There was nothing wrong with his sensory apparatus; he felt the change of pressure and the pull of gravity distinctly enough. But because he had got hold of the wrong end of the perceptual stick he referred them not to his own actions but to the action of the chair, which thus became a candidate for a place in an animistic religion.

Can we not understand the logic of the soul and its dreams in the same way? This, in its simplest and yet most sophisticated form, appears in a story by the Chinese Taoist, Chuang Tzu. "Once Chuang Chou dreamt that he was a butterfly. He did not know that he had ever been anything but a butterfly, and was content to hover from flower to flower. Suddenly he woke and found to his astonishment that he was Chuang Chou. But it was hard to be sure whether he was really Chou and had only dreamt he was a butterfly, or was really a butterfly, and was only dreaming he was Chou." Such is the exquisite power of appearances, which the Buddhists call Maya and which, they say, is the one thing in the world that cannot be understood—for when you are in the power of the illusion you are not aware of the fact, and when you are not you cannot imagine how ever you might have been.

There are various ways of dealing with this problem. In Canada, an Indian warrior, "having dreamed that he had been taken prisoner in battle, anxious to avert the fatal consequences of such a dream, called all his friends together and implored them to help him in this misfortune. He begged them to prove themselves true friends by treating him as if he were an enemy. They therefore rushed upon him, stripped him naked, fettered him, and dragged him through the streets with the usual shouts and insults, and even made him mount the scaffold . . . . He thanked them warmly, believing that

A Zapotec funerary urn, from Mexico, in the form of the butterfly god. The butterfly was the emblem of fire and of the purified soul.

Above left, a woodcut by Albrecht Dürer (1471-1528) of a Christian penitent flagellating himself before an altar. Above right, an 8th-century Mayan relief of a penitent passing a rope of thorns through his tongue—no doubt at the ritually correct hour of midnight.

this imaginary captivity would ensure him against being made a prisoner in reality." This belief is one expression of the widespread idea that the other world is a mirror image of this one—what is up here is down there, right is left, black is white. The Ainu of Japan even say that the dead think of themselves as living and see the living as ghosts—"they think of us just as we do of them." And among the Plains Indians there was a Society of Contraries, whose members obeyed every command by doing its opposite.

We find a similar logic in force wherever men mutilate themselves in the practice of their religion. Mutilations often follow some great deed, such as the killing of an enemy, and they can be seen as a way of forestalling the vengeance of the dead man by inflicting wounds upon oneself. That this prophylactic masochism can be turned into an affair of honor, with men trying to outdo one another in endurance and courage, is merely the other side of the coin; and both these psychological motives can be turned to the purely religious ends of penance and penitence, as in the Aztec practice of drawing a thread through the tongue, thorns having been knotted onto the thread to ensure a nicely judged experience of pain, or in the wearing of

Right, a Tibetan painting of Yama, the god of death, performing his horrific dance. He is mounted on a bull, which is sexually humiliating a corpse. Overleaf, shadow puppets of two sexual demons from Indonesia. Puppets are sometimes used in rites of exorcism.

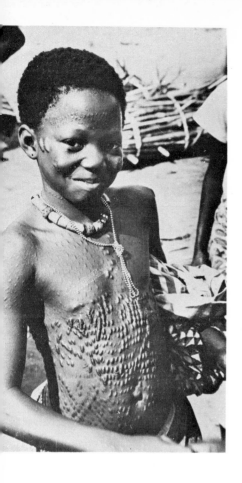

Left, a young Dahomey boy bearing the ritual scars inflicted in the course of his training for the priesthood.

Right, a New Guinea woman with a mutilated hand—she has cut off a finger joint in mourning for her dead brother.

sackcloth and the use of flagellation by desert monks. Many such practices are the result of either a dream or a vision. It is not easy to define the difference between these: perhaps the simplest way is to suggest that whereas a vision should be truthful, a dream may deceive. The interpretation of dreams throughout the ages has recognized this fact, warning, for example, that a dream of money may herald bankruptcy, and one of failure, success. But to many peoples the distinction is unknown. An Indian of the Gran Chaco of Argentina once accused a missionary of stealing his pumpkins. At the time of the theft the missionary had been two hundred miles away, but the Indian knew him to be guilty because he had seen it all in a dream. Many other stories from this part of the world show how quick Indians have been to accept dreams as true, and in similar situations have killed suspects who were in fact innocent—of the act, if not of the intention. Dreamers in this state have no touchstone by which to discern the difference between the image of reality and the reality of an image: they are like the schizophrenic in being pulled out of themselves by a strong sensation attached to figures in the outer world.

Left, an 18th-century Tantric painting of Cinnamasta, goddess of the Great Wisdom. With her attributes—sword, blood-bowl, and cobra—she is seated on a lotus that springs from the coupling of the sexual principles. Her neck is severed to denote that in intercourse she gives freely of her life.

A sculptured figure of Belam, a spirit of the Melanau tribe of Sarawak. Belam catches the souls of sick people and restores them to their bodies.

Wherever this happens we must expect to find reports of souls being lost to their owners, or eaten by powerful antagonists, human or animal, or being infected by a venomous intention projected from a distance. The first state is more commonly known as panic, the sense of being lost in an alien world and threatened by anxieties that never quite materialize: a state of dissociation precipitated by a shock, great or small. Men in this state lose their powers of speech, wander aimlessly through the jungle for months and perhaps years until they are discovered by their fellows and brought home. The cure is a shamanistic treatment of some complexity through which their awareness of the proper balance of things is restored. Panic is one of the unpleasant marks of a sacred experience, and the power of the great god Pan, from whose activities we get the term, is still known among Greek shepherds today. In ancient Greece the powerful energies that such a dissociation unleashes were sought for their own sakes and indulged in as a kind of drunkenness through which the soul might imbibe new vigor.

But where the soul is said to be eaten, a new dimension appears. In Freudian terminology, the oral complex is at work here—meaning that matters of aggression are referred to the mouth and teeth and that a carnivorous urge is not far below the surface. The powerful swallow souls to feed their spiritual resources; they are psychological cannibals. They may be so powerful because of this fact that they claim to have a familiar animal in the form of a jaguar, tiger, crocodile, or vulture, or to turn into such an animal when they die. In the arts of Middle and South America, of Europe, and of many parts of Asia and the Pacific, one may recognize the ritualized face of this oral character: a visage with protruding eyes and tongue, with four great fangs curling out of the mouth and over the lips. It is the Gorgon's mask. In Greece it seems to have been little more than a prophylactic against misfortune, placed over ovens where bread or pots were being baked, or in other places where a notice saying *Keep Out* was required. But in other regions it is the face of a god, of a power that is as reckless and devouring as Time, which is a Gorgon to the Hindus.

To trace the history of this image is by no means easy. In the Americas, Gorgon-faced gods are male. There, men have the habit of wearing labrets— plugs of wood, stone, resin, or feathers—through their lower lips and sometimes through the upper ones and the noses and cheeks as well. In Alaska, men went so far as to cut under their lower lips a false mouth, which they filled with a piece of wood representing lips and teeth. This terrifying spectacle certainly implies some fierce competition between men, but there is more to it than this. Psychoanalysts have usually explained the meaning of the Gorgon's face by referring to the *vagina dentata*, the fantasy toothed womb that can castrate a venturesome man. So in any society where we find the Gorgon, we can assume a continual underground war being waged between the sexes. In Greece, its outcome in favor of men was celebrated in temple friezes showing the battle between men and Amazons. The matter is by no means so explicit elsewhere, but it is still safe to say that wherever Gorgon-faced gods are worshiped, the battle between the sexes has come to a show-down, with men parading the emblem of their own sexual fear of women as the trophy of their victory over that fear, and over the female principle into the bargain.

We can describe this situation in anthropological terms as the consequence of certain patterns of marriage, in which men have to bargain with other groups in order to get a wife. The bargain is that the groom can have his wife as long as he pays for her with bride service to his in-laws, who treat him as a potential enemy until he has finally repaid the debt, often by fathering a daughter who will marry a man of his wife's kin. Many peoples have but one term for both enemy and brother-in-law. The Bedouin, going a step further, consider it improper for a man to marry a woman who does not come from a group with which the blood feud is in force. The image for this delicate balance between sexual desire, masculine competition, and the solidarity of kinship groupings is often found in the *vagina dentata* carried on the face of men, an image of pride as well as fear. Such an explanation fits in well with the Freudian definition of the oral stage as being an aggressive sexualization of the mouth.

The belief that a soul can be swallowed thus demonstrates a fertile confusion between two distinct parts of the body, and we can call the Gorgon the material representation of two immaterial qualities organically located. It is one metaphor compounded by another. The psychological complication of this experience allows the soul to be drawn out from the safe middle of the metaphor and, given the right conditions, to be drawn into any one of its coinciding parts, which have an equal power to fascinate the attention and eventually to immobilize it. The power of the Gorgon was, after all, that of petrification and Perseus had to look into his shield when he cut off her head to protect himself from the directness of its glare.

It is difficult to imagine the effect of this glare on those who are frightened of it. A distant analogy might be found in a curious sensation associated with the often trivial event that triggers an epileptic attack. In ethology a normal and yet automatic process of coincidence between inner state and outer event is known as "imprinting." At a very early stage in its development a young animal takes as an image of itself whatever it first sees moving about it; it follows what it sees and when adult pays sexual allegiance to

A Peruvian ceremonial vessel, of the 14th-15th century, with its handle in the form of a jaguar. In Peru, as elsewhere in the Americas, the jaguar denoted war and rivalry.

*Above, the Gorgon's head with its snake
locks, from a vessel of about 490 B.C.
found at Tarquinia. Above right, a 19th-
century European illustration of a
Brazilian Indian wearing a labret, a
nose-plug, and a collar of jaguars' teeth.*

*Right, the battle of the Greeks and the
Amazons, from a frieze at Halicarnassus
dated about 350 B.C.*

anything conforming to the image. What Freud called the Oedipus complex is perhaps a grand elaboration of this simple mechanism, for it also is a process by which a child comes to recognize its humanity through the images of its parents, and to learn its relationship to them so well that when adult it repeats the lesson upon its own children. The learning process involved here covers an automatism that is easily enough seen in hypnotism, for instance, or in the psychological disease called *latah* in Malay. Latah sufferers are in a trance that forces them to repeat everything they hear and to copy everything they see done so obediently that they can be taken advantage of by the malicious, even to the point of being led to commit murder.

The mind is a suggestible organ at the best of times, and the processes by which we think, imagine, feel, and act are based upon automatisms that can, under certain circumstances, detach themselves from the totality of our nature and lead a more or less independent existence. The function of a belief in the soul is to articulate these processes and give them a common identity, however apparently specious. This identity acts as a reference point by which intentions are created and also judged. When this reference point is lost, then the soul itself is lost, eaten, or infected, and the faculties of the mind become unable to cope with the metaphorical nature of perception, what is truly outside then being felt as being inside, and vice versa. A psychologist would call this the result of a weak ego structure. The ego itself is as curious an entity as the soul, being a way-station of consciousness that has constantly to battle against unconscious impulses, and so is divided into an I and a Me, the ability to attack or to be on the defensive.

All this implies that psychology, the study of the soul, is at bottom a study of intentions, and of how we deal with them. How one is to talk of intention is also the business of ethics, aesthetics, and religion, and science has little to say about the matter—indeed, until now the whole business of science has been to attack the very idea of intention in the natural world and to understand phenomena in terms of the properties of matter and their inescapable interactions. As we are still fumbling for a scientific theory about the nature of consciousness and those experiences of our own subjectivity where intentions are all-important, we have to fall back onto figures of speech that bear all the marks of primitive thought. Such is the psychoanalytic distinction between conscious and unconscious intentions, which can lead to the bizarre conclusion that a man can "know" what he is doing without being conscious of the fact. This is a figure of speech, not an explanation, and is as much a confession of ignorance as a number of opinions we call superstitions. Consider, for example, the Ba Ila of Africa, who hold that a man hears because of little beings called *bapuka* who live in the ear. If an

An eye in white and blue glass worn against the evil eye—an amulet still commonly sold and carried throughout the Middle East.

The Eye of Horus—an ancient Egyptian amulet. The Eye was originally a goddess, who became enraged when she was supplanted. Later, it came to stand for the moon, and for the victory of Horus over Seth.

explosion or thunderclap leaves one temporarily deaf, the bapuka have been momentarily put out of action; if one becomes permanently deaf, they have died. Bapuka are also responsible for the mysteries of procreation. It is easy to see this belief as an animistic one, but a little thought shows that it is at bottom a metaphorical way of referring to those unconscious intentions that govern psycho-physical automatisms. However different the modern frame of reference may be from that of the Ba Ila, both frames of reference still have to cope as best they can with that most slippery of concepts, an intention.

The idea of the soul as an intentional mechanism can be seen in concrete form in the traditional image of the soul as a rider and the body as its horse, an image that Plato accepted with approval. To lose one's soul leaves the horse riderless and another rider may manage to climb into the saddle and direct the mount. This is known as spirit possession. To possess means to inhabit. The question then is: what inhabits a material possession?

We know from the study of both human and animal behavior that intentions are frequently aimed with the eyes and at the eyes. A newly caged lion will eat its meat happily enough in the presence of human beings, but it will snarl defensively if you stare at it. A blackbird may perch happily upon your windowsill, and will take alarm only if you look at it squarely. Both animals and humans can fight battles of will by staring at each other, the first one to drop his eyes admitting defeat: in ethological parlance, he has taken on the submissive role, the victor occupying the dominant one.

An interesting variation upon this battle of looking is known as the evil eye. The evil eye is a look of admiration that blights the thing it looks at because it is envious, the word *envy* coming from the Latin *invidia*, "a looking upon." There are several ways of dealing with envy. In the Middle East it is still a custom for an object to be given to anyone who remarks upon its beauty. The gift not only overwhelms envy, but also puts the envious one into a dependent position vis-à-vis the giver. Gifts, as Marcel Mauss first perceived, and as Lévi-Strauss has since labored at length, are the material representations of a psychological exchange. They are ways of entering into a contract with another and thus of equalizing the social position between the contracting parties, or else a way of putting people into debt. Primitive forms of chiefship employ this latter technique extensively—the chief is the man who can bind a group to him not by force but by giving so continuously that he may appear to an outsider to be the poorest of his group. And in many societies the accumulation of property by an individual breeds envy and unrest—hence the custom of holding large feasts at which quantities of food, drink, and material wealth are vaingloriously dissipated to the greater glory of social cohesion. A Papuan, for instance, who leaves his village to work for a white trader and returns after a couple of years with his wages, cannot expect to retain them all for himself. He has to turn them over to his chief, or the family head, who distributes them among the other villagers according to a particular social logic. We can read this custom as a way of maintaining the social system and internal power structure of the village by circulating its wealth and taming envy. A classic case was described by Darwin. A couple of Fuegians had been taken to England, taught good manners, English, hygiene, and a smattering of the Bible, and then sent back to Tierra del Fuego to exert a healthful influence upon their fellows. But as soon as they disembarked, their compatriots stripped them of their possessions so completely that within two days they were indistinguishable from their neighbors, and, because they occupied no determined social position, the missionary hopes that had been fixed on them remained unrealized.

But what happens when what is admired is a person and not an object? In Mediterranean countries, to compliment a mother upon the beauty of her child is the height of bad manners, and she will either beg you to criticize the shape of its nose, ask you to spit on the ground as a combined insult and gage of good intentions, or ward off the evil eye with a formalized but still obscene gesture. For to admire a child is to imply that it could be an item in an exchange whose opposite poles are life and death. It is an act of *hybris*, or going against Fate: and Fate is Nemesis, which originally was the sharing out of goods, properties, or luck among the members of a group. To praise a child for its beauty or intelligence is to bring it to the attentions of Fate, which may then reconsider its apportionments: the belief in the evil eye enshrines the superstition that Fate itself can become jealous, and take back what it gave. Perfection is only for the gods: thus it is that Persian carpets always have an irregularity in their design, an imperfection confessing man's inability to compete with the divine.

Anthropologists looking at this state of affairs in peasant society— where any man doing better than his fellows is disliked and even thought to be in league with the devil—have accounted for it by the theory of the Limited Good. Peasant societies are closed societies, in which there is only a certain amount of wealth available at any time, so that people who take more than their share are accused of theft. They swallow wealth instead of souls; but the result is very similar and based on the same process.

The evil eye is the projection of an underhand intention. If this is to be aimed without the victim seeing the eye itself—at a distance, that is—an apparatus has to be used. A pointing stick will serve, or a very small bow

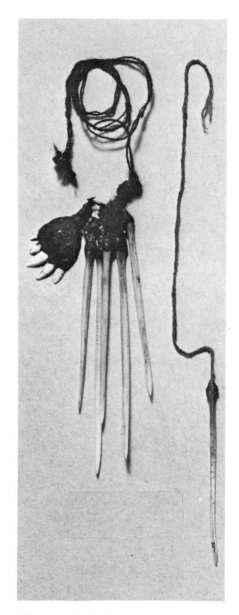

Two sets of pointing bones of the Aranda tribe of Central Australia. They are attached to human hair, which increases their deathly power. The set on the left is reinforced with kangaroo teeth bound together in the form of a hand.

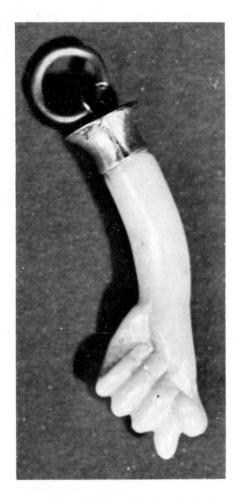

A mano in fica *from Southern Italy. To*
"make a fig with the hand" is to
distract the evil eye toward an obscenity.
It may also be used simply as an
insulting gesture.

and arrow, or a magical powder made of leaves and bones; or one can stick pins into a doll. There is a host of such methods. A person attacked by the evil eye can be cured if the intention is sucked out of his body in the form of a thorn, a piece of wood or bone, a crystal, a maggot, or a shred of meat. The foreign body once removed, the intention that placed it there is helpless. It is plain to us that this removal of an intention is a conjuring trick—one that may sometimes require considerable sleight of hand, but a conjuring trick nevertheless. Yet such a trick, played through the coincidence of an intention and an image, can settle a question of life and death.

There is no doubt that what the neurophysiologist Cannon called "Voodoo death" really does occur. A man can die out of conviction. An often-told story concerns a Maori who died when he discovered that some food he had eaten was the remains of the chief's meal. The chief's person is tabued among the Maori, and anyone who touches him or any of his belongings will bring an automatic and fatal reaction upon himself. European doctors in Africa have often been confronted with similar patients, who die despite all medical treatment. The only thing that can save them is counter-magic that convinces them that the effects of the broken tabu, or of the sorcery, have been lifted. This is not usually part of a European medical repertory.

The belief in magic, and the fact that it works, is a corollary of the general process we have been examining, by which a perception is formed out of a coincidence between an idea and a sensation, one of them (it does not matter which) located internally, the other externally. Even the most blasé of us will experience a twinge of guilt if we lose our temper with someone and damn him, and he then goes off and breaks his neck. We try to take the sting out of this coincidence by various forms of rationalization, such as the use of statistics, but even so the fit between a wish and an event may well bring on an apprehensive shudder. Magic is, of course, an operation designed to bring about such coincidences. The commonest method is to ill-wish something that belongs to your victim—a tuft of hair, a pile of nail clippings, a rag of clothing, or even the earth in which he has left an impression of his body.

We can properly call the items in this list "belongings," or possessions, although at first sight this may seem odd. They belong to a man because they are excrementitious matter—that which has grown out of his body— or else because he has grown into them by leaving his mark upon them. In both cases he has left something of himself behind. Hair, nails, and excrement are the commonest materials to do magic on because they bear within them the footprints of a man's metabolism, as it were, and are half way between being part of the body and being distinct from it.

At the same time the orifices of the body through which one takes in and puts out are also vulnerable to magical assaults. Thus the Balinese are ashamed to be seen eating in public, and turn their backs on each other during communal feasts. It is tabued to watch some African chiefs eat, the punishment being death. The labrets worn by Amerindians and others are an example of a particularly aggressive form of defense of the mouth. Shame and defiance mix in these matters, so that it is possible that the adornment of the sexual parts, though certainly an invitation in its own way, should also be seen as a protection against the evil eye; and it seems likely that defecation is a matter so little to be proud of that it is shame and little else which covers it so frequently.

But, as Freud insisted, children at least take pride in their feces, seeming to regard defecation as the simulacrum of giving birth. This imaginative experience is part and parcel of the Oedipus complex, under whose influence a child comes to believe that he can give birth to himself without the aid of a father, just as he can give birth to his feces. The magical use of feces takes its life from this fantasy, and also from its denial. Where feces are a matter of disgust, they are used in black magic, their effect being unmistakable. For feces, like the soul, are a double of the body that excretes them. Because of the tabu upon their enjoyment they may be regarded as either sacred or obscene, as a blessing or a curse.

In talking about animals, the German naturalist Bilz made a far-reaching remark. "Excrement and the image conveyed by it, frighten and even terrify the intruder [to a territory]. Is not this similar to magic? That tree trunk, scarred through being rubbed, is still potent, even though the bear fell a victim to the hunter's gun weeks ago, and the scent banner unfurled against a tree stump by a dog continues to strike terror even when the animal has long since changed masters and gone to live on another farm. Bear and dog alike have laid a ban on the district, to show it is their home. Cave! Taboo!" Scent has a less immediate effect upon human social reflexes, the object that exudes it perhaps being thought more important than the scent itself. Yet the reflex is there, and the tabu, or power of shame, adds to it an even more powerful notion of ownership. The perfect world envisaged in such different ways by Christianity and Communism insists that inequalities of wealth are maintained by social distinctions, upheld by legal prohibitions, and that without these things there would be no property or sense of ownership, and no need to bother about the health of one's soul. For he who loses his soul shall find it.

So what is a possession? Nearly all Melanesian and Micronesian languages divide nouns into two classes, those that take a personal pronoun as a

An ornamental padlock from Shanghai. It was meant to be hung from a child's neck to lock in the child's soul and prevent it being stolen.

suffix and those that do not. Of Melanesian languages Codrington said: "The distinction is based upon the notion of closeness or remoteness of connection between the object possessed and the possessor, but the carrying out of this principle in detail is by no means easy to follow." Nevertheless he distinguished particular categories of this usage, such as nouns signifying the parts of the body or a family—which last we should call kinship terms—and nouns referring to a man's equipment. All these nouns indicate a man's way of claiming those relationships that center upon himself, or in himself, but with a number of interesting reservations: for instance, the terms for husband and wife are not suffixed by the possessive pronoun because each comes from a different exogamous clan.

If the soul is a possession, it too is partly a family affair, for a man inevitably belongs to a clan or a lineage, and he is, as it were, possessed by it. The soul is, then, as much a social as an individual concern. Even in Christianity a child is held not to possess a soul until it has been christened, or named—an exercise which saves it from limbo should it die. In other religions a child is not considered to be human until it has been named, and this accounts for the apparent cold-heartedness of many tribal peoples who scarcely mourn the death of an unnamed child, and who impenitently practice infanticide. The Bakongo, for example, call a new-born infant a "grub"; it becomes a "child of man" only when it has been named in a public ceremony. This logic explains the curious story of a Fijian whose brother and sister-in-law had been killed in a battle leaving him to bring up their infant daughter. He arranged for a wet nurse to look after the infant, but when his wife gave birth to their own child he had it killed so that she could nurse instead the adopted girl, who had already been named. Newborn children, as Lévy Bruhl remarked, are merely candidates for life; they become human only when everyone recognizes them to be so.

So a name is one token of the existence of a soul in a man, and at the same time of his status or social position. Often, as among the Tupi, the achievement of a new social status is marked by the taking of a new name. But it is also often the case that a man's real name is not used to his face, even within his family. He is known rather as "the father of so-and-so," and his wife as "the mother of so-and-so"—a convention in which we may see the conjunction of name and child as a possession. But the name is also a man's sense of identity. To call him by it is not merely bad-mannered; it is a threat to his soul because it takes it out of his keeping.

Some years ago there was a story in the newspapers of a priest, who, reading the last rites over the corpse of a young woman, thought that she stirred when he pronounced her name. He pronounced it again, more

In a medieval manuscript illumination,
Jacob and the Angel wrestle together.
They fought through the night until dawn,
when the Angel conferred the name
Israel upon Jacob.

59

loudly. And this time there was no mistaking it: he had called her out of a death-like stupor, and she returned to life. In Haiti the same power can be used in reverse. If you awake in the middle of the night and hear a voice calling your name, it is imperative not to answer, or you will put yourself into the power of the magician who is calling you. And, for exactly the same reason, the real name of God has often been a closely guarded secret. A man who discovers the name of his enemies' tribal god can, by uttering it together with the right invocation, seduce that god out of his obligations and make him turn his power against his own people. In more abstract religions, such as Judaism, the name of God is still kept secret, not only because in the last resort his name is unknowable (the Arabs say that only the camel knows the hundredth and most powerful name of God, and the camel isn't telling) but because to pronounce it would be close to blasphemy, to taking the name of the Lord in vain. So the Jews may write the name of God only as YHWH and may never pronounce it with its vowels.

Secrecy is of course the concomitant of tabu: it protects something helpless yet powerful in a man's experience of himself from being shamed, mutilated, or destroyed, and turns it into a possession. And because of the symbolic nature of language, the name for this possession can be experienced as coinciding so exactly with what it refers to that it is itself the central object of identity. This can be carried so far that tribes in Paraguay put a tabu upon any word that sounds at all like the name of a man who has recently died; to utter such words is to invoke the dead, a matter with consequences serious enough to be avoided if possible. It is only later in social development that names lose the immediacy of their symbolic relevance, and can be used objectively.

But however two-faced the experience of naming may be, it is still a way of objectifying experience. As such, naming has an important part to play in the cure of psychosomatic disease, where it works by focusing ill-defined sensations onto an intellectual object. This technique is used in various ways both in psychoanalysis and in ritual performances, both of which make use of an anonymous container for a man's sense of individuality and what ails it, and by doing so enable the forces concerned to be studied, analyzed, and manipulated without confusing his identity. The psychoanalytic method can be likened to donning a fancy dress that allows its wearer to express what his own habits disguise to himself, and it is through this conversation between an intention and an appearance that a cure can be effected. Ritual performances use another kind of jargon—spirits instead of complexes, gods and goddesses instead of fathers and mothers or anger and despair. But the logic is the same. The methods are perhaps closer to the Jungian than to the Freudian system. In Haiti, for instance, a man's soul can be ritually transferred and placed inside a bottle, jar, or small animal, which is then hidden away, thus allowing him to move through the world free from the fear that magicians might eat his soul. The parallel to this in Jungian therapy is drawing a mandala, which can appear either as an opening flower or a walled-in city, and which has the same protective virtue.

The same method is also often referred to in fairy tales, where the giant has his heart hidden in an egg, which in turn is hidden upon an island; or else his life is concentrated in one of his hairs. And this doubling of the soul has a lurid application in beliefs about werewolves. A werewolf is literally a manwolf, the wolf being the form taken by the soul when it leaves the body for an excursion into the savagery of night. So close is the man-wolf connection that tradition holds that a wound inflicted upon the wolf is duplicated on the body of the man sleeping far away.

But there is a philosophical twist to this belief in the objective double of the soul. If the soul can leave the body in dreams, or inhabit an animal double, or be lost and eaten, then it cannot be the soul that keeps the body alive. Some other entity must do that. Recognizing this, the Maori have at least four words to express various psychophysical functions: the *wairua* or likeness, which is also a shadow; the *mauri* or life principle, similar to the Greek notion enshrined in the word *thymos*, "the smoke of life"; the *hau*, which might be translated as the virtue or essence of things; and the *ahua*, a kind of token personality. These definitions of native words are obviously

Above, stone carving (of about A.D. 600) from northeast India of the goddess as genetrix displaying her yoni. Similar figures are frequently used as altars.

Below, a German woodcut of 1685 showing a werewolf driven into a well, and another hanged from a gibbet.

inadequate, and the only way to understand them is to see the situations in which they are used, because this kind of theology arises as much from practical needs as from philosophical curiosity. And, because it is a theology that is foreign to us, it is all too easy to deride it. A priest writing on the Ten'a of Canada, for instance, said that they "do not conceive the spirits as really spiritual, or immaterial substances. For them the spirits have a sort of subtle body, a kind of aerial fluid, so to speak, capable of endless transformations, moving from place to place almost instantaneously, rendering itself visible or invisible at will, penetrating into other bodies, and passing through them as though they were no obstacles, in short, possessed of the qualities of real spirits. But the conception of a real spiritual substance is beyond the Ten'a intelligence." And as for that, the distinction between a subtle body and an immaterial substance is beyond anyone not trained in a scholastic argument that seems to have no practical application.

Scholastic arguments aside, the difference between a soul and a spirit in Western thought is obviously based on a particular form of experience. On a very general level it seems that the soul is a feminine and receptive function, whereas the spirit is a masculine and active one, though their exact relationship to each other and to the body is obscure. Psychology has done its best to do away with such terms, because there is no longer a practice that fits them. But it is still interesting to speculate on what such a practice could be, and for this we need to see the metaphors that once brought them alive. Of the many such metaphors, the one that Plato used has an interesting scope. Using what was no doubt a traditional image, he wrote of the soul as though it were a particular form of double to the body, and was fixed to the body by a multitude of small nails that made up the totality of the spirit— a sort of organic crucifixion. Underlying this image there is an intuition that the soul is attached to the body at the joints of the limbs, an idea also present in the shamanism of Siberia and of South America, and in the cosmogony of the Dogon of West Africa. The Greek case is instructive because the word for a joint, *gonia*, is close cousin to that for a knee, *gonu*, and both words are related to *gonad*, the reproductive glands. We have here the makings of an equation between sexuality and the spirit, which seems surprising. The sexual principle is of course worshiped or revered in many different ways throughout the world because it is the physical model for all thoughts about origination and, in mysticism, for those about union with the divine. Union, of course, means "to become one," and, to etymologize again, the Greek word *teleo* signified at once to be perfected, to marry, and to die—an idiomatic usage that is a theology in itself. It is obviously a mistake to think of sexuality merely in terms of libidinous pleasure: it has

"The soul is attached to the body at the joints of the limbs." Left, a carved Dyak figure from Borneo, showing joint marks.

definite metaphysical connotations, and the orgiastic experience it allows is rightly held to unite the faculties of the soul, to unite one person to another, and finally to unite the universe of human life to that of nature and the gods.

But if this is to happen, the relations between the immaterial faculties of the soul and its material representations must be given some intellectual standing. After all, it is not as though there is something equivalent outside for everything inside: there are disagreements between men, and within man besides. Body and soul are usually experienced as being of different enough natures for there to be a war between them—or if not a war, in Marvell's term, a dialogue. Here the soul is speaking in a dialogue between it and the body:

> O, who shall from this dungeon raise
> A soul inslav'd so many ways?
> With bolts of bones, that fetter'd stands
> In feet and manacled in hands:
> Here blinded with an eye and there
> Deaf with the drumming of an ear;
> A soul hung up as 'twere, in chains
> Of nerves, and arteries, and veins;
> Tortur'd, besides each other part,
> In vain head, and double heart?

Above, joint marks on the pottery figure of a woman—this one is from Venezuela.

It is a civil war: but, as ever, it is by objectifying such matters that a peaceful solution can be achieved. We therefore find a common tribal distinction between a head soul and a body soul, both of them equally venerated. It is something of a problem, however, to determine which one is sexual in our meaning of that word, and which is spiritual, for sexuality ritually considered stands rather against egotism than against the spirit itself. We see this in the Mediterranean gestures to avert the evil eye, the *figo* and the *mano cornuto*, both of which have obscene connotations, or in the curious figure carved upon some old Irish churches, the *sheila na gig*—a naked woman squatting with her legs apart to show her vulva. A strange sight to see on a church, one thinks, until one realizes that this obscenity is placed there in order to shock evil thoughts and evil spirits, and to suggest that all malice and envy begin as a sexual longing that has lost contact with physical reality. This longing can become spiritualized inside the church, where the individual finds his place in the body of the congregation through the virtue of the body of the Christ.

Below, a mudra—*or Indian hand gesture representing the lingam in the yoni.*

At this point we might remember the Melanesian use of the possessive suffix for words denoting the relationship of a part to the whole, whether the whole be a thing, a body, or a society. But the word "possessive" is

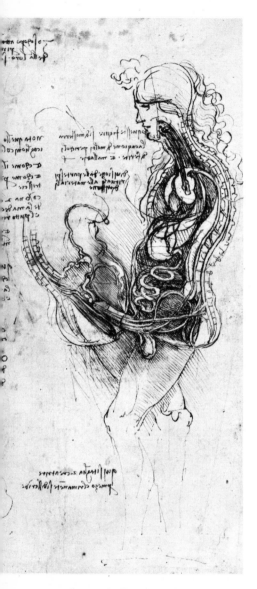

Leonardo da Vinci's anatomical drawing of sexual intercourse. He has shown an imaginary duct leading from the spinal cord to the penis to honor the notion that human semen originates in the brain.

basically a misnomer. The original grammatical term was "genitive," and it seems that modern linguists have come to favor this term once more as being both more apt and more logical. Certainly the concept of the genitive makes very good sense whenever we find the soul manifesting its powers through possession. Let us put it this way: ideas about the soul are incomprehensible until they are seen to be based upon physical models, if only because psychic functioning cannot be at all expressed without a vehicle. Freud in his way and anthropology in another demonstrate how these ideas are developed from the experience of organic functioning—or, perhaps we should now say, how they are generated. Freud looked particularly at the orifices of the body to provide him with such models, and in one sense psychoanalytic theory is an attempt to describe the often tortuous ways by which the libido—or, as others have said, the life force—is organized and translated into psychical terms through the social use of bodily parts.

How consciousness itself was created Freud could not determine, which resulted in the obscurity of two of his main concepts, one to do with the death instinct and the other with sublimation. The theory of sublimation attempts to deal with the transformation of organic energy into psychic and thence spiritual energy, which makes one suspect that the death instinct is one particular aspect of the ungraspable nature of consciousness. However this may be, the theory of sublimation was a knowledgeable reversal of the traditional way of looking at things, which holds that it is the spirit that creates matter and not the other way round. As for where the exact dividing lines between spirit and matter are to be found, or the question of which gives birth to which, that is a matter which can be argued without end. In the last resort these categories are intellectual constructions that allow one to think about certain relationships that emerge from definite practices, and, as Meister Eckhart said, the truth about all such categories is rational but not real. They have a bias, if only because they are shorthand notations for apparently opposite states in a unitary process, and as a result any system built around them will eventually come to bite its own tail.

The old term for such a process was *circulation*, and we can meet it in Plato's *Timaeus*. There he describes how those mysterious entities the Same and the Other are variously mixed and separated by god in order to create the driving force for the revolutions of the sun, moon, and planets, the motions of the crystalline spheres, and the circulation of energy in living bodies. This circulation is thus a generative function comprising the round of life, both physical and spiritual. This doctrine was developed in medieval times, and the summary given of it by Bartholomaeus Anglicus is in its own way as interesting an account of sublimation as that of Freud.

The process starts with the intake of food, which is refined by the heat of the stomach into an essence that passes along the blood to the liver. In the liver this essence is boiled, giving off a smoke that when purified is called the natural spirit. The natural spirit goes with the blood to the heart, whose poundings further refine it into the vital spirit and send it to the brain, where it is subtilized into the animal spirit. Within the brain this animal spirit turns into the intellectual functions of common sense, reason, intelligence, imagination, and memory, and the surplus goes down the spinal marrow to the testicles, where it is transformed into semen, ready to be concocted with a woman's blood into the vehicle for a new soul.

The Hindu imagination is still alive to the experience of such psychophysical processes, which are the basis for many sexual Tantric practices, not to mention the common masculine complaint of nocturnal emission, which wastes the seed of the Atman or Self without result. In such systems we see how closely knit to organic processes the soul is experienced to be, and why the principal bodily location of the soul is thought to be—according to the particular system—the liver, or the heart, or the diaphragm and lungs, or the brain, or even the fat surrounding the kidneys. In these systems, everything is both symbolic and real. The heart is a metaphor for courage. The soul is a metaphor for certain transformations that occur within the body in time with social relationships and the grand circulation of energy in nature. These systems order the world as best they can, being themselves ordered by it: through them one catches a glimpse of that tremendous coincidence which might, if all goes well, make the world outside the reflection of the one inside, and allow the human spirit (however we define that difficult word) to travel with a sense of sacred order upon the energies of the universe.

Below, four illustrations from Jacob Rueff's De Conceptu et Generatione Hominis *(1554), showing how maternal blood and paternal seed combine within the uterus to form a child.*

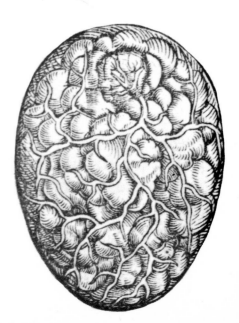

3 In the Beginning

It has long been something of a heresy to suggest that those whom we call primitive peoples think like children, just because children so often think like primitives. The problem involved is a real one, but it remains true that both ways of thinking can be remarkably similar, and that both depend on an animistic view of the world.

What is animism? A simple answer is that it is the natural way our imaginations express ideas about origins, without paying much regard to the difference between cause and effect. The Swiss psychologist Jean Piaget has collected a great number of children's remarks that show this animistic instinct. Those made by his daughter, J, are of special interest because they show how, as she grew up, they developed into a cosmological scheme that was basically the same as that proposed by the ancient Greeks.

When she was nearly three years old, J said: "I understand everything. I understand the waves: it's because there's a tree at the edge of the lake. You see that white thing in the tree, it's the waves. It's the tree that makes the waves: trees make wind."

At three years and three months she said, touching her granny's face: "Is that how grannies are made? Did you make yourself?" But the next day she said spontaneously: "Oh no, I don't think granny made herself."

At three years and four months she asked her father: "Where did that little baby come from?"

"What do you think?"

"I don't know. Out of the wood. There wasn't a little baby before."

The next month, while walking through the woods, they passed a woman with two small children. "She's been looking for little babies," said J. Three months later she thought children were bought in shops; a year later, that babies came from the clinic where there was a mummy. "All the babies in the clinic have the same mummy and then they change their mummy. This mummy gets them ready and then they grow. They have teeth and tongues put in them."

"The clouds cause rain," said Chuang Tzu, "rain causes clouds. Wind comes from the north. It now blows east, now west; and now it whirls aloft. Who puffs it forth? Who has leisure to be doing all this? I should like to know." Right, the landscape of the Yangtze River.

At five years and four months she asked: "Are you dust before you're born? Are you nothing at all, are you air?" And a month later she decided: "Babies don't make themselves, they're air. Eggshells make themselves in hens. I think they're air too."

"What things make themselves?"

"Pipes, trees, eggshells, clouds, the door. They don't make themselves, they have to be made. I think trees make themselves, and suns too. In the sky they can easily make themselves."

And two days later: "How is the sky made? I think they cut it out. It's been painted."

At five years and six months: "I think the rain's made with the sky. I think it opens and then the water comes out. Does the light come from the sky too, all the light that's here?"

"Yes."

"How is it made? Does it make itself? No, it's daddy's student (the object of her admiration at the time) who made everything, the sky and the water and the light and everything." (Quite seriously.)

A month later: "Does the moon move? Tell me what makes it move."

"You can find that out yourself."

"It's the air. I think the moon's made of air, air that gets golden at night. It's air that undoes itself like that (the crescent) and then makes itself again."

Then: "Where does the dark come from? I think it comes from the lake, or from all the little streams, because they come from the stones. That's why stones are black sometimes. The dark is dirty water that evaporates."

At six years and seven months: "The wind is air that's moving. It's the leaves and the grass and the air that makes the wind, and then above it's the air and the clouds. The clouds make the air move: the air pushes them and they then make the wind. They both help one another."

Right, the seven stages by which a tree becomes a woman—a 17th-century woodcut from Le Songe de Poliphile *by Beroalde de Verville.*

"And when there isn't any wind?"

"The cloud moves a bit by itself, because it's air. Then it makes wind."

"And what about the grass?"

"The wind pushes it and then it makes more wind."

The same day: "Earth is very fine wet sand. Sand is what comes out of the water of the lake. The sun and moon are fire like lightning." And a month later: "Daddy, will this rock grow when it rains?"

These few examples are enough to show certain fairly obvious parallels between some of J's thoughts and some beliefs that we are familiar with in cosmology and theology. The Bible tells us that there are waters above the heavens as well as below, and agrees with J that rain falls through sluice gates in the sky. And we know that until recently in Europe, and still today in Southeast Asia, minerals were thought to grow in the earth. The sky is, in many mythologies, a covering cut from the hide of an animal—our word *celestial* is akin to the French *ciel,* "sky," and both are related to the Latin *caedere,* "to cut up." In South America many an ancestor comes out of a tree at the Beginning, just as J thought babies come out of the woods.

But what particularly strikes the imagination is J's interest in the invisible movement of the wind. She was, in the proper sense of the word, an animist, believing everything that moves to be alive and breathing. Indeed the perpetual motion she saw in the world allowed her to construct a circular argument so satisfying that she left it unaltered for at least three years.

It is easy to pour scorn on animism. But the animist is not necessarily stupid or irrational. On the contrary, animistic doctrines are often notable for their ingenuity and for the subtle ways in which they use symbols and metaphors to understand what is their principal concern—the way things grow, or what the Greeks called Physis. As Lévi-Strauss has pointed out at length in his works on South American mythology, animistic thought

Below, a 17th-century alchemical illustration of the Tree of Life rooted in man and with the sun, the moon, and Mercury beneath its branches. Below left, Geb the earth being covered by Nut the sky, who is being impregnated with the stars—from the ancient Egyptian papyrus of Tamenin.

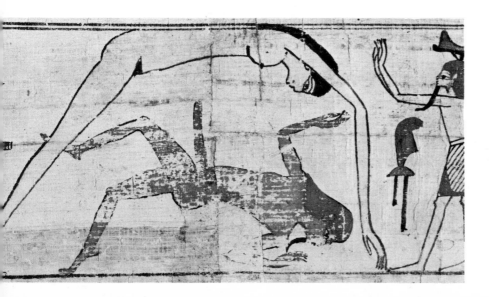

employs sensory distinctions (such as the differences between visible and invisible, fluid and solid, light and dark, moving and stationary) to create an intellectual world where these distinctions can be experienced as having meaning. As we shall see, meaning is ultimately to be found in how such distinctions are held to originate.

J's concern with Physis is quite apparent well before she is six. Her philosophical position by this time is already quite complex. She holds that things are made out of each other by reason of the movement within the air, air being a kind of lively nothing, able to condense itself into tangible entities. But she has not yet coped with the problems of fire. When she was six she said, "The sun and moon are fire like lightning." She has shelved her intellectual difficulty by lodging fire in the heavens—as she says, in the sky things can easily make themselves.

But what is the difference between the making of a door, for example, and the making of babies? J thought that both needed a human being to stand *in loco parentis* to them and therefore thought it possible that the entire world had been made by daddy's student—whom she looked up to because he was full of admirable virtues. Who made daddy's student, however, was not a problem, but a self-evident truth.

But what is self-evident is also, in some way, an absolute, and absolutes always tend to have a transcendental function attached to them. The transcendent is that beyond which one cannot understand or explain anything, but in whose activity all things come hopefully together in a center or a conclusion. J's three main types of explanation lead to three apparently different conclusions about this transcendent. She holds firstly that there is a circular transformation by which Nothing gives rise to Something and then returns to Nothing. Here the transcendent is Movement, which is part of the process it explains. Secondly, she holds that there is a state in which things make themselves without having to change their natures. Here the transcendent is in the sky—that is, above the world of relativity. And thirdly, she holds that there is a person whose intelligence allows things to be made or to make themselves, and yet who is undoubtedly part of the scheme of things. In all three of her explanations she seems to be searching for a Self who will articulate her perceptions into a single meaning.

Now a transcendent is always used in cosmological thought when an origin is being looked for, since it enables the mind to gather everything up into One, to which the Many can then be related. As we shall see, its status is paradoxical, and it often seems best not to enquire too deeply into its ontological nature—or at least not to separate the two abstract categories of the One and the Many into absolute entities.

"What is at variance agrees with itself," said Heraclitus. "It is the attunement of opposite tensions, like that of the bow and the lyre." What is self-evident here is the fact of harmony, a position which is as fundamental to Taoism as to Heraclitus. Can anything be said about this self-agreement? The Taoists say that if things move in a balance, it is essential that the pivot of this balance should be not a thing but a nothing, which is the transcendent empty of all attributes. Chuang Tzu illustrates this point with his usual humorous profundity:

"The Spirit of the Clouds when passing eastwards through the expanse of Air happened to fall in with the Vital Principle. The latter was slapping his ribs and hopping about; whereupon the Spirit of the Clouds said, 'Who are you, old man, and what are you doing here?'

" 'Strolling,' replied the Vital Principle, without stopping.

" 'I want to know something,' continued the Spirit of the Clouds.

" 'Ah!' uttered the Vital Principle, in a tone of disapprobation.

" 'The relationship of heaven and earth is out of harmony,' said the Spirit of the Clouds; 'the six influences do not combine and the four seasons are no longer regular. I desire to blend the six influences so as to nourish all living beings. What am I to do?'

" 'I do not know!' cried the Vital Principle, shaking his head while still slapping his ribs and hopping about; 'I do not know'."

The six influences mentioned here are the Yin and the Yang, the wind, rain, light, and darkness. The Yang, although invisible, has a positive movement; the Yin is what the Yang moves into, though it has a negative, or seductive, activity of its own. Wind, rain, light, and darkness are phenomena resulting from the complementary movement of the Yin and the Yang. The Vital Principle is not a thing in the usual sense of the word, but rather that by which we may understand how a process and its products are hopelessly entangled with each other: the All is the One, and its harmony comes by itself.

Chinese philosophy has made great play with the complementary opposites of the Yin and the Yang, taking good care never to give them a status independent of each other. We can see this in the diagram known as the T'ai Chi, a circle formed of two interlocked tadpole shapes of black and white, in which the white tadpole has an eye of black, and the black an eye of white—a figure that says plainly that the positive energy of the Yang still contains something irretrievably negative, and that in the end everything consists of a movement that turns into its opposite.

The T'ai Chi also evades the question of which comes first, the Yin or the Yang, in a way that reminds one of the curious entry at the very beginning of the library catalog in the British Museum: "A. See B. A correspondence between two clergymen on Regeneration and Baptism. (The letters are signed alternately: B., and A.) 1867." For Yang, see Yin: there is no better way of dealing with such opposites than by making them play pingpong with each other, the point being less to win a game than to keep it going for as long as possible.

This activity has been christened "bricolage" by Lévi-Strauss, a bricoleur being a jack-of-all-trades whose only interest is to play one contradiction off against another for as long as he has the energy. Bricolage is often a sacred activity, since it can be made to obey definite rules that work only in a closed system. The Jews, for instance, have developed a form of bricolage known as the Cabbala and interpret their scriptures by various kinds of letter play, such as *gematria, notarikon,* and *temurah.* Gematria establishes meaning through the numerical value of letters; notarikon, by making words from the first or last letters of other words; and temurah by changing the order of letters within a word so that, for instance, *oneg,* meaning "pleasure," can be read as *nego,* which means "pain."

Freud took great interest in this process. In his "Antithetical Sense of Primal Words" he noted how many Egyptian words could reverse both sound and meaning, and how others were formed of compounded opposites. Indo-European languages have a similar peculiarity in that a single root often seems to give birth to opposite meanings, as can be seen in the related verbs *to join* and *to joint,* the one meaning "to put together," the other "to separate." *Shine* and *shadow* similarly come from the same root expressing an idea of separation, and it is only logical that these two words should be related to each other by virtue of the division we make between them.

The kind of imagination required to keep two such terms joined in their separateness is constantly being challenged by causal thinking, especially in the West. To think in terms of cause is to have a partiality for one term of such an equation over another—to arrange things in a linear sequence and to trace actions and reactions to something singular at the beginning of things. Linear thinking often becomes reductionist—it explains a complicated state of affairs on one level by a physical mechanism operating on another. But it is obvious that if ever such a thing as the lowest level of all is discovered, reductionist thought will be at an impasse, for that is what cannot be explained by anything else. It is self-evident, and as we have seen from J's argument about the transformation of air into wind, trees, clouds, water, and earth, such a self-evident argument is necessarily circular.

We can see this dilemma at work in modern cosmology. There the term *singularity* is much used to indicate an event standing at the beginning of the world as we know it. It was perhaps a bang—a Big Bang—when all the matter of the universe was exploded out of a single compacted nucleus; or the continuous creation of hydrogen atoms in empty space; or the process thought to occur at the center of certain galaxies where matter and anti-matter destroy and create each other, like the Yin and the Yang. But what kind of a beginning do these theories describe? The doctrine of continuous creation says quite firmly that it is impossible for the world to have had a beginning or to have an end; the Big Bang theory holds that the world of time and space had a real start. But where did the matter come from when the start was made? One variant of the Big Bang theory answers this question by using the circular argument also found in Hinduism, that the world is periodically destroyed and created. After the Big Bang of creation, matter disperses faster and faster into the far reaches of space until it attains the speed of light, upon which it reverses direction and returns upon itself to re-collect its energy at the center and explode again. If there is a singular event that can explain the existence of the world, it is then either continuous or circular, and therefore not as singular as all that.

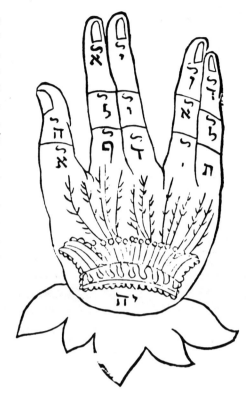

Religious thought faces the same problem, which can briefly be stated in this form: if the world was created, what was it made out of, and is the Creator to be regarded as a something on the same level as his creation? The question was put to St. Augustine in a somewhat different form. He was asked, "What did God do before the world was made?" His answer was that He created a hell for the inquisitive—a tart remark to be understood in the context of his belief that God is continually creating the world, which thus could not have a beginning. Origen inclined to a kind of Big Bang theory, holding that God had previously created many other worlds than this one, which implies their destruction. The reason for this conclusion is to be found in Scotus Erigena, who maintained that God precedes the world not in time but in idea—a doctrine on which Aquinas set his seal, holding that because God was the sufficient cause of the world, it is impossible for this creative cause not to have an effect at all times. The doctrine of the non-eternity of the world as put down in Genesis was to be believed in only in deference to authority; for if God is God, then the world can have no beginning.

How then are we to decipher those pregnant words "In the beginning God created the heaven and the earth?" There have been many explanations of this sentence, all of them interesting, many of them tortuous. Perhaps the most lucid was given by Rabbi Bunam: "The Lord created the world in a state of beginning. The universe is always in an uncompleted state, in the form of its beginning. It is not like a vessel at which the master works and he finishes it; it requires continuous labor and unceasing renewal by creative

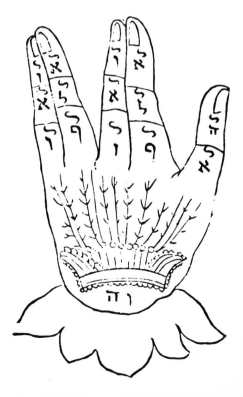

The Hands of God, showing the creative act always at work, from Shefa Tal, *by the 17th-century German cabbalist Shabbetai Horowitz. On each wrist are two of the Hebrew letters of God's name, and from these emanate the 28 letter combinations on the finger joints.*

Above, an ancient Assyrian seal showing the god Marduk, thunderbolts in hand, about to kill Tiamat.

Left, the creation of the world by divine fiat, from Robert Fludd's Utriusque Cosmi *(1617).*

forces. Were there a second's pause by these forces, the world would return to primeval chaos." "In the beginning" (which in Sanskrit is rendered by a word meaning "at the summit") thus has the same force as the phrase "once upon a time," which means that what happened once will also happen now, because it is always happening. We can see in this usage the curious psychological process that transformed the aorist tense in classical languages from the present—*this is done*—into the past—*this was done.* But what are we to make of the last sentence in Rabbi Bunam's exegesis? Is there really any difference between a state of beginning and primeval chaos?

What is chaos? The second verse of Genesis continues: "And the earth was without form, and void; and darkness was upon the face of the deep. And the Spirit of God moved upon the face of the waters." The words, "without form, and void" are a translation of the Hebrew *tohu-wa-bohu,* which in shortened form is used even now in French to indicate chaos, confusion, hubbub. The word *tohu* is related to the Babylonian Tiamat, the sea monster whom Marduk slew and from whose body he carved the earth and the firmament above. As for the word *chaos,* this originally meant a yawning chasm, something which gapes. This bottomless gullet is traditionally pictured as a whirlpool that draws everything into its maw or as the turbulent milling about of a furious crowd. And it is no coincidence that cosmology today has been forced to use the concept of turbulence in its efforts to describe the formation of galaxies. This turbulence is understood to be capable of moving so fast that it generates sonic booms of great intensity.

"Strictly speaking," writes the astronomer Jagjit Singh on this topic, "the velocity of sound is merely the speed with which infinitesimal pressure or density changes, whether audible or not, are propagated in the gaseous medium. . . . But supersonic motions are a different matter altogether. They cause violent and abrupt changes in the pressure and density of the medium." In the high-speed turbulence of a galactic cloud, myriads of these supersonic booms are clashing together; eventually the statistical irregularity of these whirling shocks creates a spin in the whole galactic cloud and the stars are born.

Well did the Hindus say, then, that the world was created by Brahma thundering out the creative syllable BHU! and that the Milky Way was churned during a tug of war between the gods and the demons, the whirling motion they imparted to the pole around which their rope was wound making the earth come into existence like butter. That they picture chaos as the Milky Way is a convention, and one of the functions of a convention is to stop the mind from going mad with unanswerable questions and thoughts of infinity. There is a magnificent illustration of this in the *Brihadaranyaka Upanishad,* where the overpersistent Gargi asks the insufferably knowledge-able Yajnavalkya what the earth is made of.

"Yajnavalkya," says she, "since all here is woven, like warp on woof, in water, on what, pray, is water woven, like warp on woof?"

"On air, O Gargi."

"On what then is air woven, like warp on woof?"

"On the worlds of the sky, O Gargi."

"On what, then, are the worlds of the sky woven, like warp on woof?"

And Yajnavalkya answers this question and six more in the same manner. But when Gargi asks him on what the worlds of Brahma are woven, like warp on woof, he refuses to play any more and tells her: "Gargi, do not question too much lest your head fall off."

Brahma is the title given to the self-subsistent, which means, literally, "that which stands beneath itself." When we put things this way we can see that it is a problem of the most exquisite subtlety to decide what this self-subsistent is composed of. This accounts for a curious remark made by Jacob Boehme, the German mystic: "In the deep the power of the stars, together with the heat and lustre of the sun, are all but *one thing*, a moving, boiling, hovering, like a spirit or matter." How strange that one cannot tell the difference between these apparently contradictory terms! He continued: "only it hath not reason, for it is not the Holy Spirit." What he is describing is therefore a kind of chaos, a primeval motion without intelligence.

Chaos, as we have said, is the turbulent yawn of matter that continually engulfs itself. We know from the Book of Job that God speaks out of the whirlwind, that forceful confusion of air turning upon itself with a void at its heart, and the metaphysical problem involved in this image is to separate God from the confusion in which He hides, and to account for the apparent solidity of the universe. We can only do it as Boehme did, by appealing to reason. Reason is light, confusion is darkness, as we are told in the first chapter of the gospel according to St. John: "And the light shineth in darkness, and the darkness comprehended it not." This gospel is Gnostic in character, which means that it is based on the primacy of knowledge, a claim that can be made of many tribal religions such as that of the Witoto Indians of South America, who say that in the beginning the word gave origin to the father of all things. But knowledge is also a reflective activity and, in the language of cybernetics, exhibits feedback from knower to known. It is not straining an image too hard to suggest that we can find just such a feedback in chaos when it yawns itself up, or that this act is the beginning of that self-reflective activity which is the mark of consciousness and the light we impute to God Himself. The voice of Brahma then turns out to be the noise of chaos; they are as indistinguishable as the Yin and the Yang.

Jung, following the Gnostics, called the Brahmanical chaos the Pleroma, the abundant totality that is One because it is Many. In all religions that play with mathematics in order to talk about God in abstract, yet understandable, form, the number one always has a catch in it. Indeed, it is no number, as Marvell said in a rather different context, and this is both because and in spite of the fact that it stands at the head of all the ordinals. For oneness implies both a unity and a totality: it is the atom of all relational thinking. The word *atom* of course means that which is indivisible, and from the time of Lucretius (who based himself on the Epicurean doctrine) it was held to be the smallest particle involved in the structure of matter. Now that it has been split, physicists have reverted to the ancient idea that one is no number, and that the solitary atom is a totality that can be decomposed into a complex of energetic particles. But the atom contains these particles in such a way that, when it is whole, they cannot be distinguished from each other; they compose harmony or relationship so perfect that they become indivisible and only the atom exists as an independent unit, a true perpetual motion machine. Quantum theory has extended this insight and, as David Bohm has said, "at a quantum level of accuracy an object does not have any intrinsic properties . . . instead it shares its properties mutually and indivisibly with all systems with which it interacts."

Atoms can exist in various levels of complexity, and they all possess the quality of totals containing mutual and indivisible properties. It was thus that the astronomer Georges Lemaître held that the universe was originally

Left, the Orphic god of light, Phanes (also called Priapos), at the center of the zodiacal egg. Above, a carved stone from Easter Island—the bird-man holding the egg from which mankind originated.

a primeval atom that exploded—the primeval atom being something nuclear that was at once singular and of a compendious totality. In mythology this atom is often an egg. It floats in the abyss until it hatches, when the top half of the shell becomes the firmament, and the bottom the earth, and from it emerges Eros (the creative principle) who populates the space so created.

At this moment we can revert to Jacob Boehme, who distinguished between a chaos with and without reason. Knowledge, as should now be plain, is a divisive act. Because of its ability to cut things in two it is often figured as a sword, like the one with which Marduk killed Tiamat, or the double-edged blade that emerges from the mouth of the Christ in the Apocalypse, a true picture of his terrifying remark "I come not to bring peace, but a sword." But this imagery is inept when we have to deal with an egg rather than a sea monster. An egg must be laid by a bird and it hatches from within, as it does in the *Vedas*. There the bird is a gander, whose name *hamsa* is traditionally taken to refer to breathing, *ham* being the sound of the inbreath and *sa* that of the outbreath. When the gander hums its own name continuously it can also be heard as *sa-ham, sa-ham, sa* meaning "This," and *ham* "I." As the gander is the animal form of Brahma, the breathing of its own name means that the world of Brahma is filled with the cry, This is I.

It is this I that emerges from the egg in the form of a multitude of creatures, each saying I. Since they all differ from one another, the utterance of selfhood

Right, an ancient Greek vase depicts one of the Dioscuri, the twin sons of Zeus, hatching out of a large egg resting on an altar. The woman is probably Leda, the twins' mother.

The Mercurial Fountain, which quickens the three kingdoms of nature, enclosed by the twin processes of condensation and rarefaction—from the 16th-century alchemical work Rosarium Philosophorum.

acts as a separator and is the figure in which is hidden the sword of knowledge that slays the dragon of chaos. But why, we must ask, is chaos a dragon? Why is it a seabeast?

In Sanskrit the word *atman* (from which we get our *atmosphere*) stands both for the breath and the soul. Through the practice of meditative breathing yogis can attain the world of Brahma, when they are called *paramahamsa*, or higher gander, and they are then able to hear the song within the name of the gander, which goes like this: "Many forms do I assume. And when the sun and moon have disappeared, I float and swim with slow movements on the boundless expanse of the waters. I am the Lord. I bring forth the universe from my essence and I abide in the cycle of time that dissolves it."

In the same way, in Genesis, the Spirit of God moves upon the face of the waters—cradled by them, indeed, as a child in the womb by the amniotic fluid. We must give due weight to this biological metaphor, if only because Tiamat is a goddess as well as a dragon: as Jungians would say, she is the Terrible Mother from whom a child is saved by being born. The image of water is used because it is a type of chaos in being maternal, formless, unstable, obedient to gravity and to the receptacle that contains it, and a container of all that swims in it. But it is also a something, and it is put into opposition with the wind because the wind is not a something. As the Welsh bard Taliessin said, "The wind without flesh, without bone, without veins, without feet, is strong; the wind has no wants, but the sea whitens when it comes out of nothing. He is in the field, he is in the wood, without age, without old age. He was not born, he has never been seen, he will not come when desire wishes. He is uncourteous, he is vehement, he is bold. He is bad, he is good. He is yonder, he is here. He comes from the heat of the sun, and he comes from the coldness of the moon."

In this collection of mythological images we can see the beginning of an association that flowers in Aphrodite, the foam-born—the meeting of air and water produces love. But, as can be seen from the passage by Taliessin, the wind—though unborn—still comes from the heat of the sun and the coldness of the moon, and we are confronted yet again with a circular argument. We must read this in the light of the phenomena of evaporation and precipitation in which, according to Aetius, we see "the fire of the sun and the stars feeding itself on the exhalation of the waters"—the moon being the regent of the dew and the rain. The wind is then the motion that turns water into light and back into water by condensation and by rarefaction.

This theory is described at length in Plato's *Timaeus*. "In the first place," he says, "we see that what we just now called water, by condensation, I suppose, becomes stones and earth; and this same element, which melted

Chaos of the Elements—an
illustration from Robert Fludd's
Utriusque Cosmi.

and dispersed, passes into vapor and air. Air, again, when inflated, becomes fire; and, again, fire, when condensed and extinguished, passes once more into the form of air; and once more air, when collected and condensed, produces cloud and mist; and from these, when still more compressed, comes flowing water, and from water comes earth and stones once more; and thus generation appears to be transmitted from one to the other in a circle." We have here a description of the activity of the four elements—air, fire, water, and earth—that was to flourish in Europe until well into the 17th century and which emerged spontaneously from the imagination of Piaget's daughter in this century.

It is, then, a powerful doctrine, which we must examine.

The early Greek philosophers were at one in believing in the existence of these four elements, though they differed in their opinions as to which was primary—Aetius holding that the divine power was in elemental moisture; and Heraclitus, that Fire was the ever-living. The quarrel between these philosophical animists (or hylozoists, as they are called) arose because a notion of final cause had entered the argument; the old theory of circularity had to be cut through at one point or another, and a bias leading back to a singularity had to be made visible. This movement led Parmenides to ascribe such a perfect self-continuity to god that no motion could be ascribed to him, so that it was a matter of the utmost perplexity to discover how the movement within the world originated. This argument was countered by the first atomist, Leukippus, who did away with the notion of the four elements and of self-continuity and instead postulated a myriad of indestructable particles that were able to move because they existed in a void or nothingness. At bottom this difference of opinion is based on the logical status of Nothingness, which, if circularity is denied, must come before Somethingness. Parmenides equated God with fire and also with origin, so that fire, being self-subsistent, must also be a Nothing: Leukippus agreed rather with Rabbi Bunam and considered Nothing to be part of the incompleteness of the world and the mark of its perpetual beginning.

The dilemma of Parmenides is also to be found in Islam, in the person of Al-Ghazzali, whose *Mishkat Al-Anwar* was an attempt to describe how plurality came into being out of the unmitigated unity of Allah. Al-Ghazzali postulated the existence of a Vice-Regent who partook of this unity while standing outside its orbit. This was thought heretical because it implies that Allah is a pantheistic spirit and brings the absolute distinction between him and his creatures to naught. Al-Ghazzali's follower Ibn Tufail tried to remove this taint of heresy by making elaborate use of the notion of reflectors. The Vice-Regent was the first reflector, being "as it were, the image of the

Opposite, 17th–18th century Chinese painting of sages displaying the T'ai Chi. They are surrounded by figures—the deer, the pine tree, and the peach—denoting long life and immortality. Overleaf, a detail from Michelangelo's ceiling in the Sistine Chapel—God creating sun, moon, and planets.

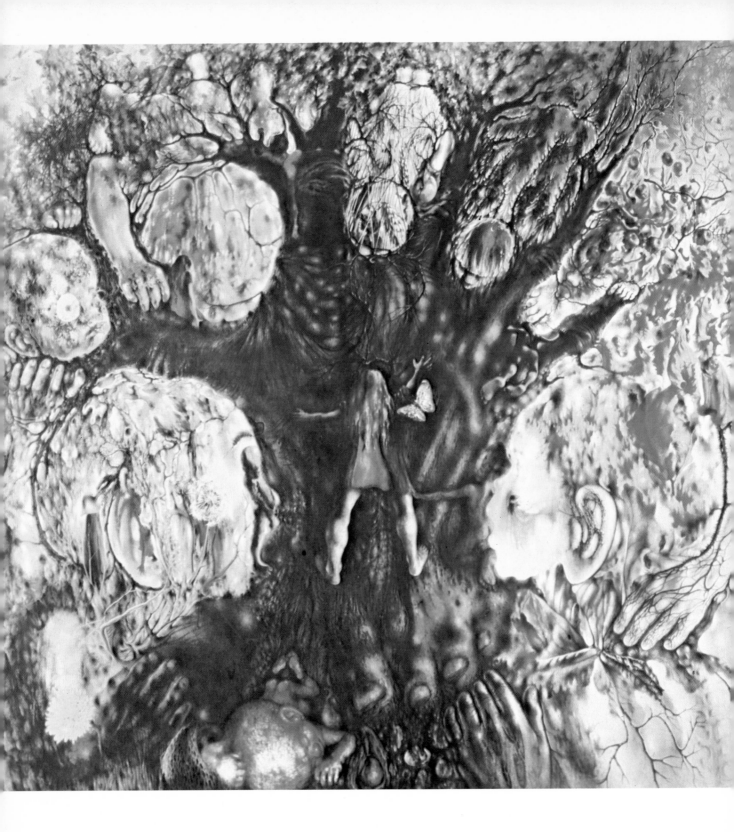

84

Above, Hide and Seek *(1940–2)*
by Pavel Tchelitchev. It is summer to the
left of the tree, harvest time is above, and
the fires of the fall burn on the right.

sun which appears in a polished mirror; for that image is neither the sun, nor the mirror, nor other than them both." This solution is similar to the Cabbalistic doctrine, that the Lord created the world by looking at his own reflection as it appeared to him on the surface of the primeval water, a reflection that turned the black and white of God into the white and black of Adam.

These logical difficulties show that we are reaching the heart of a paradoxical mystery. It has to do first with the difference between a symbol and a sign. A symbol is the image of a relationship in which the knower and the known share a common factor; a sign is rather a mark placed upon the known to distinguish it from the knower. Secondly, the relationship that is to be intuited in a symbol constantly tends to take the form of the knower, which means that it is personified. It is therefore the mark of a person who, in this context, is to be viewed as the primal atom of psychic life out of which signs emerge and within whose singleness a baffling abundance of relationships forms a totality.

It is possible, though finally misleading, to see this habit in Freudian terms—as the result of the interplay between projection and introjection. Strangely enough, however, a more satisfactory model to illustrate its peculiarities is to be found in the logical paradoxes of Bertrand Russell. The most famous of these is about the Cretan who said that all Cretans were liars, the difficulty being whether the speaker should be included in his utterance or not. Another is about the barber in a village who shaves only those who do not shave themselves. If he does not shave himself, he must then shave himself, but if he does then the definition is void. A third has to do with the librarian who catalogs all the books in his library, and his problem is whether he should enter the catalog within itself or not.

The mystery, as we can see, has to do with self-reference.

The theories of the early Greek philosophers concerning the primacy of one of the four elements suffer from the same paradoxical ambiguity, for these elements too are like catalogs that at one moment refer to themselves and at another to the elements listed within them. When any of them are also made to contain the unthinkable category of Nothingness, the logical difficulties they develop are beyond all remedy. Anaxagoras tried to get out of this impossible situation the atomistic way, by denying that the elements were to be found in matter at all: cut hair into smaller and smaller pieces and you will never come to a spark of fire. (Hair was held to be the excrement produced by the elemental fire contained in the brain.) He held that what is cannot emerge from what is not; therefore fire must be made of small particles of fire, bone of bone, gold of gold, and so on.

This tautological regress can be made use of in surprising ways: thus Josiah Royce held that Time was made of time, and that "every *now* within which something happens is therefore *also* a succession." We are thus back in the circularity of the symbol, of that totality which can also be viewed as a unit, and of the Aquinian view that the simultaneity of God's presence implies an eternal creation. But causal thought is not content with such tail-biting arguments and requires, if not an origin or an atom, at least a polarity upon which to build its systems. Thus Heraclitus, the philosopher of perpetual change within the All, could only express this situation in such a phrase as: "Fire lives the death of air, and air lives the death of fire; water lives the death of earth, earth that of water."

We have come back to the four elements, and here they are paired in such a way that the first two are ruled by the alternation of heat and cold, the second by condensation and rarefaction. Plato, as we have seen, put all these matters together in one complete cycle based upon atmospheric phenomena. But there is another way of doing this, which brings the nature of fire closer to experience. The cosmological nature of fire, as we have seen from J's speculations, is difficult to comprehend. But if it is a fire one lights oneself, the matter becomes self-evident. Cyrano de Bergerac used this image in his *States and Empires of the Moon*, and he centered it upon a log of wood, which he saw as containing the four elements. Put a match to the log and the latent fire within it is liberated: it forces out the elemental moisture of the sap, while the particles of fire bearing some of this moisture rise into the sky and are lost in the clouds. The air of the log turns into clouds as well, and when the rain falls fire and air return to the earth. The log has now turned into ash, which is a kind of earth cured of its sterility by fire. An acorn dropped in this ash, and watered by rain containing fire and earth, grows into a tree that can once more be consumed by and reborn from the same process.

This is a traditional description, which is also found amongst the Dogon people of the Congo (now Zaire). Their cosmology is one of the most complicated ever to be recorded in print, and it begins, as does the Hindu cosmogony, with an egg—the Egg of Amma, the name Amma signifying God and meaning "to hold tight," "to arrange." The Dogon are Platonists, and are much given to diagrams, number play, and geometry. In one of their pictures of the egg we see the four elements arranged in the quarters of the universe with two guide signs making an X at the center.

Because of their preoccupation with the doubleness of things, the Dogon have two signs for each of the four elements, and implicit in this scheme is the tautological factor that Josiah Royce saw in Time, where every Now implies a succession: each double element is multiplied by two five times in succession until we have the number 64 in each quarter, and adding these four together plus the original 8 of the elements and the 2 guide signs we arrive at 266, the Dogon number of totality out of which the universe is created in a most complicated manner.

The first of the guide signs is known as the sheath, and the second is pictured as a curious curve known as the "emergence of conception."

Here air blows on water to produce mist; water falls on earth to produce soil; air blows on fire to make sparks; and the fire feeds on wood and leaves ash. The products of the four elements are known as "creatures."

But where does the wood come from? The Dogon say that it came from the acacia tree, which was the first thing made by Amma. The seed of this tree is said to be neither living nor dead, to be neither plant, tree, nor person, and the tree itself to contain no water. This is because the acacia flowers and leafs in the dry season, and sheds its leaves in the wet; and its name, *sene*, is significantly the same as that used in the Bible for the burning bush seen by Moses. Out of this tree was made a top containing the seeds of all things, and it was set into motion by the singular will of Amma, which the Dogon figure as the Jackal. Just as in Plato, they picture the turning of the universe upon itself as a spinning-whorl, and the top as Amma's first effort to bring things into a system of self-circulation. But the top burst in spinning and scattered its seeds into the void, and this is the Failure of Amma.

It is this that we see in the second of the guide signs: it shows the four elements in their phase of expansion or, if you will, of their mutual destruction. It is only when they are contained within the sheath that they are able to condense into living entities, and the Dogon see this as coming at the end of a five-fold cycle, made up of three emanations or rarefactions, which also have a spiral movement downward, and two condensations or returns to the original state, which have a spiral movement upward. The four elements then become Matter; they are subject to the laws of Time and Space, and go through the accustomed cycles of birth and death.

The word *matter* has two relatives of great significance for us: the one is the Latin *mater*, "mother," the other the Portuguese *madeira*, "wood." The Greeks called this matter that is mother to all things by the name of Physis, from a word meaning "to grow," "to cause to be born," "to engender"; and what Physis most easily produces is a *phyton*, or plant, the largest of which is, of course, a tree.

The Dogon however, insist that the first Physis was devoid of water, which in their scheme is to say that it was not condensed. Here we must return to the image of chaos as a seabeast, and note that in mythology trees and dragons are often images of the same reality. Their relationship to water

*Right, an engraving, after an early
English manuscript, of Christ as the King
of Glory who—in the words of the
apocryphal gospel of Nicodemus—
"trampling upon death, seized the prince
of hell, deprived him of all his powers,
and took our earthly father Adam with
him to his glory."*

*Below, a seven-headed Naga carved on a
balustrade at Angkor Thom in the
12th century. Nagas are tree spirits who
control the rain, bestow fertility, and
cure diseases. They are also connected
with soma, the drink of immortality.*

can be seen in two ways, either they live in water, or water lives in them. We can see the first possibility in the Book of Job, where Leviathan is pictured as a burning matter within the deep, whose gaping maw was used later, in the Middle Ages, as an image of the mouth of Hell.

"By his neesings a light doth shine, and his eyes are like the eyelids of the morning.

"Out of his mouth go burning lamps, and sparks of fire leap out.

"Out of his nostrils goeth smoke, as out of a seething pot or caldron.

"His breath kindleth coals, and a flame goeth out of his mouth."

Here the dragon is an ever-burning fuel, or wood, which energizes the deep of chaos. It is slain and cut up to make the heavens and the earth. In the Vedas this killing of the primal serpent is likened to the cutting up of the World Tree into logs—an exact parallel which tells us that because Jesus was a carpenter, he must also be the dragon-slayer, as he is indeed made out to be when he is said to harrow hell.

In Southeast Asia, besides, we know that the spirits of trees are called Nagas, which are snake-divinities. But these snakes are also the masters of rain. In the related mythology of India we know that they have yearly to be cut in two by Indra, the sky god, in order to free the monsoon from their all-containing bellies. For tribes in Guyana, this freeing of the waters was originally produced by cutting down the World Tree. What puts these two images, the snake and the tree, in such close parallel is a fact of some psychological curiosity: they are symbolically bisexual.

Freud, we know, came to the conclusion that trees and snakes were phallic in character, because they were stiff, rod-shaped, and erectile. But here he missed not only the etymology of matter that we have noted, but the fact that in mythology the main characteristic of primal serpents is their habit of swallowing everything, so that they have to be killed to make them disgorge. This is traditionally interpreted in one of two ways: either the killing of the serpent and the resultant flood of waters signifies the birth of a child from its mother, or it refers to the symbolic ejaculation of the Sky Father, which produces rain and children impartially. The second alternative was held by the Australian Aborigines as by the ancient Egyptians, whose god Osiris brings much of our argument to a head. For after Osiris had been slain by Set, he was placed in a coffin of cedar wood (exactly as the Dogon place their dead in acacia-wood coffins), was dismembered by Set, and then pieced together by Isis, who found all the parts of his body except his penis. She replaced this by a wooden one with which she copulated, thus becoming pregnant of Horus, the sun god. Osiris then became the Lord of the Dead, was responsible for the flow of the Nile waters, and was pictured as a kind of Okeanos, the serpentine flow of water that rings the world.

It is perhaps surprising to reach the conclusion that the bisexual dragon of chaos, which is also a tree, and which is that Heraclitean fire of change by which the elements are continually destroyed into each other, is also a dead man. But this conclusion is undoubtedly correct, for in Greece, Africa, China, and elsewhere the soul of a dead man is regularly figured as a snake or dragon. The dragon brings children, as it does to the Aborigines, which tells us that the dead are also the unborn—that is, matter which is only in a state of potentiality.

Where do babies come from? We must now introduce another metaphor having to do with beginnings, that of sexual generation. The Platonic doctrine—which is also the Hindu one—sees this as a unitary process requiring three distinct natures. Plato describes these three natures as "first, that which is in process of generation; secondly, that in which the generation takes place; and thirdly, that of which the thing generated is a resemblance. And we may liken the receiving principle to a mother, and the source or spring to a father, and the intermediate nature to a child."

This is a new metaphor, but it is only another way of seeing the productive circulation of the four elements. The primal mother and father are no other than the dragon in its bisexuality. So we now see the answer to the problem of how to create something out of nothing—it is to cut into two the self-copulating dragon and so release the child of matter from the waters of its fertilizing birth.

Above, two Celtic coins from Bohemia (second and first centuries B.C.). The upper coin bears a dragon shaped like a torque; the lower, a coiled, eared dragon.

This self-copulation within one totality is mythologically viewed as incest, masturbation, spitting, or rubbing the hands together to make the skin of the palms flake off and form a ball of dirt or earth. It provides the basis for Freud's theory of the Oedipus complex. The child whose birth is the result of the self-copulation exists as the reflection of its father's nature. But, since the child forces the father out of the mother, it is the father's rival as well as his reflection, like the Cabbalistic Adam who, although he is given a will of his own as he is created and although he is a perfect mirror image of God, yet rebels against Him and falls.

The fall of Adam in the Bible is followed by his sexual knowledge of Eve, which makes him the father of all mankind and disperses his seed throughout the world. The One has in fact become Many through an act of generation. The secret of the dragon lies ultimately in this act, which is a recurrent subject in mythology. Plato described man as an androgyne so powerful and intelligent that it frightened God, who cut it in two to divert its energies into a perpetual search for its other half. Earlier the Greeks had told how Uranus was castrated by his son Cronos, and his penis thrown into the sea, where it created Aphrodite—the cosmological import of this act being that

An Italian Renaissance painting of the castration of Uranus by Cronos. The celestial machinery is to be reassembled around the axis marked by Uranus, who lies below the equatorial ring.

Uranus was the sky god who, by lying in a heavy embrace with Mother Earth, prevented his children from having space to move about in. What is destroyed in this—and in the Polynesian myths dealing with Maui, whose exploits were similar—is the sexual union of the primal parents who form a unity only in order to produce a third.

It cannot be fortuitous that here we are seeking a mythological solution to the philosophical problem faced by Parmenides and Leukippus, of how to account for movement within a perfectly coherent One. As J implied when she asked whether the grass was real, because it moved, life is movement; and not only does movement need space (so that Cabbalists make out that God created the world by withdrawing Himself out of space) but life ends in death and so makes room for itself perpetually. It is because of this that Adam becomes mortal after he has lain with Eve. Death necessarily enters the picture whenever there is a birth, not only because birth destroys the perfect union of the dragon parents but because the process of generation is the prime example of how the elements live and die into each other without end.

We have in this chapter seen how several different metaphors have been employed to think about opposites that are complementary halves of the same process, a process that is an apparent succession of putting things together and setting them apart. Once this process has been set in motion there is something inescapable in it from which only the dead and the unborn are exempt. All cosmologies are thus describing, in whatever images they choose, the birth of an apparently free spirit into the world of necessity. This necessity cannot be seen apart from the dragon, if we are to follow that particular image, nor is it to be seen apart from the dragon-slayer, for it is imposed equally on both. It is an allotment of functions within a totality, and it is logically prior to the gods who take up the positions allotted to them. As Scotus Erigena said, "God must be considered prior to his creation not in Time, but in Idea."

The Rig Veda says that he who is the center of creation either formed it or did not form it, he whose gaze controls the world either knows whence it came or knows not. More magnificently, the Lord tells Job:

"Where was thou when I laid the foundations of the earth? declare, if thou hast understanding.

"Who hath laid the measures thereof, if thou knowest? or who hath stretched the line upon it?

"Whereupon are the foundations thereof fastened? or who laid the corner stone thereof;

"When the morning stars sang together, and all the sons of God shouted for joy?"

4 The Death that Gives Life

"There was nothing whatsoever here in the beginning. By death indeed was this covered, or by hunger, for hunger is death."

The words are from the *Brihadaranyaka Upanishad*. Elsewhere in Hinduism this death at the heart of things, this power by which things exist, is called Vishnu—Vishnu, the all-pervader, the universal intellect that plans the world. When Vishnu falls asleep, the world dissolves into formlessness, and he is represented as lying upon the 1000-headed serpent called The Endless.

William Blake, in the *Book of Urizen,* figures the same death in life as Urizen, a self-contemplating shadow:

> Lo, a shadow of horror is risen
> In Eternity! Unknown, unprolific,
> Self-enclos'd, all-repellent: what Demon
> Hath form'd this abominable void,
> This soul-shudd'ring vacuum?

The Eternals call Urizen Death, because he has rent himself from the side of eternity by his hunger for a separate existence. Mortals, however, usually call this process birth.

As we saw in Chapter 3, the story of the dragon and the dragon-slayer is one way of describing how the birth of a child forces its parents apart in order to make space for its own activity. In his magisterial little book *Hinduism and Buddhism*, Coomaraswamy says that the Dragon Father—the Self of Hindu scripture—may either choose death for his children's sake, or have the sacrifice imposed upon him by the gods. These apparently contradictory doctrines are in fact one, for, explains Coomaraswamy, "in reality slayer and dragon, sacrificer and victim, are of one mind behind the scenes, where there is no polarity of opposites, but mortal enemies on the stage, where the everlasting war of the Gods and the Titans is displayed."

And yet, he goes on, "it is recognized that the sacrifice and the dismemberment of the victim are acts of cruelty and even treachery, and this is the original sin of the Gods, in which all men participate. . . ." Many people

An illustration from Théodore de Bry's Americae *(1634) of Tupinamba warriors disembarking with European prisoners, executing them, and dismembering their bodies. The prisoner on the right is being slaughtered without benefit of the usual rites, no doubt because he has shown himself to be a coward.*

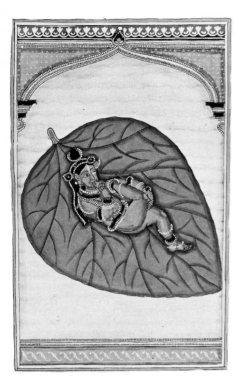

Vishnu the All-pervader, from an 18th-century Indian manuscript. New-born, he lies on a lotus leaf, with his big toe in his mouth to signify his self-absorption. In the original he is colored dark blue—the color that represents the all-pervasive ether.

make God responsible for the appearance of evil in the world—for, in the words of Amos, "Shall there be evil in a city, and the Lord hath not done it?"

A sacrifice in its most abstract sense is a commemoration of this primal act of cruelty by which death entered into matter by dividing the endless play of the elements in such a way as paradoxically to bring life into the world. We can call this death a void, or a shaft of intelligent light, or hunger, or something immovable like the axle around which the wheel of circulation turns; whichever we choose, we have a notion that is definable only in terms of its opposite. We can follow this out on the human level in another book of Blake's, *The Marriage of Heaven and Hell*:

"The Giants who formed this world into its sensual existence, and now seem to live in it in chains, are in truth the causes of its life and the sources of all activity; but the chains are the cunning of the weak and tame minds which have the power to resist energy; according to the proverb, the weak in courage is strong in cunning.

"Thus one portion of being is the Prolific, the other is the Devouring; to the Devourer it seems as if the producer was in his chains; but it is not so, he only takes portions of existence and fancies them whole.

"But the Prolific would cease to be Prolific unless the Devourer, as a sea, received the excess of his delights.

"Some will say: 'Is not God alone the Prolific?' I answer: 'God only Acts and Is, in existing beings or Men.'

"These two classes of men are always upon earth, and they should be enemies: whoever tries to reconcile them seeks to destroy existence.

"Religion is an endeavour to reconcile the two.

"Note: Jesus Christ did not wish to unite, but to separate them, as in the Parable of sheep and goats! and he says: 'I came not to send Peace, but a Sword.'

"Messiah or Satan or Tempter was formerly thought to be one of the Antediluvians who are our energies."

In these terms, the self-creation of Urizen is the story of the Devourer biting its own tail of the Prolific, slicing up its own substance into morsels that, like Plato's androgynous man after his bisection, have pity for themselves and each other and try to reunite under the cover of a tent, which is another figure for the self-enclosed. The paradox of the situation is that religion—a word traditionally taken to mean "to bind together"—is here scorned in favor of a radical separation of the sheep and the goats. But Blake, although he may have been partial, was certainly not wrong in what he said, the sacred being found in that which is set apart so that the Prolific and the Devourer may perform their necessary functions.

We find this alternation between production and destruction in many mythologies. The Aztecs believed that four worlds or suns preceded this one, all of them destroyed because of their inadequacies. The Dogon phrased the matter in terms of alternate rarefaction and condensation, ascent and descent; and their problem was whether to attribute the creation of separateness in the world to Amma on high or to the Jackal, his first-born son, below. Their argument begins with the notion that Amma is perfect because he is androgynous and the twin of himself. Creatures born without a double are imperfect and, consequently, sinful. This belief is paralleled in the *Brihadaranyaka Upanishad*. Here the self appears alone in the universe and, being afraid and without delight, splits itself into man and woman, bull and cow, stallion and mare, and ends by populating the world with reflections of its fear and love. The Dogon picture Amma as separating from himself his female half, which becomes Mother Earth. But Amma's female half, the Earth, is like his male half, androgynous. So Amma as male can couple with her only after he has castrated her. This first and lasting fault has led to every imperfection since. From this faulty union of Amma and Earth was born the Jackal, a creature deprived of half his mother's inheritance and hence a solitary. The Jackal in man, which we can equate with the Devourer, death, hunger, or even, in Freudian terms, the actor of the Oedipal role, is now continually searching for the twin female his father's act deprived him of.

Other Dogon stories have it that the Jackal was impatient to couple with his twin while still within the womb. He ate through his own placenta (which the Dogon regard as the double of a child) in order to assimilate his female half. In these stories the Jackal's treacherous impatience is the origin of all the oddities and imperfections of the world today. In fact, in Dogon myth we find a continual counterpoint between the perfection of Amma and the oddity of the Jackal, the responsibility for the creation being placed now on the one, now on the other. In the end there is no doubt that the Jackal must be understood as the mask that Amma wears in order to carry out a particular function necessary to the unfolding of the world, and the Jackal's hunger is a reflection of Amma's cruelty toward his female half when he wished to couple with it.

How to redeem the fault of Amma? The Dogon say that Amma ordained a revenge of an exquisitely painful character, by sacrificing another part of his fourfold nature. This part is figured as a fish-like embryo, and is a blameless but necessary victim. Its umbilical cord and its genitals were cut off at one stroke, and it was then crucified, beheaded, and dismembered. The blood of this sacrifice sanctified and fertilized the ground it fell on,

A wooden figure (18th or 19th century) from the Burutu Islands, Polynesia, of the god Tangarao. He is shown here with human and divine figures issuing from his progenitive power.

95

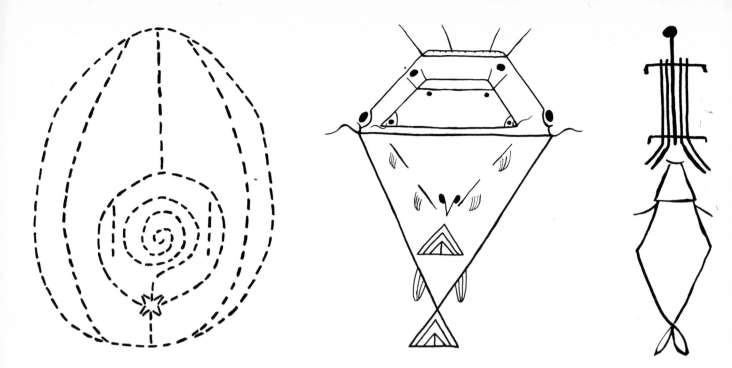

*Above, three Dogon diagrams. On the
left is the* yala *of the Egg of Amma. It
is divided into four segments, representing
the* Nommos *or four-fold sexuality of
Amma. In the center is the Seat of Amma
containing the spiral of his seminal
essence, flanked by four male and four
female souls. All these contents will
emerge through the star-shaped opening,
which is the Eye of Amma. The center
diagram is the* tonnu *of the Sacrifice of
Amma. The executioner and his victim
are both represented as* Nommos, *or
fishlike embryos, and the victim is
pictured as lying quartered within the
executioner. The right-hand diagram is
the* toy *of the circumcision of the Jackal.
The Jackal was circumcized after he had
tried to devour his female twin. Her
fourfold soul became lodged in his
prepuce, which a* Nommo *is biting off.*

and also gave birth to the planets and certain stars. The Dogon's diagram
of this act clearly represents the devouring of one principle by another, for
the dismembered fragments of the victim are to be seen lying within the
corresponding parts of the executioner. The work of the Jackal here comes
to a crux. The Devourer has assimilated the Prolific and these two opposing
forces have become united in the form of a living body, and the victim
accepts his death with the words: "My head has fallen for men's salvation."

Like the story in Genesis, where Eve was created out of Adam, and like
the Greek legend of Aphrodite's birth from the severed penis of Uranus,
the Dogon tale is strongly masculine in tone, as befits a male-dominated
society. On the metaphysical level, however, we note the reversal the
Cabbalists speak of when they say that Adam is the mirror image of God:
the fact that man is born of woman is a reflection of the tenet that in heaven
woman is born of man. The primal sacrifice is staged exactly at the moment
when the original idea is transformed into its material reflection, and it is
this act that separates creatures from God and allows them to propagate
themselves. The framework of life has been set up, and the divine necessity
passed into the creation.

The creation myth of the Dogon is extremely long and complex, and it is
made to account for the formation of society as well as for the origin of
the world. Its every stage is in fact commemorated by appropriate rites, so
the metaphysical theory is never without its social practice. The mythological sacrifice, which is also commemorated by an actual one, is central to

this religion, because it marks the moment when mankind is born and family life begins. Every *ginna*, or family house, is thus a monument to this occasion.

A family is a procreative unit and the house it inhabits is at once a shrine for husband, wife, and ancestors and a nursery for the children. The marriage upon which the family is based is not the mere coupling of a man and a woman, but an agreement between the families of the bride and the groom that has to be paid for, usually by the groom's family having to find a bride price. Moreover, there are certain relations within which marriage is impermissible. The old Book of Common Prayer included in the list of women a man might not marry not only his mother and sister but his grandmother, his cousin, and his deceased wife's sister. Prohibited relationships vary from culture to culture for a variety of complicated reasons, but they are all based on a similar logic—that those who share a community of descent, commensality, or property are forbidden to marry.

These incest tabus or exogamous regulations are in one sense the continual expression of the dividing acts of creation. (In India the castes are said to be literally "born of the Sacrifice.") Every family is in some way self-enclosed and all-repellent. Only through marriage do families become related, creating obligations between them and formal ways of resolving those antagonisms that individuality cannot help but bring about. Marriage links together what is otherwise separated. It does so on both the human and the cosmological levels, for it appears that in many places a marriage was the figure by which the principles of heaven and earth could come together. Hocart saw it also as the prefigurement of kingship, the groom being the sky king and the bride the earth queen, their ritual marriage bringing fertility to the earth and to the society they represented.

When we bring mythology down to the social level, we can also see how, in fairy tales, the dragon or giant can be understood as the father of the bride, whose defeat allows the victor to carry off the princess. Such dragon fathers are notoriously jealous of their rights over their daughters, and not only because of quite natural incestuous feelings. Marrying off the daughter decreases the size of a family, which can be an economic as well as a psychological disadvantage. One way of getting around this problem is to make the groom pay bride service. Among the Tupi, the groom hunts and fishes, works in the fields, and gathers firewood for his in-laws-to-be. He has to do this under the most awkward circumstances, for he has to show his in-laws-to-be the kind of respect known as avoidance, whereas they treat him as an unwelcome stranger, even as an enemy, and give him little or none of the food he gets for them. Even after the marriage he must continue

An Aztec statuette of Tlazolteotl, goddess of sexual pleasure, known as the Eater of Filth. She is giving birth to the maize god, who, like her, was connected with penitence and sacrifice.

A door guardian from Easter Island, covered with bark cloth and with tattoo marks painted on its face to frighten off evil spirits.

to work for his in-laws. He may be allowed to move back to his own family group after his first child is born—especially if the child is a girl, because he can then promise her to his father-in-law or one of his brothers-in-law as a wife. This repays the debt he has incurred to his wife's family by taking her away from them. It is by such interlinking of credit and debt or demands and obligations, regulated by tabus, that tribal societies function.

The dragon, then, in one aspect, represents the solidarity of the family against the outside world. As we have said, the family is a small but well-marked totality limited by incest tabus based upon the society's notions of procreation and descent. We need look at only one example of such notions to see what may be at stake. The Tupi thought that children were created by the man only, the woman being merely a receptacle for his seed, the earth in which he sowed. They therefore allowed a man to marry his sister's daughter, because she had been begotten by a man of another family line and so was of a different blood. A man could not marry his brother's daughter, however, because she belonged to his own line of descent.

The Tupi believed that an incestuous union resulted not only in leprosy for the offenders, but also in barrenness for the entire world. And here we should recall two parallel myths. One is the Dogon story of the acacia-wood top that was set spinning by the incestuous Jackal and whose contents spilled into the void without germinating. The other is the theory of the circulation of the elements, which can take place only in a similar void. Now the masculine dogma that women have only a passive role in procreation implies that to be fruitful the seed of a man must circulate through the various family communities. Women are the void in which this circulation takes place. Anthropologists, describing marriage on a social rather than a biological level, view the pattern in reverse, seeing women as the elements that circulate within the social system, being exchanged by men either for other women or for wealth and service.

Whichever view we take, there is certainly a circulation to be observed. But the importance given to marriage around the world also tells us that this circulation has definite stages and stopping places, such as courtship, engagement, marriage, sexual relations, and childbirth. Each stage is marked by what Van Gennep called *passage rites,* which allow an individual to change one role for another with the help and agreement of the other members of his society. To illustrate the basic form by which we may understand these rites, Van Gennep used the image of a house. A passage rite is like knocking at the door of a house, opening the door, and stepping over the threshold. The threshold is the boundary between one state and another, and to cross it is dangerous. Many threshold rites—such as burying an animal or child under the doorstep to protect the entrance against unwanted visitors—make this clear. Once inside the house there may be doors into other rooms, and further thresholds to be passed. But he who enters a ritual edifice of this nature must always be able to come out again, so the rite of passage ends with the visiting initiate crossing the first threshold in the reverse direction.

The Dogon would be in full agreement with the logic behind this. Their family house contains an aggregation of human beings who live together either because they were born there or because they are women who have married into it. Both birth and marriage are celebrated by passage rites in order to aggregate the newcomer into the family, and at death the final rite allows a man to go out of his house forever, thus defining the space he has left empty and allowing another to occupy it in his turn.

Marriage is the crucial rite of passage, however, not only because it joins two families, or because the initiations of boys and girls into adulthood usually concludes with their marriage, but because of the paradox that marriage is thought to be a kind of death. This thought is enshrined in the Sanskrit phrase *eko bhu,* "to become one," and the Greek *teleo,* "to be perfected," both of which also mean "to die," and "to be married."

There are doubtless various reasons for this usage, ranging from the feeling that orgasm is a little death, something that makes one die with pleasure, to the metaphors used in hunting societies that express the killing of an animal and making love to a woman in the same words. But it also has a true metaphysical foundation for, as Coomaraswamy remarked, "when 'Each is Both', no relation persists and were it not for this beatitude there would be no life or gladness anywhere." And where no relation persists, as all great traditions have it, one is illuminated because one is dead to one's selfhood or ego.

"Therefore," as Genesis has it, "shall a man leave his father and his mother, and shall cleave unto his wife: and they shall be one flesh." Flesh is commonly thought of as coming from the mother. Bone comes from the father (because it is hard, and hardness, besides having a sexual connotation, implies a degree of incorruptibility, the notion of individual immortality being peculiarly masculine). But, as we shall see later, it is common to regard a house—especially a ceremonial house—as an inhabitable body made from the remains of ancestors. Just as the carpenter fells the World Tree and saws it into logs to build the house of nature, so the ancestors contribute their bones to form the posts and beams of the sacred house. *House* is thus a collective term for the family and its traditions, and these are reminders of the origins of the human world, which are continually being reinforced by succeeding marriages where two people become one flesh in their children. The Dogon state this explicitly, by making their family house the result of the primal sacrifice; the Spanish state it obliquely, by turning the noun *casa,* "a house," into the verb *casar,* "to marry."

But the collective unity of a house is by no means exclusive, and there are other relationships between families besides those of marriage. In hunting societies, for example, a man who kills game is not allowed to keep the meat to himself and his family. Among the Urubu Indians he must not even bring the dead animal into the village, but has to leave it at the outskirts to be collected by his wife. Another man cuts up the carcass, and distributes the joints among the households of the village. The hunter is allowed to have only the head and backbone—portions that may have little meat on them but which are important because in them is concentrated the life of the animal.

The practice of distributing food between families is found all over the world and must have existed in high antiquity. In one of the Vedas we find a hymn to Brahma exemplifying it:

> I am the first born of the divine essence.
> Before the gods sprang into existence, I was.
> I am the navel of immortality.
> Whoever bestows me on others—thereby keeps me to himself.
> I am FOOD. I feed on food and on its feeder. . . .
> The foolish man obtains useless food.
> I declare the truth—it will be his death,
> Because he does not feed either friend or companion.
> By keeping food to himself alone, he becomes guilty when eating it.

Some societies regard the killing of an animal as in itself a sort of crime. They may ceremoniously ask the dead animal not to feel revengeful at its death, invite it to induce others of its kind to make themselves available as food, or place its skull on a pole, both as a trophy and to do the animal honor. But this is not the guilt spoken of in the Vedic hymn. Tabus upon the way meat should be distributed do not apply to a hunter alone in the jungle, who has no compunction in eating the choicest parts of the game he kills. This is because in the jungle he is a predator, and as much a part of the jungle as an animal. This shows us that the guilt is that of greed, or parsimony toward one's neighbors, as indeed the last two lines of the hymn state explicitly. By refusing to share his food, a man cuts himself off from his fellows and brings circulation (and help in times of scarcity) to an end.

Above, a Paleolithic engraving on bone, from the Dordogne, representing the head, forelegs, and spine of a bison lying between two rows of men.
Right, a Huichol Indian painting from Mexico of a soul penned in a corral with an angry mule, as a punishment for sexual transgressions. The soul is trying to rope the mule, but is being trampled upon for its sins.

In societies so regulated we thus find two different notions of community —one based on sexuality and marriage, the other on food. The Arapesh of New Guinea keep these two communities rigorously apart, and one of their deepest tabus is that which separates the mouth from the genitals. They have an aphorism that runs:

> Your own mother
> Your own sister
> Your own pigs
> Your own yams you have piled up
> You may not eat.
> Other people's mothers
> Other people's sisters
> Other people's pigs
> Other people's yams that they have piled up
> You may eat.

We may justifiably say that what we call the incest tabu applies to food as readily as to sex. The Nuer of the Sudan know this well. They say that a man may talk about food, but not about sex, with women whom he cannot marry, but may talk about sex only with women he can marry. Here the tabus on sexual relations and eating together go in opposite directions. This is a widespread phenomenon. It is common throughout Africa and South America for married couples to eat apart from each other, and in the Sandwich Islands the sexes even eat different foods.

Both marriage and eating together, therefore, are ways in which two can become one, and because the rules for eaters and spouses do not usually overlap in tribal society, we can see that there are two notions of community present that are both complementary and at odds with each other. The tabus that set them apart, however, also act as naming devices. Anthropological literature is full of instances of clans naming themselves after animals or plants that are held to be representatives of the clan ancestor. This has generally been held to be a mark of totemism, but the term has come to have a romantic evolutionary significance and it obscures the more general principle involved—that of distinguishing human groups from each other, by different observances and by exchanging services between them. Australian clans, for example, operate on the principle that a kangaroo-man must kill kangaroos and give them to emu-men, and emu-men must return the compliment with emu flesh and eggs. Australian *intichiuma* rites are partly ways of making reparation to animals killed by the clan, but they are also expected to increase the number of the species so that the complementary clan can continue to be provisioned. The clan system also regulates marriage, so that you may only marry a girl coming from a clan that does not eat the same food as yourself. We find similar exchanges in nontotemic societies such as the Bororo of Brazil, who divide their villages into two moieties, or halves. It is the duty of the men of one moiety to bury the dead, and to marry the women, of the other.

Such complementary regulations about procreation and food point back to Blake's distinction between the Prolific and the Devouring. It seems that both share in the formation of the incest tabu. That there is a kind of incest operating on food can be seen from the Nuba of Africa, who say that if members of different clans eat or drink milk together they will become lepers, the usual punishment for incest. But incest also brings about barrenness, and the penalty for eating prohibited food, say the Nuba, is illness, starvation, and even death, which supports the argument.

It is natural for food and sex to be ruled by the same general prohibitions, if only because both have to do with matters of incorporation. Ultimately, they also have to do with blood, which in the West is proverbially still thicker than water. The belief is shared by tribal societies, which exact no penalty from a man who, by accident or intent, kills one of his own family. A murder can be paid for only by another murder or by blood money, and a family can have no interest either in reducing its numbers or in compensating itself. But payment is always exacted for a murder committed by a man outside the family. And the matter goes even further. The Bedouin state explicitly that a man should marry only into groups with

Right, an Australian Aborigine letting blood from a vein in his arm. The blood will be used for ritual purposes, such as gluing white pigment onto the skin. Far right, an Aboriginal novice being bathed in his sponsor's blood, to incorporate him into the society of men.

which his own has blood feuds. The Tupi show the other side of the same coin. They forbid a man to marry into a family linked by a blood covenant to his own, considering that such a relationship would be incestuous.

Many societies, of course, do not rely upon supernatural forces to punish incest. The Herrero subject an incestuous couple to all the consequences of a blood feud. In Australia the penalty for incest is the same as that for murder—both the man and woman are attacked with lances until their blood flows. Women are also lanced by their brothers when they come to marry. This lancing not only allows a brother to take out his incestuous feelings on his sister, but also disaffiliates the woman from the family and turns her into a stranger, whose blood it is proper to shed.

Blood is so readily taken to be the vehicle of life and the principle holding together a family that the point need not be labored. But it is of interest that if you share the same blood with a relative, it is impossible as well as unnecessary to enter into a blood covenant with him. The Dinka indeed say that one of the greatest misfortunes is to be touched by the blood of the animal that represents the clan ancestor, or by the blood of one's mother's

brother, who represents the blood line. The result is a skin disease whose Dinka name means also "incest." An equal misfortune the world around is to come into contact with the blood of a menstruating woman, which is thought to produce debility, impotence, sterility, or death. The Urubu Indians believe that a man who has touched this blood will turn yellow, which seems to be their equivalent for being leprous.

We have already seen (in Chapter 2) the link between leprosy, incest, menstruation, and the moon. It is a curious inversion that imagines the moon, the white incestuous man, as the bringer of menstruation ("the monthlies") to women, even though the course of the moon's waxing and waning has much the same period as that of a woman. There is little doubt that there is a relationship between the shedding of blood in the primal sacrifice, the castration of Mother Earth in Dogon myth, and the menstruation of women. Freud insisted at length on the infantile idea that women are castrated men—a notion that Swift expressed in a less gruesome way when he said, "Every Smatterer in Anatomy knows, that a Woman is but an introverted Man; a new Fusion and *Flatus* will turn the hollow Bottom of a Bottle into a Convexity." The psychologist Bettleheim has noted how some of his young patients in the United States wish to be circumcised, or to undergo some painful letting of blood, just when their girl friends are having their first periods. It is their way of equalizing the score. Menstruation is so surrounded by tabus even in our society that it is certainly a sacred phenomenon on a biological level, and as both Durkheim and Raglan have argued, it may well have been one of the main factors in the establishment of the incest tabu itself. They reason that a man must not come into contact with the blood of a woman, which should give life but which is mysteriously shed as if in punishment. Certainly, the manner in which women are in many societies secluded during their periods suggests that this is for the safety of men rather than for the health of the women.

"It will have blood, they say; blood will have blood!" exclaimed Macbeth —a remark that has several applications. Among the Dinka, an incestuous couple can be cleansed by the sacrifice of a ram, which while still alive is cut in half lengthwise, especial care being taken to bisect its genitals. Much the same rite was performed by Abraham (in the days when he was still called Abram) when the Lord made a covenant with him. He divided the sacrificial animals and "as it was dark, behold, a smoking furnace, and a burning lamp . . . passed between those pieces," an event implying that God had a murderous intent toward Abram and accepted the sacrifice as a means of dividing him from this anger. "Blood will have blood" is also good talion law, an eye for an eye and a tooth for a tooth. In this sense, it is the psychological equivalent of the Newtonian truth that every action has an equal and opposite reaction. Talion law is based on the same mechanism that leads man to divide his experience into black and white in order to understand it immediately, and it has special reference to the reversing of emotional states from positive to negative. Our own experience, especially as children, shows us how difficult it often is to contain one's resentment over a slight, and how, if we are unable to reply in kind, resentment turns into a sulk. Children recover fast enough from their sulks, because their sense of continuity is untrained, but it is a different matter for grown men in whom resentment and a sense of honor combine. Social rules about honor have to do with an individual's place in society, and how far others may go in asserting themselves before they may expect a comeback. Such rules make a space in which people can live and be responsible for their actions; they also create a scale of social roles which sets apart high and low.

But honor has to do with jealousy, the *phthonos* or grudging jealously of the Olympian gods, the ever-watchful eye of Nemesis, and the plain speaking of Jehovah: "for I the Lord thy God am a jealous God." As Melville makes Captain Ahab say in *Moby Dick,* echoing one of Heraclitus's aphorisms: "All visible things, man, are but as pasteboard masks. But in each event—in the living act, the undoubted deed—there, some unknown but still reasoning thing puts forth the mouldings of its features. If man will strike, strike through the mask . . . Talk not to me of blasphemy, man; I'd strike the sun if it insulted me. For could the sun do that, then I could do the other: since there is ever a sort of fair play herein, jealousy presiding over all creations."

Ahab, who chased the white whale of ultimate significance to his watery grave, is here talking about honor, or that which makes one take things personally; and because the word *person* originally meant a mask used in Greek drama, to strike through the mask is to get behind appearances where there is no polarity of opposites. The tragedy of Ahab is that he cannot do this because he is motivated by revenge, and the enormous drama whose significance is hidden by natural appearances becomes polarized against him each time he asserts himself as an individual and attempts to call its bluff.

Tragedy is the proper mode in which to see the fate of individuals caught in the game of honor, jealousy, blasphemy, and revenge, but a simpler one may be found in children's games where one player is marked by significance and tries either to keep or to lose it. The best example is Tig, a game in which one child, the "he," tries to catch and touch one of the others, the touch transmitting the sign of the chaser onto the chased. The game may once have been part of a religious rite, for in some parts of England the "he" is called Bull, Stag, or Old Horney, names that remind us of the fertility figures that Frazer examined at such length in his *Golden Bough*. But such a rite could survive only if it appealed to something spontaneous in children, the act of chasing and touching having some curious significance for them. What this significance is can be seen from Tig games called Hospital Touch, Poison Touch, Wounded Tiggy, Doctor Touch, Germ, or the Poo. In all of these the touch is plainly felt as being infectious, and in Poo the child who is burdened with the touch at the end of the day is jeered at for being smelly. The Opies, who have studied these and many other children's games, say that children who cannot pass on the touch at the end of the day seem genuinely ill at ease, and they note that the same game is played in Madagascar, where the chaser is called the leper, and where the children sensibly gather at the end of the game and say with a spit: "Poa, for it is not I who am a leper."

Tig is, in the words of one child, "an endless game," because it consists in circulating the touch. It is in fact the most primitive form of playing scapegoat, where the infection of significance can be laid to rest only by the kind of exercise with which the children of Madagascar end their game. In the Bible, of course, a scapegoat is a real goat upon which the sins of the people are ritually laid. It is driven out into the desert, according to Jewish commentaries, to placate Azazel, the demon of the wilderness and, as it were, the owner of sin. Interestingly enough, the name Azazel appears to mean "Strong one of God," and he may have been the Jackal to the Amma of the Lord, bearing the part of the divine significance that is felt to be intolerable. In any case, scapegoating (like witch-hunting) is a sophisticated game in which someone becomes "he," either through his own fault or because of the situation he is part of, and is punished accordingly unless he can find a substitute victim to represent both the fault and himself. But the other side of the coin is that jealous accumulation of significance known as honor, which a man will die to protect.

Significance and singularity both circulate in the world of men as they do in the world of nature, at times as something to be prized, at others as an illness to be got rid of. Significance is, in logical terms, an addition to the system, rather like a game of Musical Chairs where there are more players than seats. But how are we to view singularity now? In cosmology, as well as in children's games and the serious games between families that culminate in marriage, it seems that those who are marked by significance are in some way representatives of the game itself. They stand for the group. The games are thus symbolic in nature—which means that they can be made to stand for more than themselves—and significances of other kinds may be expressed by playing with the formal one that characterizes the game.

We have traveled in an apparently devious way from the self-closed and all-repellent Urizen, whose other names are death, hunger, and jealousy, through sacrifice, marriage, the incest tabu, honor, revenge, and children's games, to representation. If there is one thing that connects all of them, besides matters of circulation and the relation between a whole and its parts, it is the existence of something deathlike. The First Principle of creation is death, sacrifice entails death, marriage and death may be called by the same name, honor and revenge are ambitious manifestations of what Freud called the death instinct, Tig is a kind of infectious disease, and representations, when fixed upon an individual, often turn him into the victim of the forces he represents. It appears, then, that these various aspects of death are crucial to our understanding of how human communities cohere and celebrate their own existence, and how, because of death, fertility rites—the action of the Prolific in face of the Devourer—came into existence.

The idea of death is indissolubly linked to that of sacrifice, and it is a truism in religious thought that the shedding of blood washes away sin and gives birth to new life. There is one form of sacrifice, moreover, which has long both fascinated and appalled civilized man, in which all the threads of our argument come together. This is ritual cannibalism. A classic example is found among the Tupi of Brazil, who have been mentioned in other contexts. We have already noted that the Tupi used the same word to mean both "brother-in-law" and "enemy." This was *tobajara,* literally meaning "the face owner," he who faces you. We are reminded of the Chinese usage of the word *face* to mean "honor," and of competitions held by the Kwakiutl Indians of northwest America in which the object was to "squelch the face" of rivals.

Rivals are always in opposition, and the word originally meant "the banks of a river." This image is important; it shows that opposites of this nature exist only when there is something that sets rivals apart from each other, and for which they compete. We noticed in the last chapter that the Sanskrit for "in the beginning" is rendered by a word meaning "at the summit," and mythological thought often shifts this image onto what makes a habit of coming down from the summit, namely a river. A river is like an upsidedown tree whose roots are in the hills and which flows—or flowers— into the sea. As we have seen, it takes part in the image of the dragon or World Tree in such figures as Okeanos or Osiris. It is in fact a stream of life (an image often used by writers on natural history in the recent past), and tribal peoples who divide themselves into exogamous or ritual moieties often

Above, the Tree of Jesse, from Hondeletius' Libri de Piscibus Marinis (1554).

call them Upstream and Downstream. Whatever specific notions this stream may come to have, on a general level they are concerned with the generative process—birth, sexuality, death, food, and the turn of the seasons. If men are rivals, therefore, they must be standing on either side of this generative flow, competing with each other for the various benefits it offers.

The word *tobajara* indicates that the Tupi rivals made war and married each other's women, so that the stream that divided them was also that which brought them together. One of their proverbs ran: "the people make league of friendship with great labor and difficulty," and we have already seen how true this was in marriage, where a man had to give lengthy bride service to his in-laws. Looking at this service in terms of talion law, we can say with some justice that the payment exacted through bride service is motivated by a sense of revenge. The woman has been taken away from the family, and the sexual connection forbidden to her brothers is to be enjoyed by the husband. Revenge was one of the mainsprings of Tupi life, balanced by what early travelers in the region noted as being a sense of great harmony within the family. Indeed, the chiefs walked around their villages every morning preaching two things, affection to one's wife and revenge upon one's enemies. But revenges occurred even within a village, for a man had the right (and perhaps a duty to himself) to avenge an injury in kind, even if caused by accident and by his best friend. If he could not do so because the man was too powerful, he would roll upon the ground in frustration, eating the earth. The Tupi would even crush between their teeth the lice that bit them, blood having to be paid for by blood. Children at the breast were initiated into the system by their mothers, who would smear the blood of a dead prisoner on their nipples and make the children suck.

As revenge goes with matters of honor, it is not surprising that the Tupi made rules about it. A man might not marry until he had killed an enemy or executed a prisoner. Men could gain immortality only by valor in war (or in the wars of the spirit fought by shamans, those ecstatic medicine men who cured disease and foretold the future), or "by dying in the land of their enemies," that is, by being victims in the ritual executions that preceded cannibal feasts.

To get prisoners, a war party would be made up of men from several villages. It would set off just after the harvest, and would travel sometimes for several hundred miles to attack an enemy village. A warrior who overpowered an enemy would clap a hand on his shoulder (the *coup* of the Plains Indians is similar) and cry: "You are my prisoner." Such was the sense of honor involved in this fatal game of Tig that the prisoner would obediently allow himself to be tied up and led off.

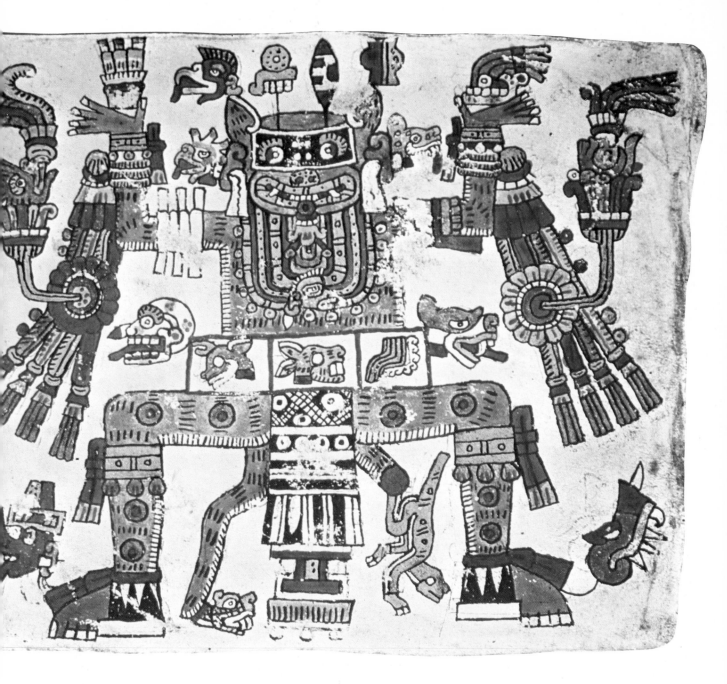

Above, an Aztec painting of the Old, Old Coyote, the Spirit of Uncertainty, with day signs on various parts of his body.

The war party would have an impromptu feast upon the bodies of those they had killed. This had nothing sacramental about it—it is the same behavior as practised by hunters, who may eat the best bits of their kill when they spend several days in the jungle. The prisoners were led back to the invaders' village, where they were met by a horde of screaming women to whom they were made to say: "I, your food, have come." Let us remember the Vedic hymn:

The foolish man obtains useless food.
I declare the truth—it will be his death,
Because he does not feed either friend or companion.

In this case, however, the prisoner can satisfy honor only by feeding his enemies with himself, and although it is his death, it turns him into a hero. But before this happens he must be turned into more than a friend; he is adopted, by giving him the wife or sister of a man who has died in war, and certain rites are carried out to make him the substitute of this dead man. As soon as this occurs he is set at liberty and leads a life that differs in one thing only from that of a young husband doing bride service—he is not treated with hostility.

The name for a prisoner was *miaussuba,* which means "the loved one." The French and Portuguese who arrived on the coast of Brazil sometimes managed to ransom some of these loved ones, and were startled to find their erstwhile captors making long journeys to visit them and enquire whether they were being treated affectionately. Some prisoners actually escaped from the Europeans and returned, not to their homes, but to the village in which they were sure to be executed, where they were welcomed with much love and joy. Prisoners in fact seldom tried to escape, not only because their deaths assured them of immortality, but because, if they did, their fellow-villagers would jeer at them for being cowards and for forgetting that their deaths would be avenged. They would have broken the cycle of revenge, and so undermined the *raison d'être* of Tupi life.

The prisoner was also loved by the unmarried women, who thought it the greatest pleasure and honor to sleep with him. But this love had a term; it ended when the time of his execution was near, when he was paraded again as a captive, jeered at by the villagers, given the opportunity to hurl clods of earth and hard fruit at his tormentors, and at last urged to escape. These rites marked the end of his adoption into the tribe and turned him back into enemy victim.

The rites leading up to his death were various and complex, their purpose being to set him apart in an even more significant way. At last he was painted, decked with feathers, surrounded by dancing women wearing

Opposite, The Close of the Silver Age *by Lucas Cranach the Elder. The men of the Silver Age were totally subject to their mothers, and were also noted for their ignorance and quarrelsomeness; hence, the painting is also known as* Jealousy.

Above, a mural from Bonampak, Central America, showing Mayan warriors, probably after a raid to obtain prisoners for sacrifice.

their menfolk's regalia, and tied by the neck in the middle of an enormous rope, the ends of which were held by two groups of men like teams in a tug-of-war. The executioner approached, vaunting his prowess. In reply the prisoner vaunted his own valor and ability, until he was clubbed to death by a stroke on the back of his head. His body was then scalded like a hog, cut up, boiled in a large pot, and eaten by everyone except the executioner, who was set apart by the fact of his having killed the loved one and retired into a small hut, his property being appropriated by those who wanted it.

These rites suggest some general conclusion about sacrifices. The Latin formula that justified sacrifice was *do ut des,* "give that you may be given to." In other words, it was an exchange between the human and the divine world. But Tupi practice shows that the exchange began between different human groups, each one thinking themselves to be human while the others were—well, brothers-in-law for a start, but since the culture hero of Tupi mythology was also a brother-in-law, gods as well. Central America gives us a famous example of such a hero in Quetzalcoatl, the stranger from over the sea who brought gifts of culture and was repaid by death. When a rival comes from a distance, bearing gifts, he can become sacred. It seems strange, then, that he must be put to death. However, there are clues to this riddle. What we know of the diffusion of culture leaves us in no doubt that cultural advances usually come from the outside and that these external contacts are often accompanied by intermarriage.

But the individual who is made a hero by this form of sacrifice occupies the same role on the ritual level as the dragon does on the mythological one. His death creates—or rather, re-creates—the organization of the world, and his blood fertilizes the earth it falls on. In the case of the Tupi it does so by ensuring that the cycle of revenge will continue—the cycle that initiates the young men who kill or execute enemies and allows them to marry, and produces the sense of honor and status that seems essential for the development of society. In this cycle the prisoner is obviously a scapegoat, but he is also a great deal more than that. He is a loved one and brings to mind those other darlings of women, Tammuz, Adonis, and Attis, the vegetation gods of the Middle East who, after their sacred marriage to the representative of the goddess, were put to death when the agricultural year came to its close. Although it is certain that the Tupi prisoner represented similar ideas about fertility, the emphasis lay in other directions, for he was the representative of what seem to be three contradictory figures or groups. First, it did not matter whether the prisoner was actually the killer of the

Above, Aztecs at a cannibal feast. They are seated in front of the dawn god, who allows the souls of sacrificial victims to join the sun. Right, a late-16th-century European illustration of the ritual execution of a sacrificial victim among the Tupinamba.

Above, a carved stone head, from Kabah, Mexico, of the Mayan god of war and sacrifice.

tribesman whose death was being avenged. As long as he came from the same group (and even, sometimes, if he came from another hostile one) he was the enemy himself. Secondly, his adoption into the village made him at one and the same time a substitute for the dead man and a representative of the village itself. Thirdly, as is shown by the fact that among one section of the Tupi the executioner took the name of his victim, the prisoner at last came to represent his killer.

The essence of tragedy seems to be that a man has to play a number of roles simultaneously, with the result that one of them comes into conflict with another. Because the roles are marked by tabus, failure to carry them out leads to death, as it did with Cuchulainn. In formal sacrifices the contradiction is forced upon the victim. We have seen that the Tupi prisoner is a kind of brother-in-law who is not only loved but also permitted to indulge in adulterous behavior. This sleeping around is enjoyed by the women and envied by the men, but puts him outside the law. This reversal of normal in-law behavior is matched by another, in which women dress up as men in a way usually forbidden. This again ultimately hinges upon the incest tabu, here to be seen as the division of labor between the sexes.

The Aztecs sacrificed prisoners in much the same manner as the Tupi, their victims also being tied to a rope that in this case represented the umbilical cord. The Aztecs held that "the hour of parturition is called the hour of death," which means that the hour of death is that of rebirth into the other world. All matters of initiation, as we shall see later, have to do with death and rebirth. Usually these are carried out only on the metaphorical level; and when they are carried out literally, it is partly because the sense of honor has become involved.

All such reversals show that death is being transformed into life. But if this transformation is to affect the fertility of the world, the victim must represent as many notions of collectivity as he can, which the Tupi prisoner did. The same pattern of thought is found among the Dinka of East Africa, who say that a sacrifice performed by a man in solitude is meaningless. The collectivity—a group, though divided by family and political allegiances, is single by virtue of its common ancestry—must participate if the sacrifice is to be effective. Among the Dinka a sacrifice first clarifies the difference between the participants, and then merges them into a common enthusiasm as the victim is ritually consecrated. The sense of duty comes to a head when the victim is killed. After this, the group falls back into its different parts, a fact given material expression by the distribution of the carcass between distinct kinds of relatives according to a traditional scheme. Though this is not a communion meal in the usual sense, because there is

Left, an Aztec statue of Coatlicue, Lady of the Serpent Skirt, mother of the war god. Her two snake heads represent the spiritual and physical aspects of sacrifice. Around her chest she wears the skin, hands, and hearts of victims. Her feet are those of the Earth Monster.

no thought that the virtue of the animal victim is passed to those who eat it, it is certainly a community meal, for each part of the society forms around its assigned portion and affirms its place within the whole by means of it.

The Tupi would have agreed with Dinka sentiment. Not only did they eat the bodies of the enemy dead on the field of battle without thinking the occasion a sacred one, but they habitually invited other villages to share the honor and guilt of the ritual execution by eating the victim. All over the world, to share a meal—or, as among the Arabs, to eat salt together—is a mark of friendship, alliance, and even communion. Christians commemorate the Last Supper in the rites of the Mass. This sharing of food, to be efficacious, must be made to represent a contradiction through which reversals can take place. Two important contradictions of this nature, which are incarnated by the prisoner, remain to be noted. The first is that in him the two communities of food and of sex, which so often help to delineate the incest tabu, come together in a strange way. Not only does he eat with his in-laws, which is against the norm, but he is loved by the women as much because he sleeps with them freely as because they may eat him. It seems that the impossible conjunction of the two communities represents a cross-fertilization of the opposites involved, which are made to bear fruit when they are separated by his death.

The second contradiction may be seen in a passage from Montaigne, who learned about the Tupi from a Frenchman with 12 years' experience of them, and had also spoken with two Morans brought over to France. "I have a song by a prisoner in which there is this passage: 'That they should come boldly, and soon, in order to dine off him; for they will then be eating their fathers and ancestors, who served as food and nourishment to his body: these muscles, this flesh and these veins, these are yours, poor fools that you are . . . savor them well, you will find in them the taste of your own flesh.' Conceit showing no sign of barbarism." The idea of eating oneself in the flesh of another is a metaphysical one of much subtlety, made possible not only through the cycle of revenge but because of those representations by which a part becomes the figure for the whole. The Mass is again an example. The congregation represents the separateness into which Adam fell when he ate the forbidden fruit. The bread and wine stand for the flesh and blood of Christ, the second Adam, who puts individuals at one with each other by feeding them with the representation of their own divine Self.

The psychological mechanism by which this can be made to work has been pointed out by the American philosopher-grammarian Kenneth Burke, who in one of his books recounts the story of a friend who had both a partiality for and a fear of heights. This showed itself in an urge, which he managed to contain, to throw himself off the tops of high buildings. One day he was viewing the city from the top of a skyscraper with his young son and found to his horror that he was contemplating pushing the child over the edge. In retrospect, he realized why he had had this urge: his love for his child had so identified him with it that "if, then, I threw him from the height, I could have had, simultaneously, both the jumping and the not jumping."

This deeply intelligent observation confirms the prime axiom of sacrifice—that the sacrificial victim represents the god it is sacrificed to. Hence the victim is usually chosen because of its symbolic likeness to the god. At the same time, the rite creates an identification between victim and sacrificer so that, like the Trinity, the identity is completed in three terms.

What happens, then, to the formula *Do ut des*? It must be that what is given to God is death, division, conflict, and sin, while what he gives back is life, unity, peace, and prosperity. This exchange can take place only through the person of a victim who represents both halves of the equation, the great reversal being effected through his death. In every such representation we are confronted with the identity of opposites, the jumping and the not jumping: one kills what one loves in order to rid oneself of the bad and retain the good.

It is thus quite logical that among the Tupi both prisoner and executioner attain immortality, because the one who has jumped carries to heaven the one who has not, an event symbolized by the executioner's seclusion after the deed. But if he is to become good, the prisoner must become bad, which, as we have seen, was what actually happened. It was by this logic that Luther made one of his more astonishing remarks: "All the prophets saw that Christ would be the greatest brigand of all, the greatest adulterer, thief, profaner of temples, blasphemer and so on: and that there would never be a greater in all the world." Blake, 400 years later, in *The Everlasting Gospel,* had similar thoughts. He questioned whether Jesus was gentle, humble, and chaste, and answered resoundingly in the negative.

Can it be, then, that God is man's enemy? There is no doubt that sacrifices are performed as much to propitiate the anger of dead men for being dead, and of gods for being only gods, as to become identified with divine principles and, by casting bread upon the waters, to receive back ten-fold. But there is no contradiction here that sacrifice cannot resolve. As Blake said, "Without Contraries is no progression." We can also remind ourselves of his remark that the Giants who give this world its life are enchained by the cunning of weak and tame minds; God may be love, as he is for Christians, or knowledge, as he was for the Gnostics, but he never ceases to be power. It is this power entering human life in the form of life and death, fertility and barrenness, honor and dishonor, that all sacrifice attempts to make a covenant with, propitiating that which has been set apart in order to make apparent that which should be brought together.

"They killed the Christ, out of anger, because he was but God," said Simone Weil. The anger of men is but weak in the face of that of God, who in the Old Testament so often repented that he had made man. But who is finally responsible for this anger in us is a question as impossible to answer as it is for the Dogon to decide which of that imbalanced pair, Amma and the Jackal, was responsible for the fatality of the creation. "I am the Lord, and there is none else. I form the light, and create darkness: I make peace, and create evil: I the Lord do all these things."

The Destruction of Sodom and Gomorrah, *by the 16th-century Flemish artist Joachim Patinir. "Then the Lord rained upon Sodom and upon Gomorrah brimstone and fire from the Lord out of Heaven; And he overthrew those cities, and all the plain, and all the inhabitants of the cities, and that which grew upon the ground." (Gen. XIX)*

Ashmolean Museum Oxford.

5 The Way of the Other Body

In the central desert of Australia stands a bare, enormous hill of stone called Ayer's Rock. It rises 1100 feet from the red plain that stretches for 100 miles around it. Over the ages, the heat of the sun has flaked great boulders off its domed surface, and the five inches of rain that fall each year—enough to sustain the grasses, shrubs, and occasional trees that grow upon the plain—have eroded it into a phantasmagoria of gullies, grooves, and caves. The runoff waters a wild garden at the base of the rock, where a number of animals have made their home.

The Pitjendara tribe live there too, for the Rock is the center of their life. The Pitjendara say that the Rock has been the same ever since the beginning, when it arose out of a vast featureless plain because of ten giant beings, whose adventures are recorded in its eroded features. These ten beings were the ancestors. All except two were in animal form, and all are now the totems of various Pitjendara groups. The poisonous Liru snake and the non-poisonous Kunia carpet snake created part of the south face of the Rock during a fight they had together; two lizard beings created the remainder of the south face. The hare-wallaby, the willy-wagtail woman, the spirit dingo, and the kingfisher woman made the northern face. A third lizard made a water hole and, together with the sand mole, much of the west face, while the southwestern face was created by the doings of the Man and the Woman.

The natural features that commemorate these beings are of many kinds. Grass growing out of cracks in the Rock represents the pubic hairs of the hare-wallaby women, and a group of large boulders the women themselves. Small rocks scattered on the ground are their children, and curiously eroded features on rock walls are their breasts. Holes high up on a cliff are the footprints made by a hare-wallaby man who danced there; small caves lower down are the nostrils through which he put his nose-bone. A long boulder is a spear-thrower. An enormous pillar of stone, separated by erosion from a cliff-side and connected to it only at top and bottom, is a ceremonial pole.

Northern view of Ayer's Rock.

A tree growing high up is an old man calling candidates to an initiation ceremony. A dead bush overhanging some water stains is the body of the tribal leader. A huge stretch of eroded guttering down a cliff-side marks the place where a sand-lizard man dug for water, a cave is a tree under which he sheltered from the sun, and the curving edge of a rock-hole is his boomerang. Another rock-hole is where a carpet-snake woman was murdered by a sand-lizard man, and long boulders are her body. A willy-wagtail woman, who was speared by a poisonous snake man because her mother had killed his brother, lies on the ground as a large cylinder of stone, two small holes marking the places where the spear entered and left her body. Nearby is a small cave containing four boulders, the children of the willy-wagtail woman, and a white mark that is their urine. These four boulders contain an inexhaustible supply of *yulanya* or spirit children. When one of them wants to be born, it leaves its stone and searches until it finds a suitable mother—a woman with large breasts and a kind face—into whose belly it crawls and becomes incarnate.

Pieced together, the stories associated with the features of the Rock make up a succinct, detailed, and enigmatic history of the Pitjendara. No doubt there was a battle once between the Liru and the Kunia snake people; no doubt a lizard man did once murder a Kunia woman. But just what kind of battle and murder they were is a nice question. For myth cannot only be taken literally; it must be taken metaphorically as well. It describes an experience truthfully, but does so in terms whose real significance you can realize only when you have had the experience. Thus a myth is like a dream; indeed, sometimes it is a dream. The Aranda Aborigines call the original time—during which the world was fashioned—*Alcheringa* or "the Dream-time" and other Aboriginal tribes use similar names. It is also not uncommon for ceremonies to be changed according to what an individual may have dreamed about them.

The ability to dream about the world and then to immortalize the dream by acting it out in company is an important element—perhaps the most important—in the creation of a mythology. Ayer's Rock is a monument to this capacity for dreaming. It is a sacred place because the intentions within the collective dream of mythology are there enacted in the form of rite, when the dream becomes actual and is taken to be history.

It is convenient to think of these mythologized collective dreams as the scenario for a drama. It is a historical drama, in that it shows men moving from their beginnings to their ends. It is historical also in the psycho-analytic sense; it says something general about the psychic development of individuals, and how biological energies of all kinds are articulated and made use of to create social persons. But the details of individual actions are submerged in the general pattern of the drama. Mythology is thus both the prototype of history and, as Malinowski insisted, a charter for social actions—a tradition that people can appeal to when they are in disagreement and against which their intentions may be judged.

Because mythology constantly makes use of natural phenomena to express human intentions—or, rather, tells its story without distinguishing between the two—the charter for action that it represents is firmly rooted in the landscape, the fauna and flora, the weather, and, if need be, the movement of the heavenly bodies. At Ayer's Rock the various clans of the Pitjendara tribe lay claim to various areas and substantiate their claims by performing rites at the significant places in their religious territory. Certain caves are used for initiation ceremonies; there the men cut the veins of their arms and let the blood spurt over the walls—an act declaring that they and the spirit of the cave are of one blood. Because one function of these initiation ceremonies is to separate young men from their mothers and incorporate them into the society of men, this ritual act also identifies the cave with the female principle. In turn, this identification enables men to celebrate the origins of the world, the ancestors, and themselves without the presence of women. That this is important not only to the Pitjendara can be seen from the widespread exclusion of women from participation in—and particularly from the direction of—religious ceremonies all over the world.

But many of the places on Ayer's Rock that have a story attached to them are inaccessible, and so cannot be the scene of such rites. They are incorporated in the rites, however, because it is the Australian Aboriginal custom to approach main ritual sites following the path of the original ancestor, and to show novices the various stages of the way and their significance. Sticks may be thrown at such and such a rock where a mythical event occurred, a salutation made at another. To find a comparison with children's games once more, this is a mixture of Tig, Sanctuary, and Follow My Leader—the leader, of course, being the ancestor who turned this landscape into his sanctuary by touching it with his adventures.

This is the equivalent of a religious procession, of following the Stations of the Cross within a church, of circumambulating a sacred site, or of going on pilgrimage. All these are ways of reenacting a piece of history so that what happened once will happen again. Dreaming is another way. Among the Wikmunkan Aborigines the rites are passed from one generation to the next only by men who have dreamed them in their entirety, the dream showing that the rites have become alive and are making their own procession into the imagination.

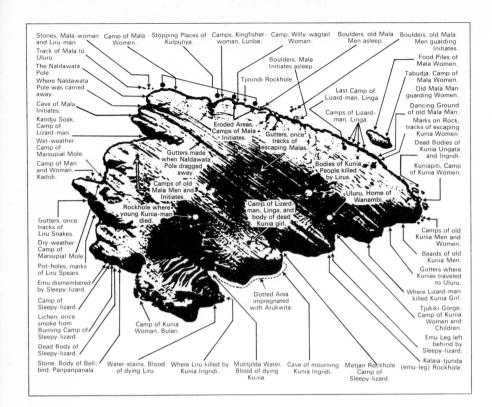

Stones, Mala-woman and Liru-man.
Track of Mala to Uluru.
The Naldawata Pole.
Where Naldawata Pole was carried away.
Cave of Mala Initiates.
Kandju Soak, Camp of Lizard-man.
Wet-weather Camp of Marsupial Mole.
Camp of Man and Woman, Kadidi.
Gutters, once tracks of Liru Snakes.
Dry-weather Camp of Marsupial Mole.
Pot-holes, marks of Liru Spears.
Emu dismembered by Sleepy-lizard.
Camp of Sleepy-lizard.
Lichen, once smoke from Burning Camp of Sleepy-lizard.
Dead Body of Sleepy-lizard.
Stone, Body of Bell-bird, Panpanpanala.

Camp of Mala Women.
Stopping Places of Kulpunya.
Camps, Kingfisher-woman, Lunba.
Boulders, Mala Initiates asleep.
Tjinindi Rockhole.
Camp, Willy-wagtail Woman.

Eroded Areas, Camps of Mala Initiates.
Gutters, once tracks of escaping Malas.
Gutters made when Naldawata Pole dragged away.
Camps of old Mala Men and Initiates.
Rockhole where young Kunia-man died.

Boulders, old Mala Men asleep.
Boulders, old Mala Men guarding Initiates.
Food Piles of Mala Women.
Tabudja, Camp of Mala Women.
Old Mala Man guarding Women.
Dancing Ground of old Mala Man.
Marks on Rock, tracks of escaping Kunia Women.
Dead Bodies of Kunia Ungata and Ingridi.
Kuniapiti, Camp of Kunia Women.

Last Camp of Lizard-man, Linga.
Camps of Lizard-man, Linga.
Bodies of Kunia People killed by Lirus.
Uluru, Home of Wanambi.
Camp of Lizard-man, Linga, and body of dead Kunia girl.

Camps of old Kunia Men and Women.
Beards of old Kunia Men.
Gutters where Kunias traveled to Uluru.
Where Lizard-man killed Kunia Girl.
Tjukiki Gorge, Camp of Kunia Women and Children.
Emu Leg left behind by Sleepy-lizard.
Kalaia-tjunda (emu-leg) Rockhole.

Camp of Kunia Woman, Bulari.
Dotted Area impregnated with Arukwita.
Water-stains, Blood of dying Liru.
Where Liru killed by Kunia Ingridi.
Mutitjilda Water, Blood of dying Kunia.
Cave of mourning Kunia Ingridi.
Metjan Rockhole Camp of Sleepy-lizard.

Left, plan of Ayer's Rock, showing totemic sites.

Right, a broken length of rock—the legs of a Kunia woman killed by a lizard man. Far right (top to bottom): the eroded walls of a cave shelter, representing the breasts of hare-wallaby women; rocks on a cave floor, representing the children of the hare-wallaby women; and grass sprouting above the shelter, representing the women's pubic hair.

Right, cave paintings from Ayer's Rock. The paintings illustrate mythic events, but have no ritual value and no particular order. Two snakes can be seen at L and O; at A is a dingo, which has left its tracks at several places; two human figures are at D and E and there are smaller ones at the bottom. At P, Q, and W are maps in which concentric circles show where mythic heroes camped; the lines joining the circles represent the heroes' tracks.

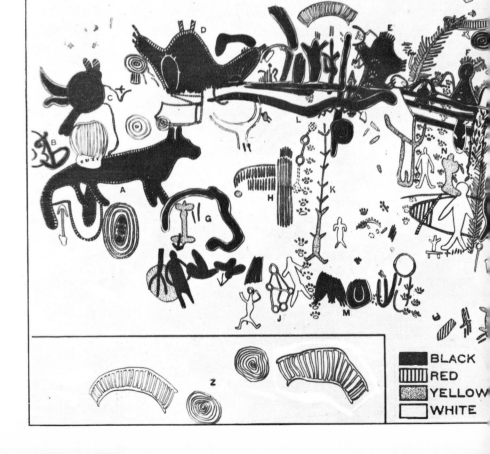

BLACK
RED
YELLOW
WHITE

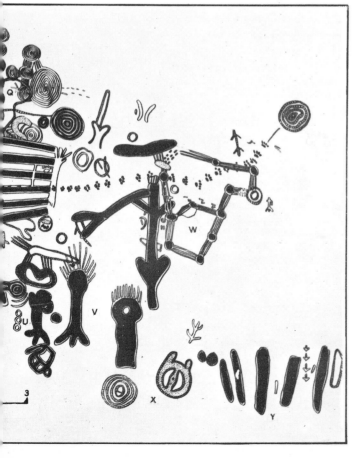

Roheim, and other psychoanalysts who have interested themselves in this subject, have argued that dreams cannot be at the origins of rites because rites are always stereotyped, because they have to be made traditional and collective. Roheim suggested that daydreams, rather than dreams, are at the root of the matter. He offered in evidence a game played by women and children of the Aranda tribe. It is called *altjira*, which is also the word for a dream. The game is an active daydream. The player, or daydreamer, strikes with a stick at leaves, which represent people, notices the way they fall, and interprets the result. A boy might say, for example: "I marry my wife, then I get another woman, the two women fight, another man steals one of them," and so on.

Only when a game has more than one player will a traditional form result— a form that is dramatic because it takes into account the disagreements as well as the agreements between the participants. The Dutch historian Huizinga, indeed, saw all formal social behavior as an outgrowth of play, and the sacred precinct as a kind of ritual playground.

Now there are boundaries and boundaries, fitting into each other like Chinese boxes: a hut within a camp, a family within a clan, a clan within a tribe, a tribe within a territory; and each boundary implies an idea of ownership. Let us here take the largest manageable boundary, the tribal territory. Australian Aborigines are nomadic, hunting game where it lives and finding food where it grows; they do not like to stay long in the same place unless something is happening to keep them there, such as a rite whose performance may take weeks or even months. When this is ended they who have come together separate and begin their wanderings again, a habit that European settlers called "walkabout."

The ancestral happenings dealt with in Aboriginal myth concern the forming of a pool here, a cave there, a tree and a rock yonder. All these places are linked together by the walkabout. Each clan in every tribe owns the part of the tribal history that happened in its own lands. The entire story of the ancestral beings is thus fragmented into innumerable pieces, many of which have disappeared with the extinction of the tribes who owned them, so that it is now probably too late for us to discover that continental walk-about of the ancestors that we should call a migration. Even within the myths of individual tribes there are curious gaps, where the ancestors are said to travel from one site to another, only the direction in which they traveled being known, at least to the initiated.

It is here that we must make the distinction between the ancestors of particular tribes or clans, who created particular totemic animals and plants and were turned into particular rocks, trees, or pools, and the Great Ancestor whose life is the life of everything. He is known throughout Australia, and indeed throughout the world, by different names, and he is commonly figured in the form of a great snake—a python whose scales gleam like the rainbow. At Ayer's Rock he exists as he has immemorially, in a rock pool that never dries up. He is many hundreds of feet in length, and his enormous head has great staring eyes, projecting teeth, and a beard. Charles Mountford, to whom we owe our knowledge of the sacred topography of the Rock, had the rock pool pointed out to him but was forbidden to go close lest the python should turn itself into a rainbow, suck the spirits from him and his guides, and dry up the water holes for miles around.

The great snake controls the waters, below the ground as well as in the clouds; its voice is the thunder; the lightning and the rain its lovemaking; the drought its sleep. In Murngin mythology, it rises out of its pool at the advent of the rains—a celestial erection provoked, in mythology, by the approach of two women, one carrying a newborn child, the other menstruating, who pollute its waters with the smell of their femininity. The snake emerges and swallows the women and sometimes its own children too. Eventually, a hero comes and makes it disgorge them. This sequence of events is the model for the cycle of rainy and dry seasons, and also for initiation rites in which the old men threaten to give the youths to the snake and let it smell their foreskins—the foreskin being used to symbolize the female because it encloses the *glans penis* like a small womb and must be cut off if a boy is to be detached emotionally from his mother.

In Northern Australia the snake is often called a crocodile. In the Purari Delta, initiation rites involve the destruction and recreation of wicker monsters that were first built to house the ancestors and now house the initiates, who are thus eaten by the monster and yet are able to emerge safely from it. Everywhere the snake is connected with rain, fertility, erection, orgasm, and spiritual powers owned by shamans and rainmakers. There is no doubt that it is phallic in nature, though it is a phallus with a real head on it that can swallow people. Because of this it naturally lives in water, which in some Australian languages is linked etymologically with the words for "milk" and "women."

Because of this, too, it can travel underground, that is, inside the earth symbolized as a woman. The Urubu Indians of Brazil tell a story of just such a giant penis that traveled underground whenever a woman summoned it to have intercourse, in the days before men had penises. An inquisitive young boy, who followed a woman to see what she did, cut its head off. Mair, the hero of the tribe, cut its body into pieces and sewed them onto the men, where they became penises. The head he kept for himself. The

Below, a rock painting of the Walbiri
tribe of Aborigines representing the
Rainbow Snake.

Opposite, a painting on hardboard of the
Snake of the Marinbata people of
Arnhem Land.

St. George, St. Martha, and the
Dragon, *painted by Paolo Uccello.*

128

giant penis is said to have been originally Mair's own, which is perhaps only another way of saying that Mair was originally nothing less than a penis. Mair was also the first victim of a cannibal execution, which had the double effect of turning him into the thunder and his executioner into an initiate. All this, together with other equivalences, shows the universality of the image of the ancestor as a snake associated with rain, with fertility, and with initiation.

Snakes hiss, but are otherwise silent. When they figure as ancestors they have to be given a voice. This is achieved by the use of a bullroarer—a flat piece of wood tied by one end to a string and whirled about the head, the wood turning rapidly and giving off an eerie and sonorous vibration. Bullroarers were until recently used by European herdsmen, to protect livestock from lightning and to scare mares away from herds of sheep that they might disturb. Their sacred nature can be seen from the belief that one in Kintyre, in Scotland, was thought to have fallen to earth from the planet Jupiter. Their ritual use is to make rain, to warn women not to approach sacred ground when rites are in progress, and to invigorate the men.

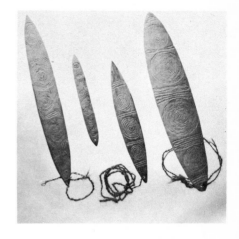

Australian Aboriginal tjurunga, with hair-string cords, used as bullroarers.

The bullroarer is an ancient instrument and has a very widespread distribution today. Tradition varies as to how it was first discovered. Some Australian Aborigines say that it was once the plaything of women, but others hold that it was given to men by the little people who were the original inhabitants of the country. That is, a bullroarer can be thought of either as a ritualized penis or as the children—"the little people"—it produces, and its voice as the creative word of the ancestor.

But no man is an ancestor until he is dead, and it is commonly held that his word becomes truly fertile only when he or his substitute is made to bellow in his death-throes. Thus the Dinka of East Africa sacrifice cattle in a particularly cruel way in order to make them bellow loud and long and infuse everything that may hear with their energy. The same logic underlies the story that Mair turned into thunder after he had been clubbed to death. Since Mair is also a serpent, and this serpent has a phallic nature, it is plain that his death is an orgasm as well as an agony, and that his thunder is fertilizing. This utterance is like the Logos in Christian theology, in being the Word of God incarnate, and we have the etymological demonstration of its nature in the close relation of the words *speak* and *sperm*, through a root meaning "to sprout," "to strew," "to scatter," "to sprinkle."

This relation between speech and semen on the one hand, and death and orgasm on the other, is one of great ritual importance, and the four terms that make up the meaning of the bullroarer must be distinguished before they can be comprehended together. Thus Freud had a point when he declared that children who indulge constantly in sexual intercourse are unlikely to learn anything. This truth is recognized in all those societies in which novices are forbidden to indulge in sex and other sensory pleasures. To be initiated means to sublimate sensual desires into an intellectual simulacrum that allows one to see the difference between speech and sperm while yet knowing their affinity. Novices are thus separated not only from their mothers, but from the immediate gratification of their desires, usually at the time when these desires make them most restless.

The walkabout of the Australian Aborigines is a symptom of this restlessness and is connected with the wanderings imposed on youths who are being initiated. They are forbidden to live with their own kin but must wander through the country, hunting as they go, singing and swinging their bullroarers as a mark of their new status. This taking to the bush is a common feature of initiations; another is the seclusion of the novices in a confined space, symbolized in the Purari Delta as a water monster who is also a house. In Haiti, the seclusion of novices being initiated into voodoo serves such a purpose: it dissociates the mind from normal preoccupations and lets it absorb the purpose of voodoo through the songs and rites that enshrine it, thus providing us with a classic example of what the ancients called "incubation." This is a process by which a sick man would sleep in the temple of Aesculapius, the god of healing (whose sign was a staff with two snakes twined around it), in order to have a dream that would reveal the cause of the disease and so allow the priests to prescribe its cure. In incubation, what is restless in the body takes form in the imagination; the effect is similar to that produced by sensory deprivation, when people shut up for a time in a room where there is nothing to see, touch, hear, or smell often end up by having vivid fantasies. The crucial difference, of course, is that such experiences are not guided by ritual forms or expectations, so that these waking dreams disturb the mind without also composing it.

To be dissociated is to be disjointed from the body of habit that links man with his fellows and his normal life, and if there is no prospect of being joined together again in a new body or new order, the result of a dissociation may be only panic and breakdown. To use van Gennep's image of a passage rite, it is like standing on the threshold of a house without knowing there is a door one can enter. In initiations, this door is the mouth of the snake, and the house is its body. Australian Aborigines can thus say: "I know Wonambi (the snake) because I have been inside his stomach"—which means that, having been dissociated from their childhood, they have been incorporated into a system of knowledge and action that gives a new sense of direction.

Aboriginal bark painting from Arnhem Land showing the Two Sisters being swallowed by the Rainbow Snake.

Such a snake, and such a system, may be termed a *copula*, meaning "that which binds together." It binds man to nature through the proper use of his natural functions, both man and nature being seen in the light of what they have in common. It works by swallowing the many so that they may become one, and then disgorging them again piecemeal and transformed. A beautiful example of this universal image can be found in the mythology of the Dogon, who say that the snake ancestor swallows his twin and regurgitates him in the form of a pattern of stones. These stones represent the main skeletal joints of the swallowed twin and also the marriage clans through which exogamy is practiced. The largest stone of all is identified with the ancestral skull and the chief. Here, as always, *dissociation* and *reincorporation* must be understood literally, as having to do with the body—dissociation having to do with dismemberment, and incorporation with the provision of joints or articulations for organized action. It is significant that in Dogon mythology the motif of becoming jointed is repeated several times—for instance, the Blacksmith, who is their demiurge, originally had only one bone in his body; it was broken into joints when he descended from heaven.

Joints are often marked in body painting and in art, and in general they serve as the model for the articulation of the soul with the body *via* the spirit. But why should joints also be associated with stone? The Australian Aboriginal's ancestor snake, like the Dogon's, vomits up stones as well as initiates. These stones are white quartz crystals, and they form one of the snake's treasures. They form also the treasure of shamans—those men who go into ecstatic trances after dissociation in order to cure disease, kill enemies by magic, foresee the future, and make rain fall. A shaman's initiation comes when he is able to look the rainbow snake full in its glaring eyes as it swallows him. He also experiences himself being cut into pieces by an elder shaman and filled with quartz crystals, after which he can ride the rainbow snake and make it rain. We find the same pattern repeated in many parts of the world. In South America, for example, shamans project crystals, flakes of stone, or pieces of wood into the psychic bodies of their adversaries in order to cause their death.

Stone, of course, is a figure for permanence; it grows, many people believe, too slowly to be seen, from earth and water. The stones vomited by the snake, however, have a different significance. They are all small ones, and the best way to understand them is to think of them as seeds containing the principle of life and power, which can continue to operate however often they produce their effects. These seeds can both make rain and appear as lightning—a notion that we can also trace in the common equation between a stone and a thunderbolt. They are prototypes of the adamantine

Aboriginal bark painting of Mamarangan, the lightning spirit, showing joint marks.

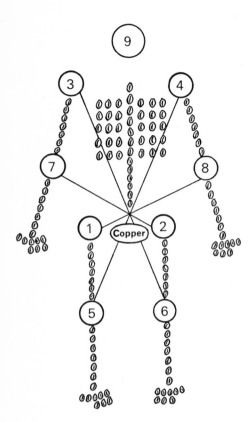

In this diagram of the Dogon social system, the skeleton is made of cowrie shells—the money of the Dogon. The joints are occupied by the eight clans, who intermarry in such a way that the two numbers involved always total 9, the number of the head and the chiefship.

nature of the spirit, like the jewels of light experienced in ecstasy or in certain drug-induced states. On the organic level, they represent the ancestral principle that creates children out of the confluence of soul and spirit, or of blood, breath, and intelligence, or of whatever symbols one uses to describe the incarnation of life in matter.

We have noted in passing that Aboriginal women feel themselves to be impregnated with the soul of a child that emerges from a stone in a cave. In other myths, these soul-children may be stored within a sacred tree or pool, or at a sacred site where one of the ancestors acted out a transformation. Animals also come from stones. In increase ceremonies, whose object is to induce the totemic animal to multiply, the central act is to rub with a small stone the rock that represents the animal, the resultant powder being the symbolic equivalent of its progeny. The same custom was once prevalent in Europe and Asia, and in Brittany barren women still go by night to rub various dolmens and standing stones in order to be given children.

But why a stone? We might again look for sexual associations, hardness being equivalent to tumescence; but this will hardly do, for stones can be inhabited by goddesses as well as gods. The hardenss of stone, however, fits in well with the process of dissociation and dismemberment. Stone is a representation of the skeleton, the part of a dead body that remains when the flesh has decayed and that is felt to be the lasting foundation of the body in all ecstasies. And, equally important, stones provide an external object to cling to whenever one passes through a crisis and stands upon the threshold of something new, in two minds as to which way to go. Thus, when a Pitjendara child is born, the father brings a sacred stone from the sacred storehouse of the ancestors, and lays it by the child as a kind of welcome. A boy does not see his stone again until his initiation. It is brought out of its hiding place once more after he has undergone ritual torments that separate him from bodily attachments and show him the power of the spirit. These torments may be circumcision, tooth evulsion, or the tearing off of the fingernails. Only when the novice has completed his course of education, and proved himself responsible and worthy, do the elders give the stone into his possession. For it is the body of his ancestor and from it emerged his soul, and that of others in the past.

The stone is called a *tjurunga*, or "other body." The word *tjurunga* also means: sacred ceremonies and sacred chants; wooden ceremonial objects, the large and the small bullroarer, sacred ground paintings, and poles; earthen mounds; and two types of ceremonial headdress. All these things may properly be called "other bodies," that is, they are concrete analogies that link man's social and natural functions together by means of images given by the outside world. They are also Platonic, because they are held to exist outside their material copies, being exemplars of that which is laid up in eternity. Thus a man can possess his other body only when he has learned the corpus of ritual action of which he is part. On his death his very own tjurunga, the object from which his soul emanated, is returned to the sacred storehouse, where it remains until it sends out a new soul to be born.

Tjurunga are made of wood as well as of stone, and although most of them are cylindrical or leaf-shaped, some are spherical, bringing to mind eggs, testes, fruit, and other ripe swellings. Cylindrical tjurunga are associated with phalluses. Leaf-shaped ones are shaped just like bullroarers, except that they have no hole for a string to be attached to them. They are of one family with the bullroarer, boomerang, and throwing stick—all of them being projections of generative power on the one hand and projectiles to cause death on the other, and by this double function showing in little the acts of the ancestor. The same paradox occurs in highly developed religions. In Hinduism, for instance, the god Shiva, whose emblem is the lingam or stone phallus, is both Creator and Destroyer.

Australian mythology in fact holds that the ancestors often used their tjurunga to kill people. Nowadays tjurunga are never used as weapons and are distinguished from them by being decorated with stereotyped patterns— concentric circles, horse-shoe shapes, straight, curved, and zigzag lines, and rows of dots. These figures represent an enormous number of different things—trees, waterholes, caves, ceremonial grounds, animals, windbreaks, ancestors, tracks, and limbs—according to the fancy of their makers. They show diagrammatically where the action of the tjurunga took place, who performed it, the tracks they left, and the parts of the body they used.

Here we must note that the signs representing tracks can also stand for limbs and for the patterns of scarification made on the skin during initation. We have thus in the tjurunga a marvelous example of how the human body is identified with the landscape through an object, the wanderings of the ancestor and his halts at sacred places being engraved upon both the body and the object. The tjurunga as the offspring of the snake is thus also a copula in which this sacred adventure can be recognized and remembered. That such a journey is the life of man can be seen in many rites in which the place names of the tribal territory are recited in due order. Dogon funeral rites, for example, end with a recitation of every journey the dead man made in life.

The idea of a journey puts us in mind of the word *way*, whose meaning can be seen in the ideogram for its Chinese equivalent, *tao*. This is made up of a sign for a head with hair on it plus that for "to go," which is itself

The Hammer of Thor—a Viking hammer set in a ring and used as an amulet—from Uppland, Sweden.

composed of two signs standing for "to step with the left foot," and "to stop." The explanation of the ideogram is that "it is the way not only for the feet to walk in but also for the thoughts to move in." In this it resembles the Latin word *sentis*, "a path," which is closely related to the verb *sentire*, meaning "to feel," "to sense," "to scent." This journey of the mind and the body thus parallels the use of the word *tjurunga* to mean rites as well as objects; it comes to mean a way of doing things. Its meaning is based on the insight that the ancestor is the forerunner who planted his footprints upon the ground so that his descendants, physical or spiritual, might know the Way, the Truth, and the Life. Buddhism also has its way, and in early carvings the Buddha is represented only by his footprints. In India today footprints are still engraved on tombs as the proper image of the person who lies within. Wherever we find footprints carved in rocks we may be sure that they mark the place where someone passed beyond, and in doing so showed the way there.

The rainbow snake is also a way. It is often painted in cave shelters, and during rites men run their hands over its long undulations from one end to another. But the way of the snake is not merely on the flat; as we have said, it also moves up and down. Trees often mark the upward movement, and so for ritual purposes, may a lopped tree or pole, decorated with bullroarers and tjurunga. A pole may also be used as a headdress by an actor masquerading as the snake. (This pole is the greatest of all tjurunga for the Aranda.

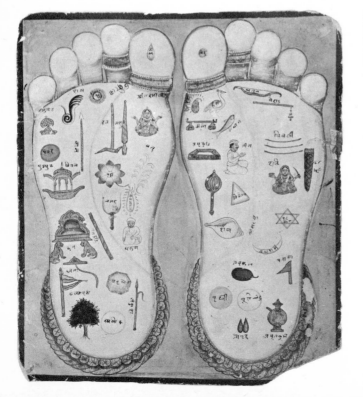

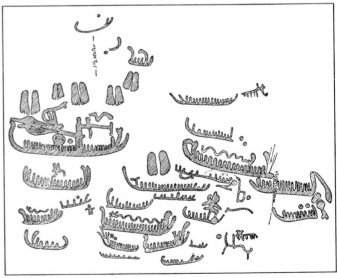

Left, the Footprints of Vishnu—an 18th-century Indian painting from Rajasthan. Above, footprints—together with ships, snakes, and other animals—on an ancient Scandinavian rock engraving in Bohuslän, Sweden. Right, the Pathway of the Dead shown as a snake on an Australian Aboriginal bark painting.

They say it has tormented them during the months of their sacred toil on the ceremonial ground, and at the end of the rites, they violently uproot it and dance with it to exhaust its strength, and at last fling it into a deep gutter.) The downward movement of the vertical is a hole in the ground, symbolizing the womb.

In Australia ceremonial sites are called "big places." Roheim, who traveled in the central desert, did not at first understand what this meant, thinking that a big place must be one where there were many people, as we mean when we say "a big city." "But lo! we arrive at Ltalaltuma, a very big place, a kind of mythological capital, and not a soul is visible. It is the same with rivers in Central Australia: the map indicates a river, your native guide may tell you that there is a river, but you see only a straight row of eucalyptus trees and two sandbanks. That is the place where the river does flow, after the rainfall." A big place is like such a river in being full of life at particular seasons, when there is game and water in abundance, so that the tribe may congregate to carry out what may be lengthy rites of fertility and order.

The serpentine way is by no means confined to primitive religions. The fact that the ancestral serpent has to be killed to release the potentialities of existence identifies it with the devil. It follows then, that the dragon-slayer is the emissary of God. Krishna defeats the hydra-headed snake who has poisoned the river Jumna; Hercules kills the Hydra, and Apollo the Python. In this last example the basic myth is overlaid by a historical event—a new

religion took over the sacred sites of a defeated people and relegated the old gods to the status of demons, who provided a political as well as a ritual purpose for the new god. Christianity is full of such reformations of belief. Their original forms are often visible in folklore, in which we find the old serpent still winding his way in and out of human life. The French folklorist Dontenville and his colleagues have recorded a number of ancient sites, such as wells, trees, and mountains, that have had chapels and churches built over them, and where the legends of the new patron saints reflect the nature of the old divinities. There are also spectacular monsters—such as the Tarasque of Tarascon, the Graouli of Metz, and the Gargouille of Rouen— that have been adopted by the Church and are still brought out processionally every year in an atmosphere of carnival.

Let us look for a moment at the Tarasque. He has two festivals—one a sober Church festival commemorating his captivity by St Martha, the other a boisterous occasion when young men splash the girls with water and the monster is wheeled about the town, clashing his toothy jaws at the spectators while his great eyes stare lugubriously. Now, Tarascon is situated just below the confluence of the Rhone with the Durance, and as a result is especially

prone to floods. The Tarasque thus appears to be the incarnation of the engulfing waters. He is awakened so that he may be placated.

The tradition is older than one might imagine. On the same spot, Hercules defeated a Gaulish monster called Tauriscus or, as Strabo spelt it, Tarusco. The word may be connected with the bull cult, which also has to do with water, and which has a long history around the Mediterranean— as we know from evidence of the cult of Minos in Crete and from bullfights in Spain today. If this is so, Hercules' monster has probably been grafted onto something still more ancient, from a religion whose underworld was called Tartarus and whose lord was placated with human sacrifices. The statue of such a carnivorous god in animal form—a kind of one-headed Cerberus with a human head under each forepaw—has in fact been discovered not far from Tarascon.

But we can perhaps go back even further than this. At Baume Latronne there is a cave overlooking the Garde River, which, like the Durance, flows into the Rhone just above Tarascon. Here there is a paleolithic painting of a serpent with what seems to be the head of a bear. (The bear cult once had a wide distribution over the Northern Hemisphere. It was practiced till recently

Right, the Tarasque of Noves—a pre-Roman Celtic carving at Bouches-du-Rhône, France. The ithyphallic monster rests its forepaws on two human heads.

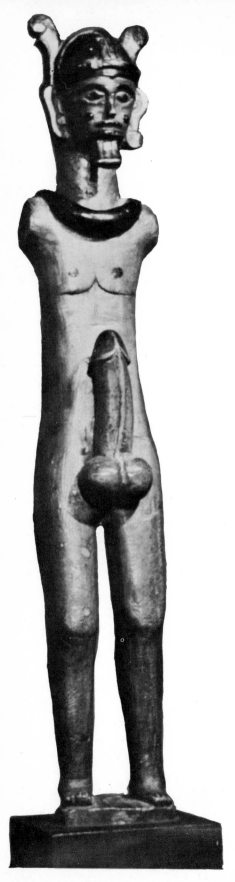

by the Ainu of Hokkaido, and prehistoric evidence of it has been discovered in Switzerland at a place called Drachenloch, "the Dragon's Hole.") The painting at Baume Latronne is the first example we know of that curious monster called a *chimera*, a compound of goat, serpent, and lion symbolizing the three seasons of the ancient year. The second example is perhaps Tiamat, the Babylonian water monster, with her serpent body and antelope head.

The Tarasque with its human head is also a chimera, as is the Gargouille, and the Graouli with its duck-bill. The Baume Latronne snake is well placed to be a representation of these water-monsters. It lives in the underworld of a cave and is—as the name Gargouille also suggests—liable to swallow up the world. As such a lord—and here we can remember what happened to Persephone or to the two Aboriginal women eaten by the rainbow snake—he lusts after women. Indeed, Gervase of Tilbury, in around A.D. 1200, wrote that these water-monsters had a special appetite for nursing mothers. They would entice them into their clutches with golden rings or cups and drag them into the depths of the river to wet-nurse dragon children.

There is a parallel in Celtic mythology, which tells of a woman who drank the water inhabited by a water-monster in the form of two worms, which she swallowed unknowingly. She became fecundated and gave birth to the great hero Conchobar, who appeared holding the worms one in each hand— a reminder of Hercules, who strangled two serpents while still in his cradle. And all this reminds one of that genial giant Gargantua—immortalized but not invented by Rabelais—who, after a gestation of two years, was born from his mother's mouth as a human-headed eel, 10 feet long—the Tarasque himself.

We must understand Gargantua and his Rabelaisian deeds as being that chimera of the imagination or, if one prefers, that genius of a people, that shapes the earth by pissing rivers and shitting hills. The hills he makes in this way, or by scraping off the earth from his feet, are typically called Gargan mounts, and he has been christianized under the unlikely name of St Gorgon. This saint is curiously connected with Rouen and its Gargouille by a custom that endured until the Second Empire. On his feast day, September 9, the girls of Rouen went to his chapel to buy small amulets called Gargans, to wear with a green ribbon and a red-headed pin. The Gargans were in the form of little men sporting great erections.

Gargouille, Gargantua, Gorgon—all words associated with *gorge*. Gargantuan's father was *Grant Gosier* or "Big Throat," his mother *Galamelle*, "the greedy one"; they were made for King Arthur by Merlin who, like Blake's Los, turned blacksmith for the occasion and—with an anvil, three hammers, a phial of Lancelot's blood, the nail parings of Guinevere, and the bones of

"The Father of the Tribe," a carved wooden figure, with huge genital organs, from Indonesia.

two whales—forged them on the summit of the highest mountain of the East. The French for "whale" is *baleine*, which puts one in mind of the name of the island where Galamelle died and was buried—Tombelaine, a corruption of the Tomb of Belisama. Belisama is the consort of Bel, the sun god, who, by another happy coincidence, has his name peppered about the environs of Rouffignac, where there is a grotto known as Gargantua's tomb. But Bel in the form of Gargantua is buried at "le mont Tombe," otherwise Mont St Michel, which rises close to Tombelaine. Mont St Michel was once called Mount Gargan and was taken over by the dragon-slaying St Michael when the country was converted.

It is no accident that Monte Gargano in Italy is also under St Michael's patronage. Here St Benedict founded a monastery on the site of a temple to Apollo, the sun god—subduing a giant, a dragon, a bull, and a horse in the process. There is a volcano nearby, fit forge for a divine blacksmith. Benedictines also took over the French Mont Gargan, and it seems that the Christian pilgrims going from one sacred hill to another spread Gargantua's legend along the way, or at least retold it in a jocular manner whenever they came across a place connected with one of his many exploits. The name *Gargantua* in fact seems to mean "the people of Gargan," who appear from chronicles to have been a particularly rowdy lot upon their journeys.

That this Gargan was ultimately called *Gorgon* also seems no accident. It seems that he is connected with that highest mountain in the East, Ararat, where there is a Mount Gorgan made of black volcanic basalt, and it was of course on Mount Ararat that Noah's Ark came to rest after the water-monster of the deep had done its worst with the Deluge. And who is the Gorgon? The Gorgon was a prophylactic mask placed wherever strangers or the uninitiated were to be warned off, and was particularly associated with hot springs, those rivers from the volcanic underworld. The head had petrifying powers, and once it had been struck off Medusa's body by Perseus it was, according to one account, buried in the center of the city of Argos, while from the trunk issued Chrysaor, a golden giant, and the winged horse Pegasus, whose hoof formed a well (in Greek, *pege*) on Mount Parnassus.

Pegasus, the winged horse, on a fourth-century B.C. stater from Corinth.

Gargantua had a famous mare, who (like her master) also pissed rivers, and her hoof marks—or the marks of other fabulous horses—are to be found imprinted on rocks and hills throughout France. Some of these horses haunt swamps, like the water-monster himself; others—such as the legendary Bayart—have the strange property of being able to lengthen their bodies to accommodate as many people as will mount them. It is fatal for anyone to do so, for this dragon-horse is the horse of death that bears the souls of the dead to the Other World, especially during the autumn when Herne the

An ancient Egyptian painting of Ammon-Ra, with four rams' heads, holding the ankh and the scepter of Set.

Hunter is on his Wild Goose Chase and his Gabriel hounds, the migrating geese, fill the sky with their foreboding cries.

The horse in India is one of the forms taken by the creator when he sacrifices himself to make the world, and it is connected with the sun, like the god Bel, as well as with water. We can apparently see its chimeric form on old British coins, or in the White Horse of Uffington, which has a dragonish head. And Herne the Hunter is also a dragon of a kind. One of his old names was Cernunnos, "the horned one." On the Gundestrup bowl he appears with a torque in one hand and a snake in the other; on Gaulish monuments he holds two snakes, each of which has a ram's head. The Dogon also know this *criocephalus*, or ram-headed serpent, for he is the image of their god Amma, who turns into a four-colored rainbow when he is not haunting the bogs and watery places at night, as a will-o'-the-wisp, a Puck, or a bog-spirit.

How are we to make sense of this chimerical medley of fact? For we are indeed dealing with a chimera—one who is like the Australian ancestor in having meteorological lusts and in fecundating women who are the ultimate cause of his downfall. It is a conflation of two apparent movements, the fall into generation and the rise into the regenerated spirit, both of which can be figured as dragons. One dragon lives in water, like the Tarasque or his female counterpart the Melusine, who every Saturday beats the waters she swims in with her tail. The other breathes fire, like the fiery steed of the sun or the treasure-guarding dragons that haunt the tombs of famous men. This fire-breathing dragon is associated with what the Greeks called the *genius* of a man—the ancestral principle embodied in his head, brain, spinal marrow, and penis. The Greeks believed that when a man died his genius took the form of a bearded serpent that haunted the *omphalos* or navel tomb where he lay buried. They worshiped the serpent in the shape of a phallic herm.

Many African peoples hold much the same view. Their herms stand in market places and contain the lower jaws of the dead men, who supervise the exchange of goods and money. In olden days, the money was in the form of cowry shells. These, according to the Dogon, were vomited up by the serpent ancestor at the same time as he disgorged the stones representing the joints of society. The Celtic equivalent of this dead but undying genius is Cernunnos, as the sack of coins he is often pictured with suggests. But the analogy goes much deeper. The largest stone vomited by the Dogon serpent was, let us remember, the representative of the head or chief, and the Celts, too, had an especial concern for heads. It is astonishing to find how many French saints are said to have been decapitated during their missionary activities and to have walked, head in hand, to say goodbye to their women-

Above, a detail from the Gundestrup bowl (probably second century A.D.) showing Cernunnos, the Horned God, holding a snake and a torque and being attended by a stag.

Right, an Etruscan vase painting of Jason and the Golden Fleece. Instead of slaying the dragon, Jason is being disgorged by it, while Athene looks on.

folk and to find their last resting place. These acts are modeled on the exploits of more ancient heroes. The Breton giant Hok Bras fell at one place and broke his head at another several miles away. Other giants are said to have had their heads turned into stone when they died. Others still are supposed to have ordered their heads to be carried to some far-off place: the British god Bran, for example, had his head carried to Tower Hill in London and it was buried there, like the Gorgon's at Argos, to be the luck of the realm.

When we piece together such legends we find a common pattern: the saint, hero, or giant dies in one place, crosses a river or marsh, and climbs a hill where his head is either buried or turned to stone. This adventure has been pictured for us in several Gaulish monuments. One at Bourges depicts a horned god flanked by two figures standing on snakes—Apollo, the sun god, on the god's right, and Mercury, conductor of souls, on his left. Now we know the Gaulish name for Apollo; he was Bolvinnus or Borvo, and, like the Gorgon, he was the patron of hot springs. And from place names in Gaul we can deduce that places sacred to Mercury were customarily sited on low ground, as befits the god of the underworld, and were

Left, 17th–19th-century herms from Nigeria. Somewhat phallic in form, and emphasizing the navel, they represent dead heads of clans. Above, a reconstructed Celtic gateway, with trophy heads set in niches, from a site near Marseilles, France.

separated by a stream or marsh, home of the great serpent itself, from the sacred places of Apollo, which were high up. Here, then, are the three beings that form our chimerical whole: the phallic god, or serpent, on one side—the lower—falls into mortality and the womb; on the other—the higher—its head becomes the solar god and the spirit rises rainbow-like into the sky.

As for the rainbow, it is a grand conception in the Bible to make it the token of God's first covenant with men, so that when the flood of his anger had abated, and the ark was grounded upon Ararat, he told Noah: "And the bow shall be in the cloud: and I will look upon it, that I may remember the everlasting covenant between God and every living creature of all flesh that is upon the earth." But it is not in the Bible that we shall learn why this jeweled bow of light is the token of such a covenant, or how it is that men try to hold God to his word by constructing a rainbow of their own in chimeric form and wheeling it about the streets of Metz or Tarascon. We can learn more from the Dogon, whose rainbow is a ram-headed snake that drinks the waters it has just poured down; or from the Bretons, whose rainbow is a serpent with a bull's head and staring eyes; or from the Australian Aborigines, in whose ceremonies the ancestral serpent is seen to give birth both to every clan's totemic animal and to human children. What comes down as cold and wet must go up when it is hot and dry. This is the covenant: that the living and the dead, the cold-blooded snake and the hot-blooded bull or ram, are joined in a great copula in which one is born where the other dies. We can see this cycle wherever the Forerunner has placed his feet or lost his head—in a cave, well, river, tree, stone, or mountain. These places, and the rites acted out at them, are what the Australian Aborigines call the *tjurunga,* or "other body," of the great ancestor, whose intangible and heavenly form is a snake cloaked in many colors and masked in a head of power. It is said that dragons have a jewel in their heads, like the great emerald, later carved into the Holy Grail, that Lucifer lost from his forehead when he fell; it is said also that there is a pot of gold waiting for us at the foot of the rainbow or, as the Hungarians put it, in its throat. These are different ways of saying the same thing—that the dragon of chaos is made to disgorge his riches in orderly and prismatic form when he dies, the instrument of his death being the thunderbolt of the Word that he utters in his agony and which seeds itself in the earth. The dragon is a boisterous fellow whose anger is joined to mercy and from whom, as Christopher Smart implied, one may well learn wisdom:

For THUNDER is the voice of God direct in verse and musick.

For LIGHTNING is a glance of the glory of God.

Dragon by Hokusai.

6 The House of God

A dragon is a tree; from its bones man builds a house, in the form of the world, in which he can be at home. This metaphorical statement epitomizes the main lines of the creation story so far. But the associations between real and imaginary things that such a metaphor makes are so numerous and diffuse that without a sense of direction it is easy to lose one's way. Consider just the words *home* and *house*. *Home*—which comes from a root meaning "to lie down in one place," "to settle"—originally meant a house with an estate, so that in various European languages variants of the word have come to mean "family," "farm," "village," or "world." But the word *house* goes in another direction, being related to *hide*—both as a verb meaning "to cover" and as a noun meaning "the skin of a beast." This relationship between *house* and *hide* is the same as that between *ceiling* and *celestial*, which are connected through a root meaning both "to cover" and "to cut off." The matter that is cut is, symbolically, the dragon's body and, literally, timber—whence the German word *zimmer*, "a room."

It was to control such profusions of verbal images that medieval scholars devised a system for the interpretation of metaphors. Dante, who inherited this scholastic tradition, advised his readers to frame what they read in four different aspects—the literal, the allegorical, the moral, and the anagogical. He gave an example of the method in the letter in which he dedicated the *Paradiso* to Can Grande della Scala. He took a passage from the Psalms: "When Israel went out of Egypt, the house of Jacob from a people of strange language; Judah was his sanctuary, and Israel his dominion." Then he explained, "If we consider the literal sense alone, the thing signified is the going out of the children of Israel from Egypt in the time of Moses; if the allegorical, our redemption through Christ; if the moral, the conversion of the soul from the grief and misery of sin to a state of grace; if the anagogical, the passage of the sanctified soul from the bondage of the world to the liberty of everlasting glory." The story we are pursuing can be interpreted by the same method. The literal sense is to be found in

The Kaaba at Mecca, encircled by pilgrims at their prayers. The photograph was taken in about 1901.

الصَّلوٰة حَوْلَ الكَعْبَة

A spirit house, with attendants—a prehistoric rock engraving found in Camonica Valley, Italy.

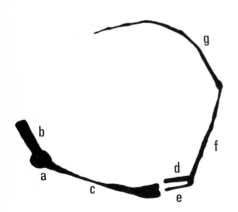

The House of Amma: a is the courtyard, b the house, c the house post ending in the hearth, d and e the life and soul of the house, f the wind, and g the water.

what we know of human behavior. The allegorical sense can then be found in myth and ritual, and on these is based the moral sense that is implied in all social relations. Finally, the anagogical sense leads one to a unifying view in which action, feeling, thought, and intuition combine or, in Dante's words, are sanctified.

This method is impractical to use in all its details, simply because its four aspects are not really separable. Dante confessed as much when he followed the passage we have just quoted with these words: "It is clear that the subject in relation to which these alternate meanings have their movement is duplex." That is, every story has an inside of meaning as well as an outside of action, and the art of story-telling lies in guiding the reader to and fro until he can understand the nature of the issue. The four aspects thus seem to be only convenient fictions; but, as we shall see, the proper function of the number four is to make things sacred.

With this in mind, we can return to the topic of the house that opened this chapter, and look at it through the eyes of the Dogon. Basically, they follow the same method as Dante. It is schematized by them as a fourfold process that defines how the imagination becomes actual. The first stage the Dogon call *bummo,* a shadow or reflection, by which they mean the first stirrings of an idea in the mind. Next comes *yala,* meaning both point and number, which fixes the idea onto the material in which it will be worked, just as one stakes out the four corners of a house before laying its foundations. Third is *tonnu,* the outline plan. Finally comes *tŏy,* the stage of constructing the house, the finished object.

The Dogon equate these four stages with the four elements. Tŏy is the earth, and by one of these paradoxes now familiar to us, its sign is said to contain those of the other three. Because of their elemental nature, the four stages of creation apply to things that make themselves as well as to things made by man. Thus the bummo of a child is its life-force, the yala the seed or semen it springs from, the tonnu its appearance as a fetus, and the tŏy is the new-born child. So it matters little whether one thinks of material things in spiritual terms or of spiritual things in material terms. A child is a house for the spirit constructed by means of an inborn plan; equally a house is a body born from the same conjunction of mind and matter that created the universe. These are the duplex aspects of the same subject, the plain fact of one forming the allegory of the other.

Allegory is important to the Dogon, who have many allegorical diagrams. The one they call "The House of Amma" is of a particular interest to us. It differs from the Egg of Amma as the tonnu does from the yala, the Egg being a geometrical abstraction conceived in terms of number, the House a pictograph. The House consists of two segments. One—the solid segment—depicts the House as a square in a round courtyard, known also as "the crossroads," from which grows a long wooden housepost ending in a hearth. The other, "liquid," segment forks from the hearthplace. The thicker end of the fork is the soul of the House, the thinner its life-force, and the two ends come together again as wind. This wind meets a bow of water that curves backward and returns to the Source.

The House of Amma is the master plan of the world. In it the four elements circulate in an orderly way between heaven and earth. The nature of this order is represented dualistically, both in the twosomes of heaven and earth and of soul and life-force, and in the fact that the House itself contains another house that is to become the world of men—or, rather, in honor of Amma's bisexuality, of men and women, who form the unit in which dualism is reflected. This human house is at the crossroads, which is also the center of the world, and the housepost grows from this center to become the axis around which the whole revolves. All this makes an interesting parallel with the Chinese diagram of the T'ai Chi, because T'ai Chi means, literally, "the Supreme Ridgepole," the wooden beam that turns the heavens into the roof of the world.

The idea that the House contains a house is like the Ionian notion that gold is ultimately made out of tiny particles of gold. In both cases the image is the product of a dualistic idea doing its best to come to the point by reflecting upon itself. The Dogon evade tautology by making the outer House a circle—the Egg—and the inner one a cube—the Seat of Amma. In the cosmogony of the Dogon this cube moves out from the center to make the eight corners of the universe.

We find the cube elsewhere in Dogon custom. In one of their villages stands a cubical stone. Underneath it are drawn the 266 signs of the Egg of Amma, arranged in concentric circles. Around the periphery are the primary bummo signs, a series of disjointed zigzags signifying air; next comes a circle of dashes, the signs of yala and fire; then four arcs, signs of tonnu and water; at the center is a circle of joined zigzags, the signs of tŏy and earth. The number 266 is the Dogon number of totality, which perhaps alludes to the ideal length in days of a human pregnancy. It is generated by the formula $4 \times 4 \times 4 \times 4 + 10$. The Babylonian equivalent was, of course, 360, which signified the number of days in the ancient calendar and of degrees in a circle, and was generated from the number six. The number six is also favored by the Dogon, apparently because it refers both to the Egg and to the House—there are six faces to a cube and six is the number of times the circumference of a circle is divisible by its radius. The

Sumerians, from whom the Babylonians got their wisdom, have a Deluge story in which Utnapishtim, their Noah, builds an ark in the form of a cube whose sides are 360 cubits long. The bringing together of a cube with a systematically round number is, then, not an accident. We must take it to mean that the cubical stone of the Dogon is a kind of ark, its contents being the four elements whose signs are drawn on the earth beneath it.

This stone is an ark because it is the foundation stone on which the earth is created. It has its own number, 60, the number of years that elapse between celebrations of the Dogon foundation ceremony. Upon it, in Dogon cosmology, the House of Amma descends as a granary and as a spinning whorl. The granary has a round base and a square top, associated with the numbers six and four respectively. It is the mirror image of its heavenly prototype, which has a square base and a round top. This reversal, in which the inside also becomes the outside, takes place during the descent,

Right, granaries in a Dogon village; they have a round floor plan and the thatched roofs are squared off.

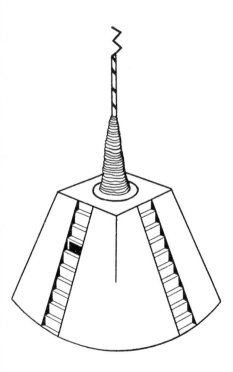

Above, Dogon diagram of the world as a spinning whorl. The interior is a granary for the eight seed crops of the Dogon; it has a square top and a round base.

which is made down the rainbow, in a sevenfold spiral. Here the spinning whorl enters the Dogon picture. Plato, in *The Republic,* used the same image as the model of the universe, which revolves upon the knees of Necessity, the spindle piercing the earth at its axis, and the rims of the whorl representing the orbits of the sun and moon, the planets, and the fixed stars.

Necessity is a goddess—for it is the woman who spins in these cultures. She spins, measures, and cuts the thread of life, which is then woven into the fabric of the body like a web to entrap souls. Her spinning whorl thus transmits the stuff of life just as does the granary, which stores the seed both for food and for next year's crops. For seed is also semen, that which you sow. The Dogon believe that everyone is born with eight seeds stored within the collarbones, four coming from the mother's line and four from the father's—a prototype, in symbolic terms, of modern genetic theory.

But seed is also number. (A similar usage has given us the word *calculus,* originally a "little stone.") And number corresponds to yala, the geometric points that fix the outlines of a drawing. In defining the Egg of Amma by the number 266 the Dogon are saying that the Egg holds the seeds of the entire creation and that the ark is a granary of number as well as life.

By moralizing upon allegory we have thus cube, ark, granary, and spinning whorl. All four belong with the dragon of the creation story, because all four contain potentiality within them and all four travel over water to reach land. That this is symbolically important is demonstrated by Utnapishtim's ark, which could not possibly have sailed upon real water. It was a boat by courtesy, to allow parallels to be drawn between the waters of birth; the birth of the sun at the end of the rainy season; the sun's nightly journey back to the east upon the stream of ocean encircling the earth; and the various connotations of a snake living in a well. Utnapishtim's ark was an image of the world. It had seven decks each divided into nine sections, rather like a ziggurat—which was also built in seven layers, each painted a different color related to one of the seven planets. (The significance of the ninefold subdivision we shall see later). Seven is traditionally the sum of three and four, usually thought of as being male and female, round and square, heavenly and earthly. It is thus both duplex and cyclic. Particularly interesting is the Dogon belief that the ark descended through 22 stations in a sevenfold spiral—22/7 is the simplest fraction to give an adequate approximation to *pi,* the ratio of the circumference of a circle to its diameter, that is, a commensuration of the curved and the straight. In any case, the traditional meaning of the number seven allows the conclusion that Utnapishtim's ark makes its descent upon the earth through the seven decks that divide it horizontally. The imagery needs only a further shake to bring to mind

A Viking stone from Sanda, Gotland, showing a boat under three solar disks. Two of the disks are wrapped by opposed serpents.

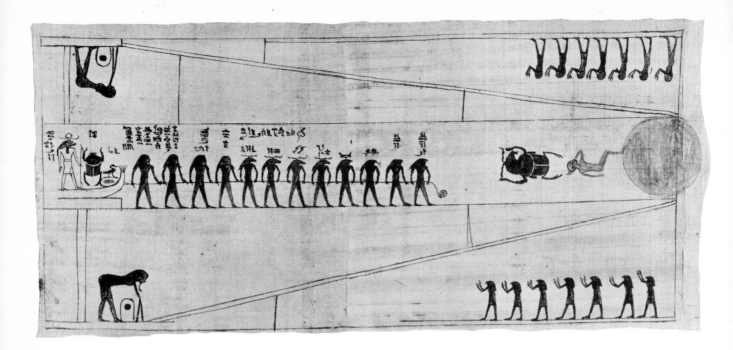

Above, the Sun Boat, drawn by 12 gods and bearing the goose, the world egg, and the scarab—from the ancient Egyptian papyrus of Queen Nejmet.

another cubical building, the Kaaba, the holy place at Mecca into whose walls has been built the black stone from heaven—in fact, a meteorite. Moslems complete their yearly pilgrimage to Mecca by circling the building seven times, three times at a run, four times walking. Legend has it that the Kaaba was originally built, in the form of a pyramid, by Seth, or by an angel in heaven; that it was destroyed by the Deluge; and that it was rebuilt by Abraham, who was led to the place of its foundation by the Divine Presence in the form of a snake. When Abraham had finished the rebuilding, the snake coiled around it, a circle about the square.

All these cubes are close cousins to the Philosopher's Stone, the perfection of matter that the alchemist sought, whose journey by water is one from heaven to earth, from vision to accomplishment. The Philosopher's Stone is an ark of the spirit that journeys in two directions, from God and to God. We can see the two-way movement in the myth of Osiris, whose coffin was launched upon the waters and washed ashore at Byblos. There its wood grew into a great tree, which was felled by the king of Byblos, who had the trunk trimmed and made into the main pillar of his palace. In esoteric interpretations of this myth, Osiris, the dead god, is equated with Ra, the sun god, the image that holds them together being the ship in which both travel, Osiris to his pyramidal tomb, Ra to his western setting.

Here the ark has truly become a ship—and as such is often used in burial rites. The Vikings, for example, buried their dead in gravemounds shaped like boats, or sent them off to sea in boats that had been set ablaze. A traditional explanation for practices of this sort is that the soul of a man is a ray

of the sun, and that when he dies the ray must be returned to its source. This may be one reason why the nave of a Greek basilica is called the *narthex*, for narthex is literally the giant fennel, the plant in whose hollow stem Prometheus hid the fire he stole from heaven.

The word *nave,* of course, means "ship," and in it the baptized make their worshipful journey to heaven. The Christian church harks back to three traditional forms, the Tabernacle, the Temple, and the ark of Noah. The Tabernacle was a moveable shrine, divided in two by a veil beyond which only the High Priest might go, containing the Ark of the Covenant; the Mercy Seat of gold, from which God might speak and on which the blood of the sacrifice was poured; and two golden cherubim. The Ark of the Covenant housed the testimony given by the Lord, which the orthodox hold to be the Two Tablets of the Law, but which scholars of the higher criticism hold to be the brazen serpent called Nehushtan, which was a prophylactic against snake bite and against the hot breath of the desert wind. Later the Ark was kept within Solomon's Temple, in the Holy of Holies, which was a cube whose sides were of 20 cubits. It was thus an ark housed within an ark, a house within the house.

Some ancient pictures of the Tabernacle show it mounted on wheels. It is then like the Merkabah or Chariot of God in Ezekiel's vision, whose wheels were made of cherubim, those chimeras that put Man, Eagle, Lion, and Bull into one image. It is similar also to the sun chariots of India, and their Bronze Age counterparts in Europe. The Ark has taken to land, perhaps because the Jews were never a seafaring people. But the connection

Left, a Maori grave in the shape of a canoe, loaded with Tainui's anchor stone. Tainui owned the canoe that brought the Maniapoto tribe to New Zealand from Polynesia. Above, a Viking grave in the form of a boat at Klintehamn, Gotland.

The Brazen Serpent of Moses, alchemically pictured in the 16th-century Livre des Figures hieroglyphiques *of Abraham le Juif.*

151

between the Temple (whose measurements must have had an esoteric significance) and the sea remains. The Temple is said to have been founded upon the threshing floor of Araunah the Jebusite. Araunah sold the floor to David, and it was later consecrated as an altar for burnt sacrifices; it now forms the center of the Dome of the Rock. It is an ancient holy place, covered with cup-marks such as often date from Paleolithic times. Legend has it that it was the plug with which the Lord stopped the entrance to the lower depths of the sea, thus putting an end to the Deluge. In its immediate neighborhood there seems to have been a cave connected with an initiatory cult commemorating Jonah, who spent three days in a whale's belly before being cast up on dry land—a story remembered by the Christ when he was asked for a sign, and which stands for his resurrection. As for Solomon's Temple, it housed a huge vessel called the Brazen Sea—a reference, apparently, to the Mesopotamian Apsu, consort of Tiamat. All in all, then, it is not too wild a notion that the Temple was founded after a sea voyage.

But the Rock was a threshing floor, which brings us back to the Dogon idea of the ark as a granary. The rainbow down which it descended is, in the Bible, the sign of the first covenant made between God and man, and this, together with other implications, some of which we have looked at, led St. Augustine to describe Noah's ark in the form of the New Covenant.

The floor of the Dome of the Rock, Jerusalem, once the threshing floor of Araunah the Jebusite.

By his exegesis the ark is "a figure of God's city here upon earth, that is, his church which is saved by wood, that is by that whereupon Christ the mediator between God and man was crucified. For the dimensions of the ark do signify man's body, in which the Saviour was prophesied to come, and did so; for the length of man's body from head to foot is six times his breadth from side to side, and ten times his thickness from back to front . . . whereupon the ark was made 300 cubits long, 50 broad, and 30 deep. And the door in the side was the wound that the soldiers' spears made in our Saviour . . . . And the ark being made all of square wood, signifies the unmoved constancy of the saints: for cast a cube or square body which way you will, it will ever stand firm." Noah's ark here becomes the model for Christ and his Church in all things.

This duplex model is the house of the Lord. The actual building is constructed according to the principle that man and the universe correspond to each other; and the rites celebrated within it are designed to turn the worshipper into a bodily temple for the Lord. As we have said, a temple is a space cut out of reality in such a way that what happens within its framework can be read as an indication of what must happen outside. The problem for its builder is to find a combination of geometrical forms that will make the correspondence between God, man, and nature visible and comprehensible. To achieve this, all classical systems have employed a harmonic scheme based on proportion—a scheme that allows dissimilar things to be put together and that can be applied to number, rhythm, music, symbolism, and indeed the growth of living things. The harmonic rules of the scheme differ according to the units held to be primary and to the methods by which the units are permuted, but not in their basic theory. During the Renaissance, when the thought of Plato and the Pythagoreans was brought to bear on the architectural relics of the ancient world, proportion and its derivative, perspective, were treated as simulacrums of the act of creation. Platonic doctrine, like the Dogon's, starts with the sphere, the original and perfect form that is both the world and a blessed god. The proportions of the Self and the Other that go to make this sphere, the symbolic properties of triangles, the mixture of inner and outer light to produce colors, and other such systematic theories propounded in the *Timaeus*, are all examples of the way a sense of proportion can build up meaning out of the bits and pieces of human experience.

There are various canons of proportion, such as the one based on the Golden Section. Related to this is the Gothic master-scheme, founded on the pentagon. In general, harmonic systems emerge from the interplay of the square and the circle. Palladio, however, who had a partiality for building

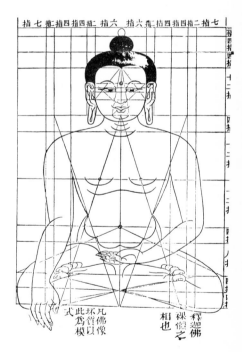

The canonical proportions for images of the Buddha according to an 18th-century Chinese drawing.

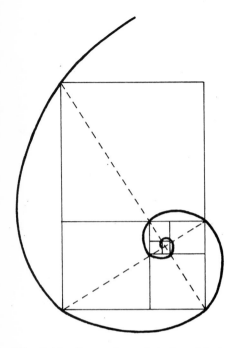

The Golden Rectangle, and the logarithmic spiral derived from it.

churches on a circular plan, explained his preference thus: the circle "is enclosed by one circumference only, in which is to be found neither beginning nor end, and the one is indistinguishable from the other; its parts correspond to each other and all of them participate in the shape of the whole; and moreover every part being equally distant from the center such a building demonstrates extremely well the unity, the infinite essence, the uniformity and justice of God." We must put alongside this the theory of Vitruvius that the proportions of a temple should reflect those of the human body; the harmony of the body being shown by the fact that a man with arms and legs extended can be made to fit within a circle or a square, the ideal figures of heaven and earth.

Vitruvian figures, of which the one by Leonardo is the most sophisticated, have a stiff look. They are laid out within their circumscribing circles and squares as if crucified upon the geometric idea in the form of a St George's or a St Andrew's cross. They are in fact strangely like the earliest Christian images of the Passion, which show Christ not suffering but victorious—as he should be, whenever the cross is given its original meaning as the sign of heaven's victory on earth, and the Passion becomes the way in which the body images the form of the world. Vitruvian figures imply the same meaning. Moreover, their astrological counterparts, which identify various parts of the body with the signs of the zodiac, harmonize man with time as well as with space, with movement as well as with fixity.

The Kogi Indians of Colombia make this same harmonic identification in a very different way. Their priests wear a headdress whose feathers, and their arrangement, form a calendar of the solar years and thus represent the cycle of time. They have a men's house with four doorways that stand for the solstices and equinoxes. It is modeled on the house that emerged in the ninth age of their world, from the World Egg created by the Mother. This house rested on the branches of a great tree that stood alone above the flood, and within it the ancestors of men danced until the waters receded and the earth appeared from below. The dance is plainly a calendrical rite and the disappearance of the flood signifies, as it does in so many mythologies, the birth of the sun and of the new time.

The ancient Tupi had a similar dance with another meaning. At certain times the Tupi, seized by a messianic impulse, made a long and dangerous pilgrimage through the lands of other tribes to the seashore. There they built a house and began to dance, for days and even weeks, in the hope that their bodies would become light enough to walk on the waters—rather than through them, like the Israelites—and so reach their promised land, which was the house of the sun beyond the horizon. Like a dead Viking in his blazing ship, they were reaching for immortality. Yet both the Kogi and the Tupi rites are basically at one with the story of Noah and his ark. The Kogi believed the world to be made maternally from the bottom upward and their dance encouraged this movement, just as elsewhere leaping dances are used to encourage the growth of crops. The Jewish and Dogon belief is the other way round, that the ark descends from God the Father in heaven. But up or down, all have it that life and death must go across the waters.

We can press the analogy further. The dance of the Kogi has the same function as Plato's spindle of Necessity, which defines the motion of the heavenly bodies and creates the music of the spheres. Plato's image, too, is that of a round dance. There is another striking example of the image in the Gnostic Acts of John. There the Christ says: "Before I am delivered up unto the Lawless Jews, who also were governed by the lawless serpent, let us sing a hymn to the Father, and so go forth to that which lieth before us. He bade us therefore make as it were a ring, holding one another's hands, and himself standing in the midst he said: Answer Amen unto me. He began, then, to sing a hymn and to say:

Glory be to thee, Father.
And we, going about in a ring, answered him: Amen.
Glory be to thee, Word: Glory be to thee, Grace. Amen
Glory be to thee, Spirit: Glory be to thee, Holy One:
Glory be to thy Glory. Amen.
We praise thee, Father; we give thanks to thee, O Light,
wherein darkness dwelleth not. Amen."

The hymn continues with the admonition: "Whoso danceth not, knoweth not what cometh to pass." The tradition was still alive in the Middle Ages. There was the Bernardine song:

Jesus the dancers' master is,
A great skill at the dance is his,
He turns to right, he turns to left,
All must follow his teaching deft.

St Basil the Great spoke of the dance of the angels, and Dante, in the *Paradiso*, described a dance of the stars—an image that Leonardo translated into a pageant in which the cosmic order became choreography. The tradition is alive today among the Mevlevi dervishes, who have a dance in which a semicircle of dancers represents the emanation of life from the godhead and another semicircle represents the return of life to its origin. Rumi, the founder of the Mevlevi order, said: "Whoever knows the power of the dance resides in the god, for he knows how love kills." The tradition

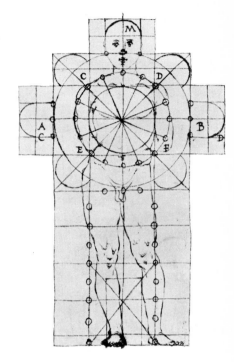

A plan for a church, drawn by Francesco di Giorgio, with the circular and rectangular schemes harmonized by the proportions of the human body.

Right, Botticelli's drawing of Beatrice and Dante in the Primum Mobile. They are viewing the dance of the stars of the nine heavens.

Below, a fifth-century B.C. terracotta figurine (from the city of Priene in Asia Minor) of Baubo, the nurse in the Eleusinian Mysteries.

is also alive in India—notably in the superb image of Shiva Nataraja, King of Dancers, who tramples upon the demon of ignorant matter to save mankind.

Christianity has lost its dances—except for relics such as the dance performed yearly before the high altar in the cathedral of Seville. Consequently it has also lost that ecstatic ordering of motion that manifests the world of the spirit in matter and which was described by an old man of Halmahera, in Indonesia, in a notable metaphor: "My dancing, my drinking, and singing weave me the mat on which my soul will sleep in the world of spirits." (It is notable not because it identifies life with movement and immortality with stillness, but because it suggests that this immortality is based on a square, the mat. Indeed, it has been thought that the idea of the square was first recognized through weaving, which consists in placing withies, or strips of reed or thread, at right angles to each other so that they hold firm.) But Christianity has at least kept, in its processions, one similar form of social mobilization. A procession is of course a pilgrimage of a kind, as can be seen from the pilgrimage ways, with Jerusalem as their center, often marked out in mosaic on the floors of old churches. These pilgrimage ways are labyrinths, like that in which Theseus killed the Minotaur. This is clearly spelled out in the church of San Michele in Pavia, where, beside the labyrinth, are the words: *Theseus intravit monstrumque biforme necavit* ("Theseus entered and killed the two-natured monster"). The

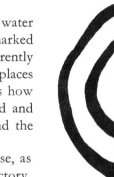

monster, as we have seen earlier, is the dragon of matter and soul, water and rainbow, and the tradition is incalculably old. Ancient mazes marked out in turf or with stones are often called after Troy, itself a word apparently meaning "to turn." These Troy mazes are connected with dances at places held to be entrances to the other world. This is why he who knows how to follow or make the diagram has his passport to the other world and resides in the god—or, rather, because the maze honors woman and the belly, the goddess.

It is difficult to make any firm equation in symbolic matters because, as the Kogi and Judaic systems have shown, symbols often seem contradictory. If we say that a goddess represents the earth, we have the Egyptians to prove the exception; if we say that the god represents the heaven and the sun, the Egyptians and the Japanese both refute us. That the earth is female, however, is a very widespread tradition, and one that we still dimly follow when speaking of nature. Nature is the Yin to God's Yang, although both are contained in the one revolving axis of necessity. It is in this light that we can take R. H. Marrett's remark: "Unlike the other animals born in the mud, only man refused to remain stuck in it. So he dances through life as though he wanted to dance till he collapsed, and thereby discovers that he is able, through his rhythmic dancing, to develop at the same time a second spirit." The mud is nature and the second spirit is man's awareness of something apparently transcending her. The same intuition can be seen in the Aborigines' habit of dancing around a pole and calling it Father.

In fact, we find poles that themselves dance, and they are connected with houses. Carl Schuster, in a beautifully ingenious piece of work, has interpreted a housepost from a Tukano Indian tribe in this manner, suggesting that it is at once the ancestor (who in so many South American mythologies emerged from a tree), the chief, and the dancer who represents the meaning of this conjunction. The figure has a mouthless head, a fourfold

Above (reading clockwise): the Troy maze as Labyrinth, on a fourth-century B.C. coin from Knossos; a Babylonian terracotta of Humbaba, Lord of the Cedar Forest and of the Fortress of the Intestines; 13th-century maze from the floor of Chartres Cathedral; and a prehistoric cave engraving of a maze monster from Italy.

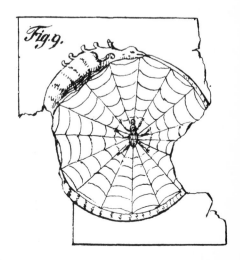

A Brahminical diagram from India of the maze as spider's web: Maya, the weaver of illusion, is within the circle of Time.

pattern centering upon a navel halfway down his zigzag backbone, testicular forms to imply his virility, and a fringe that probably stands for a grass dancing skirt such as the Tukano wear. The small rectangles within the fourfold torso, according to Schuster, show the members of a branch of the family tree, linked vertically and horizontally by blood and marriage. Since there are four such groups it seems likely that they also depict marriage clans. The figure is thus a compendium of knowledge about origins and the social order, the tribe being a man and a man having the tribe within him.

Houseposts are often erected upon a human sacrifice. (The Hidatsa of British Columbia, for example, followed the custom until recently.) The image of the ancestor thus becomes founded upon the life of one of his descendants. But the ancestor can be the house as well as the housepost. The Maori said of their ceremonial houses that the rafters were the ribs of the ancestor, the frontal boards his outstretched arms, the mask at the pinnacle his face, and the ridgepole his spine. They also carved the posts supporting the ridgepole into human figures representing the captains of the canoes in which the Maori made their journey to New Zealand. A variant of the same metaphor is used by the Dogon. They see their houses as representing a couple, not an individual. The four houseposts are the couple's arms. The woman is lying on her back, with her head at the hearth and her genitals at the inner door; the man is above her, with his skeleton forming the beams and his genitals at the outer door. And the village in which the house stands is also formally identified with the ancestor, whose head is the men's house, whose chest is the houses of the village families, and whose bisexual parts are the village altar and the oil-crushing stone.

"Jesus the dancers' master is," who stands at the center of the ring: ancestor here, housepost there, he who keeps the sky from falling, in fact the axis of the world. Astronomically, this axis points to the Pole Star, which during the Middle Ages was also called by the same name as the North Wind—*Tramontana*, literally "beyond the mountain." The mountain is that upon which the gods live, and it is called Meru by the Indians, Olympus by the Greeks, and Himinbjörg by the Norse. It is the housepost of the universe around which all things revolve.

All our analogies show that we are dealing with a very general principle of organization—one in which the ideas of movement, of container, and of things contained can be put together in different ways, according to the process being moralized upon and the allegory used to illustrate man's place in the order of things. By its means biological acts come to be framed in their social context, and social acts are given a spiritual meaning in which an anagogical sense can be made out and where things bodily and things mental come to the same point. The scholastic method of reading a text is in fact a form of initiation, during which the reader passes through the door of understanding and approaches that of experience. We can see this in the story of the Buddha, which contains many of the elements we have been considering. Coomaraswamy has insisted that this is the story not of a man, but of Man. The Buddha is "a solar deity descended from heaven to save both men and gods from all the ill that is denoted by the word mortality." His spirit entered Maya's womb in the form of a celestial elephant, and he was born at the same time as "the seven connatural ones," among whom were his future wife, his horse, and his disciple Ananda: that is, a family of eight carried in the one ark. He himself became enlightened —the title *Buddha* means "the Awakened One"—while sitting under the banyan tree, whose Naga spirit protected him during his meditation by spreading out its sevenfold hood. This has obvious reference to the practice of yoga, where the spinal cord is the tree or Mount Meru of the body, around which is coiled Kundalini, the snake-like energy of desire. In turn this imagery harks back on the one hand to the creation story and on the other to the tenet that those who are dead to the world return to their solar origin by dragon ship. According to the Vedas, suns are serpents who have sloughed off their dead and reptilian skins.

Buddhism is, as it were, the monastic version of Hinduism, from which it developed, and both religions draw on the same fund of symbolism to attain what may be called indifferently enlightenment or immortality. Now the original model for this attainment is described in the Vedas as the Fire Sacrifice. It was celebrated in memory of the Relaxation of Prajapati, who in one variant of the myth created all things by running a race with his desire and coupling with the forms of his imagination until they took life and he became as empty as death. This emptiness is his Relaxation, the exhaustion of a runner whose limbs are unstrung by fatigue. The duty of the sacrificer is to rebuild Prajapati from his parts, and to refuel his desire for himself by pouring water into fire. This fire is called *Agni,* the guest in all men's houses and also the messenger of the gods who consumes the first offerings and turns them into a sweet savour. The water is called *soma,* the deathless juice of life known to the Greeks as *nectar* ("the death overcomer") and *ambrosia* ("the not-mortal"). The fire and the water are the appetite and its food in all their symbolic guises; they are the Yang and the Yin and their circling into each other—the circling being the race that Prajapati runs with his own shadow. We know this race also from the Greeks, who performed funeral games and races in honor of the dead, who were then burned on a pyre while offerings of wine were poured into the flames. The soul of the dead

The head of a tree spirit carved on the branch of a sacred tree in India.

159

man reached back to heaven in the column of smoke the Hindus call the One-Legged Goat, which is another name for Agni and is also the fiery half of Capricorn and the Goat-Fish.

Though Prajapati scattered himself throughout creation, we find in the Vedas that he is also embodied entire within the udambara tree, when he is called Vanaspati, Lord of the Forest. Furthermore Prajapati and Agni are described as being each other's fathers. This is part of the scheme in which the four elements are contained inertly within wood until the wood is dismembered by one of its elements, fire. The mystery is reenacted every time fire is made with firesticks. The wood is first cut in two, as Prajapati divided himself into two sexes. One piece, known as the female, is laid on the ground and receives the point of the other, the male, which is twirled between the hands until friction gives birth to flame. The metaphor involved goes some way to elucidating the myths that say that fire was originally stolen: so it was, from the experience of sexual intercourse. Thus some say that fire originally lived in the vagina of an old woman, who was as dry as a stick. Others say that fire was stolen from heaven within that wooden ark the narthex, which makes the fire in its hearth the earthly counterpart of the sun in its chariot or boat. This puts the sexual and the spiritual at opposite ends of the same axis, which can be seen as either wood or smoke. The process can be summed up in four somewhat enigmatic lines from Christopher Smart's *Jubilate Agno*:

> For the Centre is the hold of the Spirit upon the matter in hand.
> For FRICTION is inevitable because the Universe is FULL of God's Works.
> For the PERPETUAL MOTION is in all the works of Almighty God . . .
> For the ASCENT of VAPOURS is the return of thanksgiving from all humid bodies.

The humid body in the Fire Sacrifice is Vanaspati, the udambara tree. This is a species of fig, like so many of the sacred trees of India and the Middle East. All these trees are nourishers, in that they have a milky sap. Some—including the udambara—are parasitic; they sprout in the branches of other trees and let down aerial roots that send up trunks of their own wherever they strike the gound, and their prodigious power of growth eventually strangles the tree that once bore them up. Like the mistletoe, which Loki the fire spirit caused to be thrown at Balder in order to kill him, the strangler fig signifies the immortal spirit that descends into the mortal body and kills it—a death that can also be called immortality. Its peculiar habit is the concrete model for the tree of heaven, which grows upside down. The *Katha Upanishad* explains: "With its roots above and its branches

Indian mandala. This support for meditation is based on a lotus—the outer circle—that symbolizes the Buddhist nature in all things. The square represents the City of the Spirit. Within it is the pyramidal World Mountain and a central lotus of spiritual powers, at whose heart is a deity.

below, stands this ancient fig-tree. That indeed is the Pure; that is Brahma. That indeed is called the not-dead (the immortal). In it all the worlds rest and no one ever goes beyond it. This, verily, is That." The same image is figured in Yggdrasil, perhaps the Horse of Ygg or Odin, and the World Tree of the Norse. This was a giant ash supporting the heavens; its roots plunged into the nether waters (except for one that reached back into the sky), serpents gnawed its roots, and an eagle perched on its branches.

As Agni is said to be the messenger of the gods, so Vanaspati is called the interpreter between heaven and earth. For it bears the sun in its branches; it rises out of the earth at dawn, reaches its full height at noon, and sinks at night. If we substitute mud for earth, the same is true of the lotus flower of the sun and of the enlightened soul. But this vertical movement must also be circular. Paralleling the way in which fire is made with firesticks, the Hindu variant of the myth says that the world was created when the gods and demons coiled a snake about the tree and pulled at it alternately, using it as a churning stick to turn the ocean of milk into butter, the solid that becomes food for the spirit—ghee, or clarified butter, being the first offering made to Agni during the Fire Sacrifice.

This churning stick then became the pillar that upholds the heavens and at the same time blocks the passage between heaven and earth. The gods placed it point down into the earth; man's duty is to unearth it and replace it point up. This is done ritually by felling the Vanaspati fig tree, whose branches trail downward, while the officiating Brahmin says: "I crush the head of the enemy of the sacrifice." The tree is then hewn into an eight-sided pillar and set up, with a cap of wood upon its head, as one of the posts to which sacrificial victims are tethered. The felling and resetting up of the tree accomplishes the reversal that allows men to ascend to God by the same path as that by which he descended to earth. The symbolism is also weighted with meteorology, for Vanaspati is King Soma himself, the dragon who is responsible for the rains. Heaven and earth are united by his thunderbolt, which is simultaneous with the felling of his tree. Accordingly, the sacrificial posts are also called thunderbolts.

The symbolic identifications then follow the pattern we have seen elsewhere. The posts are cut in lengths corresponding to the height of the sacrificer, in order that he may become the thunderbolt when wielding the sacrificial knife. In the same way the fire altar is also made according to his measure, in materials that correspond to the dismembered body of Prajapati. Indeed, throughout the description of the rite there is the closest correspondence made between Prajapati, the sacrificer, the seasons of the year, days of the month, quarters of the compass, parts of the natural world, and parts

Horus and Set turning the axis—a 12th-dynasty Egyptian stone relief.

The Whim of the Young St. Francis to Become a Soldier, *by 15th-century Italian painter Stefano di Giovanni. The cubical fortress in the air is beflagged with the emblems of the Red Cross Knight.*

163

A South Indian wood carving of Agni and his vehicle, the ram. Agni's two heads signify the inner and the outer fire.

of the altar, by whose means the substitution of god for man can take place.

This fire altar is built as a square, the form of earth, with bricks termed the children of Prajapati. At the same time it is said: "He makes the tomb of one who builds the altar after the manner of a fire altar." On this altar soma is offered to Agni, as a libation to the dead. But the dead man is alive in his children, who form themselves into an image of his body so that they may become immortals in the same way. A house is one such image and is traditionally founded upon a sacrifice; the victim's soul becomes its guardian just as that of the first man buried in a cemetery is its guardian. To take but two examples, legend has it that Oran, a monk under St Columba, either chose or was chosen to be buried alive under the monastery of Iona, and in 1871 Lord Leigh was accused of walling a man up within the foundations of a bridge at Stoneleigh in Warwickshire. We can see this as clearly in Buddhism, where a relic of the Buddha is enclosed within that burial mound called a *stupa*, whose geometrical forms are meant to symbolize the four elements and the construction of the world.

But for every death there is a birth. So the firepan of the Vedic altar is called the womb of Agni. The kindling wood is its embryo, the reed grass and hemp laid as a mat on the firepan its inner envelope, and the ghee feeding the flames its outer one. The altar itself is the navel of Agni, the place of attachment where the spirit holds the matter in hand at its center. And inside the altar is the small image of a man—made out of gold, the sun's metal—to which the breath of life passes through spaces left between the bricks of the altar. In this way the child of man, the child of fire, and the child of the sun are all equated. In much the same way the Dogon granary contains at its center four jars symbolizing the womb, the fetus, the soul, and the double nature of man and divinity, the granary being a tomb in the sense that those who lie there are not dead, but sleeping. And in both cases soma is the water of life that feeds the ascending flame of the spirit on its journeys over these waters.

These are the opposite motions of Vanaspati, interpreter of heaven and earth, who is also King Soma. Christianity knows of these two ways also. It has the two trees that stand in the Garden of Eden and are associated with the serpent. It has the two pillars Jachin and Boaz—the one green, the other dry—that stood outside the Temple of Jerusalem. Moreover, the Cross was erected on Golgotha, where Adam's skull was reputed to be buried, and which thus became the replica in reverse of the Garden. That the Christ is the resurrected form of Adam is a basic mythical truth, showing that there is but one path by which the descent and the ascent are made. These are, in the terms used by Dionysius the Areopagite, the affirmative

164

and the negative way. In his *De Mystica Theologia*, Dionysius says: "In all the other books our enditing descended from the highest things to the lowest; and, according to the quantity of descending, it spread out to a great multitude." This multitude is the branching of the tree of Brahma, whose roots are in heaven, and whose twigs spring up from the earth in the likeness of their parent. But these likenesses can not only be misleading in their multiplicity, and in the shadows they cast; they are also, in the end, inadequate to express the truth they represent. This truth can only be reached by the negative way, that of the destruction of images, which, Dionysius went on to say, "ascendeth in this book from the lowest things to the highest; and according to the measure of the ascension—the which is sometimes suddener than other—is made strait. And after all such ascension it shall be without voice, and it shall be knitted to a thing that is unspeakable." It is by this logic that the Aborigines destroyed their ritual mound, that boisterous fellow, at the end of their ceremonies; thus, too, that Prajapati as fire altar is apostrophized: "A well-built bird art thou, fly to the heavens! fly to the light—go to the Gods!"

Above, a 19th-century French woodcut of the Crucifixion. The Cross is set on the Place of the Skull.

Below, a North American Sioux Indian painting, in an oval pottery dish, of a woman in childbirth.

The place of this duplex and biformed activity is marked, both in Christianity and in the Vedas, by a cross. For the vertical motions imply those of extension and contraction as well: the center is up, the circumference down, and the round horizon bears up the sky as if it were a dome. This is the belief of the Sioux, one of whom declared: "Everything the Power of the World does is done in a circle. The sky is round, and I have heard that the earth is round like a ball, and so are all the stars. The wind, its greatest power, whirls. Birds make their nests in circles, for theirs is the same religion as ours. Our tepees were round like the nests of birds, and these were always set in a circle, the nation's hoop, a nest of many nests, where the Great Spirit meant for us to hatch our children." But in the religion of those who are settled in cities, the dome of the sky rests on pillars at the corners of the four-square earth, and this means using the cross both in symbolism and in geometry.

The cross is that image of dismemberment that quarters the world into the form of a square oriented to the cardinal points. (The word *quarter* is cousin to *quarry*, that place where cubical stones are cut for masonry.) If the circle is the form of that which has neither beginning nor end, the square is that which measures this movement, and it is on this measure that temples are founded. The traditional method is simple. A pole is planted in the ground, a rope is tied to it, and a circle marked out. The pole then becomes the gnomon of a sundial, and its shadows falling across the circle at dawn and sunset give east and west. From these points two arcs are

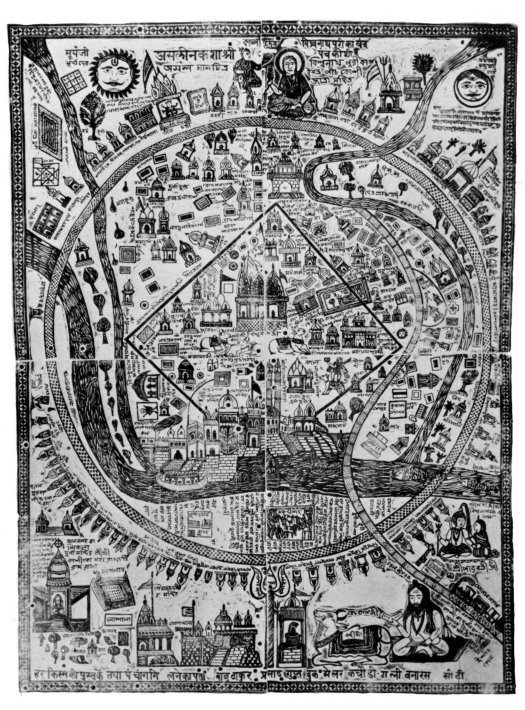

The square within the circle—an Indian
map of the holy city of Benares.

drawn to form what the Hindus call a *Fish* and Christians a *vesica piscis*, the arcs intersecting at north and south. The process is repeated at these points, and the end product is a square overlapping a circle, to mark out the temple's foundation.

The purpose of this operation is also to cleanse the earth. This is done by the plow, one of the early Christian symbols of the Cross, which breaks open the ground after the manner of the sacrificer's knife. During the Fire Sacrifice, after seeds have been scattered over the ground, the altar is plowed through five times, once through the middle from north to south, and then round its edges. The earth is then readied, or sanctified, for the crops. Romulus performed an identical rite when he founded Rome. After purifying the ground by fire, he dug a circular trench in which he and his companions placed clods of earth from their previous home. This trench was called *mundus*, the clean place, and, by extension, the world itself. It was the dwelling place of the *manes*, the spirits of the dead who were brought to their new home in the clods of earth. At the same place Romulus built a fire altar, the *prytaneum* or city hearth. About it he marked a square with the plow, and upon this square he built the walls of the city, the temple of the city divinity. Because it is sacrilegious to overstep a tabued enclosure (Remus, Romulus's brother, died for having done so) the plowing was interrupted at certain places so that doors could be built within the walls.

The Romans had a god of the enclosure, because that which divides things, be it a hedge between fields or the twilight between day and night, is sacred. Therefore every house or piece of land was marked off from its neighbor by means of a waste strip, and with termini or boundary stones at crucial places. In *The Laws*, Plato said: "Our first law should be this: Let no person touch the bounds that separate his field from that of his neighbor, for this ought to remain immovable—Let no one attempt to disturb the small stone that separates friendship from enmity, and that the landowners have bound themselves by an oath to leave in its place." Roman law was savage in defense of these stones. Any stranger who touched one was "devoted to the god," that is, immolated to expiate his sacrilege. For, just as the first altar is the body of Prajapati, so the fields are those of the individual houseowners. Prajapati literally means "Lord of Progeny," who is the same as the Genius. In ancient custom the oldest descendant of the Lord of Progeny administered the family religion, his eldest son being regarded as a debt paid to the manes to assure the priest of his own eventual immortality. It is in this way that ritual thought gave birth to the principle of land tenure. The dead were buried on the family land, originally under the floor of the house and later in the fields, where the burial mound formed the central terminus of the domain. Because of this a man's lands were inalienable and could not be sold, even for debt.

In Greece the family head was called *demspotes*, "house father" (whence our *despot*). He had absolute power over his family. He could kill his wife or sell his children into slavery. The various forms that the word *dems*, "a house," has taken make a significant pattern: we find *dome*, architecturally the house of the sky, *domain*, the territory of the house, *timber*, what it is made of, *dominus*, "lord," and *madonna*, "lady"; and what lives within the house becomes *domesticated* or tame. The taming is done by religion, through which the members of a community coinhere in the same body of worship. For this reason, in patrilineal societies, a woman abandons the gods of her fathers when she marries and becomes mistress of a house—her sacrificial rites then being to take into herself her husband's gods and to produce children in which the ancestor is reembodied. Her altars are therefore the bed and the hearth, and her function is to produce the life that her husband must turn back into spirit. And it is because a house is a temple that ideally, as Lord Raglan has pointed out, neither birth, death, nor cooking should occur within its walls, because all these are activities that need to be consecrated on their own terms, and thus defile an already sacred place. The Kogi go so far as to tabu eating and sexual intercourse within the house, but they are perfectionists and, although they worship the Mother, they would prefer women to exist only as an idea.

Of these two altars, the bed and the hearth, the hearth is symbolically the more important. Robert Graves has suggested that Hestia, the hearth goddess, was originally the heap of glowing ashes in every man's home, and that the shape of this heap was translated into stone as the *omphalos*, the navel shrine that is both burial mound and place of birth and that is ultimately connected with the Indian stupa. Traditionally the hearth is circular and associated with the number three, which is also the number of Agni in his triad of fire, thunderbolt or wind, and sun, whose totality is called Prajapati. In the Hebrides this number was remembered every time the fire was "smoored" at night; three new peats were laid in the name of the God of Life, the God of Peace, and the God of Grace, and the ashes were heaped over them in the name of the Three of Light, to keep the fire alight till next morning.

We also find this three in the triple enclosure of the Celts, which was an image of the center of the world, and which has come down to us in the form of a gameboard. Its three squares are boxed inside each other and linked by the four arms of a cross, which have been made to stand not only for the four cardinal points, and the four castes of Indo-European society, but for the four rivers of Paradise as well. But there is another way; three squared produces nine, which can geometrically be arranged by dividing a square into nine smaller ones, just as the decks of Utnapishtim's ark were compartmented. This grid gives us the simplest form of magic square. The best-known has the number five at its center and adds up to 15 horizontally, vertically, and diagonally. Less well known, but perhaps more ancient, was the square centering on 9, and adding up to 18 along its four axes. This is associated in the Chinese book of divination, the *I Ching*, with the layout of a settlement: the eight outer sections being the domains of eight families and the central one that of the lord of the settlement and of the well. As the text says: "The town may be changed, but the well cannot be changed. It neither decreases nor increases," and "The well means union." Here we may remember a passage from the *Tao Te Ching*:

> The Valley Spirit never dies.
> It is named the Mysterious Female.
> And the Doorway of the Mysterious Female
> Is the base from which Heaven and Earth sprang.
> It is there within us all the while;
> Draw upon it as you will, it never runs dry.

This doorway is the well, out of which comes the Tao, the T'ai Chi, and the Dragon.

What then is this doorway? Architecturally, it is both the cutting of earth into a square, and the quarrying of stone into a cube. We can see this in Indian tradition, where the subdivision of a square into segments reached enormous complexity. There were two main forms, even and uneven, with 32 minor types, but the most favored were those composed of 64 or 81 lesser squares. These numbers are related to specific astronomical and symbolic matters, and their multiplication in the form of $64 \times 81 \times 5$ gives the total of 25920, the number of years for a complete precession of the equinoxes. More significant for our purposes is the fact that the central square, whether formed of odd- or even-numbered sections, is consecrated to the god of the temple and over it is built a cubical chamber called the Station of Brahma, and also the Chamber of the Embryo—of the Golden Embryo, in fact, who is built into the fire altar in the figure of a golden man, and who is born by contemplation as the Jewel in the Lotus. As for the cube, this is its womb and the three-dimensional door by which it issues out of nothing to fill space and give it measure.

Like the Jewish Holy of Holies, this cube has no windows but only a door leading into the temple hall. Now, "He that entereth not by the door into the sheep fold, but climbeth in some other way, the same is a

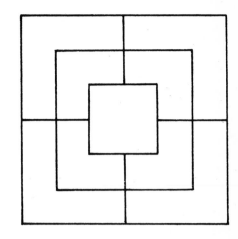

Above, the triple enclosure of the Celts. (The diagram is sometimes known also as "the Mill.")

Below, the magic square of Saturn based on the number 5, which appears in the center square.

8	1	6
3	5	7
4	9	2

thief and a robber." With the cube there is apparently no way in other than through the door. Yet here we may remember the Areopagite and the ways of affirmation and negation, where every image is a door through which the understanding may pass toward God, that "sovereign-shining darkness of wisest silence." It is because the cube is an image that it provides a way in that is not through the door itself, like those other images of arks, temples, ships, birth, death, and the new Jerusalem that is the way of the intellect alone.

What, then, is the right way? The affirmation of Christianity has built its churches on the counterpart of the square, the cross, and the exegesis of its foundation is in terms that are by now familiar to us. The Church is built in heaven of living stones, who come together in their earthly churches to praise God. Here, as St Paul said, we come "into the unity of the faith, and of the knowledge of the Son of God, unto a perfect man, unto the measure of the stature of the fulness of Christ . . . from whom the whole body fitly joined together and compacted by that which every joint supplieth, according to the effectual working in the measure of every part, maketh increase of the body unto the edifying itself in love." It was not long before the sublimity of this passage was translated into architectural doctrine, which held that a church was built in the threefold image of the Christ, of man, and of the universe. The apse could then be regarded as the head of the crucified man and, as such, as the Holy of Holies where the spirit dwelt. The altar was his heart, that center of the emotions; the transepts his arms; the nave his body and legs and the place where matter is made reasonable.

Barring the way from nave to apse was the rood screen, where Christ crucified was displayed. It had the same function as the *iconostasis* in Greek basilicas, a wall on which sacred images were placed and which prevented the body of the congregation witnessing the operation of the Mass performed by the head of the service, the priest. The object of the Mass is the transubstantiation of its elements, so that bread and wine may stand for the mystical flesh and blood. It is hidden from sight and veiled by images because truly there is nothing to be seen when it occurs, the affirmative way coming to an end where matter can no longer picture the truth.

The iconostasis has three doors, the side ones being used by the deacons, and the central or royal door by the priest when bearing things consecrated. It derives ultimately from the Greek stage, drama originally having a sacred function in which the profane could also find its place, and rites being nothing unless they are dramatic. In churches this stage has been transferred to the main entrance of the church itself, as we may see from the Royal Portal of Chartres Cathedral, where the right hand tympanum shows the

The Christ in Glory, according to the Revelation of St. John—the tympanum of the Royal Door in the west front of Chartres Cathedral.

Virgin and Child, the left-hand one the Ascension, and the central one the Christ in Glory according to the text of the Apocalypse.

The Christ in Glory is the Christ as Judge, sitting on the right hand of the Father and being the regent of the keys of heaven and hell. As tradition requires, he is surrounded by the four creatures of Ezekiel's Chariot—man, lion, eagle, and bull—which also signify his Gospels, and he is enclosed within the vesica piscis. This aptly commemorates the Christ as Fish and Fisherman, victim and sacrificer. But the tradition of the savior being a fish is more ancient than Christianity. It is found among the Sumerians, whose Oannes, half fish and half man, taught men all the arts and sciences that lead to salvation. It is still to be seen among the Dogon, in whose mythology Amma becomes a fish in order to be born as man, the fish being their symbol for the fetus. It is thus no surprise to see the vesica piscis used to denote the Incarnation, the Virgin often being pictured with it drawn upon her belly where it encloses the newly conceived child. This double usage tells us that the Judgment is for the last to be first, and that only by becoming as little children may we enter the Kingdom of Heaven.

It also tells us that the vesica piscis is properly the sign of the Mysterious Female, the doorway from which heaven and earth sprang—as it can be seen to be geometrically when it is used to open up the four cardinal points for the foundation of a temple and the purification of the earth, and iconographically when it discloses the principal mysteries of the two-natured Christ. Yet it was he who said: "I am the door: by me if any man enter in, he shall be saved." These must be opposite interpretations of the same fact, and the appearances are saved by the fundamental assumption that Man and the world can be identified in the same figure, this figure expressing the nature of what it signifies. This statement is built around a synecdoche, the grammatical term for an expression in which the part stands for the whole and the container for the contained. It is by synecdoche that the Christ is coeval with his Father on the one hand, and the door he is born from on the other. It is also by synecdoche that the operations of the sacred may be intellectually understood, even though they may not be realized in experience.

Therefore, the vesica piscis being the Virgin, who is also the Holy of Holies, the mundus, and the Ark, she comes to be what she contains by expressing it immaculately. At this royal door, which is the door of the sun, the affirmative and negative ways turn into each other. It is therefore said that when a man knocks at this door he may not answer "It is me" to the question "Who is that?" lest he separate himself from the unity. It is only those who reply "It is Thyself" who are allowed in, for then they become the door they would go through, and are the child who judges.

A 15th-century French woodcarving, "la Vierge ouvrante," in which the Passion and the Trinity are shown as the contents of the Virgin's body.

7 The Measure of Time

Once upon a time—but what is time? It moves, that is certain, but often in mysterious ways—eddying like a river, flying straight as an arrow, and going in circles when the right time comes around. It is Janus-faced—an old man at one time and a child at another. It has a forelock to be caught, as if it were a horse, and grows like a tree even when pictured as a stag, its antlers branching out like wood, as the French say. It is relative when contrasted to the eternal, though final in its effects in this world. It is the realm of Fate, accident, and opportunity, and it lies under the sway of the goddess Fortune, whom Shakespeare called a strumpet. It has duration, though some of the things it brings about happen in no time at all, and it generally speaks in riddles with a twist in their tail. To see its face naked, as Arjuna did that of Krishna, is to experience a holy terror at the multitude of independent activities it performs, which yet seem to have a common purpose. And, as Plato said, it is the motive force of the universe, and presumably the action of the First Cause itself, which can never properly be known.

How then are we to find the meaning of time? We can begin by putting ourselves into the picture and telling, or acting out, a story so that our fatality for drama corresponds in some way to the natural course of events. This gives us one kind of meaning, the once-upon-a-time of mythology that is the precedent for all custom and regularity. But time also brings about accidents, seemingly meaningless events that fall out differently from our expectations. To find what these portend involves the kind of gambling known as divination. This limits the play of chance according to a set of objects, such as a pack of cards, whose meanings are pre-determined. The moment chance is put into a context it becomes possible to make a decision about it.

Somewhere inside our experience of time, therefore, we find the idea of choice, which lets us take one branch rather than another when we come to a fork in the road. Every such fork is a temple in little, a place so marked out that we can read the will of the gods in what otherwise would seem to be a natural event, and see a personal dilemma illustrated in impersonal terms.

A 17th-century German engraving of the alchemical cycle, showing the principles of transformation.

But, whenever a coincidence of two events occurs, it is only when we know the meaning of one that we can read the import of the other. To find this meaning we have first to erect a system, by dividing our experience into characteristic parts that we can use as classifiers.

It is thus no surprise to find that our word *time* comes from a root meaning "to apportion," "to divide," and that the Latin equivalent, *tempus*, comes from a cousin root—from which our word *temple* also derives—with the special meaning of "to cut," "to mix two things together," "to temper." Hence, of course, the original association of *tempus* with the weather, because weather is the mixture of the elements that expresses the mood of the gods. When their mood is bad, tempests arise and winter comes. A change of weather thus comes to mark a season and a time of year.

External time, of course, has other rhythms, which have first to do with the day and night, whose measures are given by the sun, the moon, and the stars and to which the inner rhythms of sleeping and waking correspond. There are two major ways of reckoning the 24-hour cycle—from the moment of dusk or that of dawn. The Jews measure their days from nightfall. So did many of the Plains Indians, who measured a long journey by the number of nights it took. The Tupi tribes managed things the other way, by reckoning time from sunrise. Their journeys were counted in suns—one sun, one day; two suns, two days. For short journeys, they pointed to the part of the sky where the sun would be when they arrived at their destination, using an arm as a clock hand. For a very long journey the moon or month was the convenient measure. As for the year, the Tupi named this just as they did a day; it was one sun. The Aztecs developed this idiom; to them "one sun" could also mean a world age. Many peoples, of course, have used the stars for measurement also. The times of their rising at dusk or dawn, and sometimes their position at the zenith, provide good indicators for the seasons. The heliacal, or dawn rising, of Sirius timed the flood of the Nile, and the Pleiades seem to have been used as an indicator for the seasons right from the moment when agriculture was first practiced, and perhaps before. Unfortunately for simplicity, but very much an advantage in the development of man's intellect, these various time-keepers are not always in phase. The moon takes 27 days, 7 hours, 43 minutes, and 11.42 seconds to circle the sky and return to the same spot in relation to a fixed star, while the interval between new moons averages 29 days, 12 hours, and 44 minutes. For ease of reckoning this is often taken as 30 days, giving 12 moons in every year. But a year is 365 days long, not 360, which means that the moon cycle and the sun cycle never correspond for any length of time. The sun also has two distinct measures: the sidereal year, the time it takes to return

A medieval manuscript illumination of the conversion of St. Hubert while out hunting on a Good Friday. The stag is an emblem of time by reason of its antlers, which make yearly growth.

to the same fixed star, and the tropic year, the time between one vernal equinox and the next, which is some 20 minutes shorter than the sidereal. Such complications (and there are others even more exasperating to those wanting a quick and easy measure for time) show some of the difficulties involved in trying to put the time of the individual into step with that of the world—difficulties that have, in the interests of common sense, to be resolved by a number of compromises.

We have seen that the word *sun* can refer to a day, a year, or an age. All these terms refer to different life spans of the sun, in each of which the sun is born and dies, even though it is always the same sun. In the Metonic cycle, for example, 365 day-suns make up a year-sun and 19 year-suns complete the age. The number is chosen because over this number of years the solar and lunar cycles can be made to approximate. It is, in fact, a proportion concerning time, formed out of two different ratios, just like an architectural proportion. Because the same modulus is used on various levels, the same story is relevant to all.

Since time is a measure, it has to do with the cutting up of a duration, and, since there is a story concerning it, we must expect this cutting up to be done metaphorically as well as literally, and to find Time personified in human, animal, or vegetable shape. Let us then recall the once-upon-a-time of the Golden Age when, according to the Greeks, men ate honey, and fruit picked effortlessly from the trees, with no care for the morrow even when that morrow brought death. Among the Urubu of South America this same Golden Age was the time when the women did all the work and grown men lay in their hammocks like young children. As we have already seen, the head of the one penis the men had between them was cut off by an inquisitive lad. The length of this giant member was measured and it was cut into portions, which were sewn onto all the men of the village. Attached thus to an individual span of life, the men then had to work for their living, make love to their women, produce fire, and finally die.

The Greeks told a similar story about Cronos. Cronos cut off the penis of his father, Uranus, while he was lying at night with his wife, and pushed him up into the sky to make room for himself and his brothers and sisters. Here we may remember that, according to the Vedas, the gods imposed on man the duty of uprooting the post they had driven into the earth at the creation and of replacing it point upward to prop up the heavens. Cronos plays the same role as the sacrificer in the Fire Sacrifice, who cuts the posts he is to use according to his own measure; in one action he embodies the paternal erection in his own upright posture and steals the fire of sexual intercourse from the gods.

The Crucifixion as the source of fire. The Cross stands on the solar sign of Leo, and flames pour from Christ's wounds in this 14th-century window at Königsfelden, Switzerland.

The Origin of the Milky Way, *by
Tintoretto. The painting shows
Hercules sucking so greedily at Hera's
breast that her milk spurts into the sky.*

Cronos, however, devoured all the children his wife Rhea bore him and so was little better than his father. In the end, at the birth of her sixth child, Zeus, Rhea deceived Cronos by giving him a stone to swallow in place of the child. Zeus gave Cronos an emetic, causing him to vomit up stone and children, who were still living, and with the help of the Titans attacked his father, castrated him, and occupied his place as chief of heaven.

This was the downfall of Cronos in more ways than one. His penis fell into the sea off Cyprus, where the foam of its plunge gave birth to Aphrodite. Cronos himself fell to the bottom of the universe or to an island in the far west of Ocean, while his powers took various forms in the heavens. The stone fell at Delphi, where it was tended by men, covered in strands of wool, and used to make it rain. It must have been a meteorite, like the Black Stone of the Kaaba, and the fact that it was a substitute for Zeus tells us that it was regarded as a thunderbolt—the kind that falls out of a clear sky with an astonishing noise. We may remember the bullroarer said to have fallen on Kintyre from the planet Jupiter—the link being that the bullroarer is a rain-making instrument and rain is heavenly paternal fertilization. Since the bullroarer is the voice of the ancestor *in extremis,* and a stone marks the place of the ancestor's immortalization, we can see how proper it was to consider Delphi the center of the world and to mark it as such by a stone called the *Omphalos,* the navel shrine embodying the spirit of the ancestor in serpent form.

Cronos is traditionally assimilated to *Chronos,* Time, although the words come from different étymological roots—*Cronos* perhaps from *Coronis,* "the crow," and *Chronos* from a root meaning "to grind," "to wear out," or "to erode." As Cronos is often figured as a miller, this conflation of meaning makes sense. Moreover it is plain that if Time is the Great Reaper, the corn he cuts has to be threshed and ground. Then, too, Cronos had a Latin counterpart, Saturn, whose name probably comes from that of an Etruscan god but is traditionally supposed to come from the verb *serere,* "to sow." This folk-etymology is worth taking seriously, simply because those who took over the worship of Saturn did so. It then becomes clear that we inherit the notion of time as both reaper and sower, which makes Cronos the god of the harvest.

Here we have come upon another measure for the year—one that has to do with the growth of plants. Some peoples use a calendar that runs only from the planting season to the harvest, the rest of the solar year being unreck-oned. The rites that these peoples perform—at first to encourage the growth of plants, and at harvest time to exorcise the growth spirit that might other-wise poison the eaters of the crop—make it plain that the year spirit is the

The Omphalos at Delphi, which marks the center of the world.

Saturn as Moloch, and his alchemical transformation, from the 17th-century French Mutus Liber.

crop spirit. Society Islanders talk about the breadfruit season and Melanesians the yam season, using the terms very much as we use the word *year*. The same holds good for animals, especially those sacrificed at set times throughout the year. Domestic animals in particular tend to be called after a word meaning a year, or an age. *Wether*, for example, means "a yearling." The Greek *khimaira* is a nanny goat that has had its first kids. *Khimaira* comes from Greek *kheima,* meaning "winter," and gives us that year animal, the chimera—a monster made up from the parts of several animals standing for the seasons of the year, beginning with winter.

In many parts of the world the year is divided into only two seasons, the dry and the wet, or the hot and the cold. Where this is so, it has a marked effect on the social organization and ritual of the people. The Kwakiutl of British Columbia, for example, split into individual families during the summer and go off to fish and hunt. When winter comes they return to their villages to perform the winter festival, for then they have enough food to spare for the serious purposes of being a tribe, initiating their young men, and serving the Powers. The Australian Aborigines, as we have seen, also hold their long festivals when food is plentiful. Times of hunger and satiety go with the seasons, and in themselves are no bad timekeepers.

In Rome the feast of Saturn took place on December 17 and 18, and that of his wife Ops (the equivalent of Rhea) on December 19 and 20; the popular celebrations lasted for another three days, the whole being known as the Saturnalia. This was the time of plenty at the year's end, when slaves and servants sat at the same table as their masters, who indeed often served them. During the Middle Ages the Saturnalia had a second lease of life as the Feast of Unreason, when what to our eyes look like blasphemous rites were performed in the churches—a boy bishop officiating, the celebrants braying like asses, and the host in the form of blood puddings or sausages. Whatever the origin of the Feast of Unreason, it signaled the end of one age and the beginning of another, with the old one being blamed for its shortcomings in typical scapegoat style, and with typical reversals—high becoming low, and last first.

It was of course Cronos who became low after being high, rather than his father Uranus, who is now occupied in being the heavens; and it was the stone, the last thing swallowed by Cronos, that was the first to be regurgitated. Interestingly, too, the Saturnian age is the golden one, although the metal traditionally associated with Saturn is lead. This paradox gives us the mythological frame for the alchemical transmutation of metals, a process that often uses for its motto the remark that the stone the builders reject finally becomes the head of the corner. All such reversals occur at the major turning point of the year, the winter solstice, which falls at the beginning of the zodiacal sign of Capricorn, the original chimera itself. There are two other significant dates at this time: New Year's Day, which starts the month of January, and Christmas. January is named after the two-faced god Janus, who looks into both the past and the future and is the doorkeeper of the solar year. Christmas, whose present date was fixed only in the fourth century, signalizes the birth of the Christ child as the Victorious Sun from the Virgin Mary. Capricorn is in fact one of the two "gates" or solstices of the sun. It is the Gate of the Gods, when the fiery spirit ascends to the skies.

Capricorn is the winter sign of the sun, or the house in which it hibernates. In Europe, two animals in particular were noted for sleeping away the winter. They were the snake and the bear, which we have seen chimerically joined together in the Paleolithic drawing near Tarascon. Bears were traditionally supposed to retreat into their caves at the winter solstice and to emerge six weeks later at Candlemas, on February 2. In the United States that diminutive substitute for the bear, the ground hog, is still used in folk weather prophecy; if it sees its own shadow on Candlemas day, it retires underground for another six weeks, during which winter will still reign.

Christianity has always done its best to edit pagan festivals and to bring them in line with the Christian calendar. It is no surprise, therefore, to find that Candlemas—which is still observed in Catholic countries—falls 40 days after Christmas, since 40 days is a sacred period in both the Testaments, being first noted as the length of Noah's Flood. Greek myth makes a similar

Above, Saturn and his sickle falling from heaven—from Albumasar's 14th-century Introductio in Astrologium.

Above, Janus-head carving from a Celtic sanctuary at Roquepertuse, France.

association with the turn of the year and the Flood in the story of Lykaon. Lykaon served up his grandson Arkas upon a stone called *Trapezium*, or little table, for Zeus to eat, and was punished for his pains by being turned into a wolf, whence his name. Arkas survived this episode and later, when hunting in the woods, came across his mother, Kallisto, disguised as a bear. He pursued her to the sanctuary of Zeus on Mount Lykaon. It was the law that all who entered the precincts must be put to death, and that nothing might cast a shadow there—which comes to the same thing. (We may understand from this that the ground hog who casts a shadow on Candlemas is still in his old body, and that the year has not yet been renewed.) In any case, Zeus removed Kallisto and Arkas to the heavens as the constellation of Ursa Major and the star Arcturus, in Boötes. At the same time he sent a great flood to destroy mankind, whose habits revolted him. The only survivors were Deucalion and Pyrrha, who built an ark on the advice of Deucalion's father, Prometheus.

The Greeks called the Great and Little Bears the Hands of Rhea. In Ursa Major the two stars alpha and beta are the pointers of the Pole Star, which in turn is the tip of Ursa Minor's tail. Rhea's hands are therefore engaged in twirling the invisible spindle that pierces the earth from North to South and accounts for the revolution of the heavenly bodies. The same idea is to be found in other names for the seven principal stars of Ursa Major, Charles's Wain and the Chariot. The oxen that, urged on by Boötes, draw the Chariot are also figures engaged in turning the pole of the earth. There are of course many stories connected with every constellation, told by different peoples for different ritual purposes, though the basic function of the constellation remains constant. We can see this in the old name for Ursa Minor, Cynosura or the Dog's Tail, which the Egyptians knew as the Jackal of Set; to them the Great Bear was the Car of Osiris, or the Bier. As Osiris was castrated by Set, this makes him the Egyptian Cronos, though, as we shall see, Osiris is ultimately located elsewhere in the heavens.

The Charles after whom the Wain is named is Charlemagne, an imperial figure like Osiris. It is often said of men like these, who occupy great offices, or who are valiant heroes, that they will return after their death when most needed. Hence the title *Rex Quondam et Futurus*, the Once and Future King, by which Arthur is known. The name *Arthur* also implies as much, for it means "Bear," and like a bear he is now not dead but sleeping in his Isle of Avalon; just as Bran the Blessed sleeps in Hy Brasil, or Cronos in the isle of Ogygia in the Cronian Sea far to the west, place of the setting sun. The funeral car of these lords of the world moves around the Pole Star waiting for their return or, in Osirian style, for succeeding incarnations of the kingship.

The bear itself was the object of an ancient cult which until recently was still observed in Siberia and amongst the Ainu of Hokkaido. The bear is sometimes called the Lord of the Mountain, and, although dangerous, it is also a fatherly figure, since many stories tell of how it couples with women. The Siberian tribes kill it in a hunt, but the Ainu rear it as a cub and kill it at the end of the year. Whether wild or tame, however, the flesh of the animal is shared out in a festival of communion, and it carries back to God prayers for a plentiful future and the request that it should speedily incarnate itself into another bear, to be treated in the same fashion.

In Thrace the bear god was called Salmoxis, and the Thracians sent a messenger to him every four years by throwing a man into the air and catching him on the points of their spears. The Greeks made over this practice into the legend of Zamolxis, who returned home after accumulating great wealth—that is, no doubt, in the autumn—and built a banqueting hall in which he entertained his fellow citizens and preached the doctrine of immortality. He then disappeared into an underground chamber for four years. What this means in mystical practice can be seen from the Greeks having made Zamolxis the slave of Pythagoras, who preached the doctrine of immortality. Pythagoras's most famous disciple was Apollonius of Tyana, who followed in the footsteps of Zamolxis by consulting the oracle of Trophonius. This was the only oracle in which the consultant did not need the intermediary of a priest or pythoness. Dressed in white and bearing honey cakes to feed to the guardian snakes, he had to descend by ladder into a small cave and then slip through a tiny hole into a secret chamber below, where he awaited the revelation. Consultants usually emerged in a state of such terror that it was long before they laughed again. Apollonius, however, mastered his fears so well that after seven days he emerged as the reincarnation of Pythagoras, bearing with him a new edition of his master's teachings.

However, a tale similar to that of Zamolxis is told of the House of Athamas, of which the eldest son in every generation was forbidden to enter the banqueting hall on pain of being sacrificed, although every such son did so. This implies that the bear mystery is also a Cronian one, and could be connected with the royal succession. For Cronos is said to have been the only god who lived openly among men, which we may take to mean that he is the type of sacred king who begins his reign by putting his predecessor to death, has his title from his marriage to the queen, and is himself killed at the end of his reign. The evidence for this was first set out at length by Frazer in the *Golden Bough*, and lately has been much elaborated upon by Robert Graves. The theory, in brief, is that the king ruled for half the year and his rival for the other half; that this period was lengthened to a whole year, and that eventually the king sacrificed his own children to prolong his reign to four or even eight years. This would explain the legend of Cronos swallowing his children, or of Lykaon eating his grandchild Arkas.

The age of Cronos is certainly characterized not only by the reign of women but by cannibalism. The reasons behind the practice of cannibalism range from the need to incorporate the virtues of the dead man by eating him in a communion, which may have various ritual justifications, through hunger and the acquired taste for human flesh, to a systematic indulgence in revenge upon one's enemies. The Tupi are a good example of the last motive. Although they developed the practice of cannibalism in a most complex way, its basic justification was to kill and eat a man in revenge for the death of one of their own villagers, whose ghost would otherwise plague his relatives. To this was added a sense of honor such that only those who killed an enemy victim, or who were killed and eaten in their turn, could hope to attain their paradise. Prisoners of the Tupi seldom ran away from their captors' villages, for fear of being called cowards by their own folk and losing their chance of immortality into the bargain, and there is an obvious similarity here between their situation and that of a sacred king, who also knew what was in store for him.

The Tupi prisoner was called *miaussuba*, the loved one. He was executed at a time of year when food was plentiful, and there were connections between his death and the general fertility of the tribe—certain myths make it plain that the victim represented the original benefactor of mankind, or culture hero as he is often called, who gave the Tupi their ritual adornments, their weapons, their food crops, and their customs. Had the Tupi developed a calendar, such a victim might have come to represent the living and dying year, as did Adonis, the darling of Ishtar. As it was, his death merely marked time in the tos and fros of vengeance, and kept rivalry alive.

"Kill me, and my relatives will kill you: eat me, and you will be eating your own relatives whom I have eaten"—with such mocking words did the Tupi prisoner taunt his captors in his last moments. And thus the whirligig of time brings in his revenges or, as Anaximander said, "Things perish into those things out of which they have their birth, according to that which is ordained; for they give reparation to one another and pay the penalty of their injustice according to the disposition of time." Among the Tupi, the souls of those who competed in this game of injustice where two blacks make one white, and who perpetuated succeeding cycles of honor and revenge, went to the sun, which has cycles of its own to complete. We can see this also among the Aztecs, whose sacrificial rites were similar to those of the Tupi, but who also had a calendar. They fed the sun with human hearts lest it stop in its tracks and go out, not only at the winter solstice but also at the end of the 52-year age that brings the cycles of the sun and of planet Venus into coincidence. At these moments a fire was kindled in the breast of the victim, whose heart had been torn out and offered to the sun, while the priests ate certain parts of his body. From this we may see how the sun may become the Great Cannibal, the Cronos whose time devours the world it sustains. The Dogon are of the same opinion; every winter solstice they pray to Amma that he should abstain from drinking the blood of men.

The wars bred by these cycles of revenge are holy ones, marked by jealousy, honor, and great deeds. It is the same war that Herbert Spencer attributed to the Darwinian theory of evolution by natural selection, which he termed the survival of the fittest, or that which is subsumed under the idea of Maya or Illusion by Hindus and Buddhists, among whom the belief in reincarnation is fundamental. The victors in this battle of survival go to the unmoving center of the wheel of time, becoming its overseers, and may then move out again into other incarnations, as Pythagoras did. But the difficulties involved in this are great, as is recounted in the *Matsya Purana*. The story concerns the godlike and holy sage Narada, son of Brahma and an adept in devotion to Vishnu, who one day appeared to him. Narada asked to be given an understanding of Vishnu's Maya, and though warned against such an attempt Narada insisted.

"Plunge into the water here," said Vishnu then, "and you shall experience the secret." Narada plunged in and emerged in the form of Sushila, the daughter of the king of Benares. As Sushila, he married the son of a neighboring king and was supremely happy in their mutual love and the children born to them. Years later, however, a war between Sushila's father and husband led to the deaths of her father, husband, and children. Sushila laid their bodies on a funeral pyre and threw herself into the flames as a last act of devotion. But the moment she did so the fire turned into cool water and she became Narada once more. And there was Vishnu extending his hand to help him out of the waters. "Who is this son whose death you are bewailing?" he asked mockingly. "This is the semblance of my Maya, woeful, somber, accursed. Not the lotus-born Brahma, nor any other of the gods, can fathom its depth. Why or how should you know this inscrutable?"

This is the nightmare of history from which human beings constantly try to awake, though this awakening has its own terrors. In the same *Purana* the tale is told of another sage, Markendaya, who in the course of his meditations experienced himself slipping out of the mouth of Vishnu and found himself first in a dark illimitable sea in which he saw a sleeping giant, and later playing with a divine child beneath the Cosmic Tree. This child, who was

Drawing of Kala-makara, the leonine head of Time as the sun, with flowers growing from its jawless mouth.

A 16th-century alchemical illustration depicting the green lion of matter devouring the sun of spirit.

Vishnu, announced that he was the primeval cosmic man, the lord of the waters and of the sacred fire, the cycle of the year, and the whirlpool that sucks back all that it has once produced and is the Death of the Universe.

After this, Vishnu put Markendaya back into his mouth and swallowed him—for, after all, the realm of nonexistence is not suitable to human beings, however much they may try to escape from the pleasures and pains of existence. The point is that Vishnu is a Cronian figure, who keeps an eternal Sabbath while the world he creates has to labor through the other days of the week. At the same time the planets that give their names to the days are his emanations, and it is they who, by tradition, form the conditions under which the creation is ordered. Like Cronos, too, Vishnu is not dead but sleeping, or rather in a dream, and he returns to earth at the end of every cycle to create a new age. In India the different forms in which Vishnu returns are called his Avatars or Incarnations. There are 22 of them in all, the first being the divine child, the third the sage Narada, the 10th Matsya the Fish, the 18th Rama, the 20th Krishna, and the 21st Buddha, to mention only the better-known ones. Each has its particular function in the progress of the world ages, with its own ritual and its own timely message concerning salvation. But all of them are also manifestations of the Self that lives in fire and water, and that orders the time in which the world is made and destroyed.

Christianity has but one Incarnation, who is both Fish and Lamb. He, too, has to do with fire and water—the water of baptism, and the fire of judgment. "I have cast fire upon the world and see, I guard it until the world is afire"— so says the Jesus of the apocryphal gospel according to Thomas. The Fish has partly to do with the fact that 2000 years ago the Spring equinox fell in the time of Pisces. As for the Lamb, its significance goes back to the time of the Exodus. This occurred in the month Abib, the first month of the Jewish year, and is celebrated by the feast of the Passover with its roast lamb and unleavened bread. For the month Abib was the equivalent of the Accadian month Bar-ziggar, "the sacrifice of rightcousness" which we call Aries. Since the invention of the zodiac, Aries the Ram has always been the leader of the months and the first-born of the year.

It is significant that both the kings in whose lands the Christ and Rama were born ordered a massacre of the innocents, in an attempt to rid themselves of their divine rivals. Similarly, the last of the plagues put upon Egypt by Moses just before the Exodus was the smiting of the first-born throughout the land. For every age starts with a sacrifice, even the age of individual men and women. As the Lord said to Moses, "Sanctify unto me all the first-born, whatsoever openeth the womb among the children of Israel, both of man, and of beast: it is mine." Children, however, could be

Vishnu and his wife Lakshmi resting on Sesha, the thousand-headed serpent of eternity, in an interval between the cycles of creation.

redeemed by the price of a lamb, or by circumcision, which was the sign of the covenant cut into the flesh. In spite of this, the practice of making the children over to the king by fire had its resurgence amongst the Jews from time to time and was retained by the Ammonites.

The Ammonite king was, of course, Moloch, into whose fiery mouth babies were thrown. Without going into the complexities of the rites, the connection between circumcision, swallowing, and fire deserves some explanation. The myths of the Australian Aborigines say that boys at one time were circumcised not with a stone knife but with firesticks, many of them dying as a result. Likewise, the Urubu Indians say that in the Golden Age women had no genital organs and neither men nor women had anuses. These orifices were produced by a benefactor called Anawira (the name of a nut-bearing tree), who used firesticks as drills. As a result, human beings could enjoy sexual intercourse and no longer had to vomit up the remains of their food. The use of firesticks thus brings the Cronian age of childhood to an end, and inaugurates the adult one of sexuality.

In Greek mythology there is a definite connection between Cronos and Prometheus, the fire-stealer: in an Orphic hymn they are in fact identified by name. Prometheus is usually taken to mean "forethought," but his name comes perhaps from the Sanskrit *pramantha,* meaning "firesticks." We can see therefore that the Cronian age is celebrated by the Fire Sacrifice, in which the offspring of the primal man are formed into an image of his body, and the firesticks are used to recreate the First-born, in whose maw the sacrificial offerings are placed. The major traditions have it that the world is created from water, and destroyed by fire only to be recreated by water. The Fire Sacrifice repeats this course of events, as do all sacrifices of burnt offerings at the spring equinox, when the zodiacal year ends in the watery sign of the Fish and begins in the fiery sign of Aries.

The New Year is thus started with a new fire, which comes from heaven. Various Cronian figures, such as Lucifer the light-bearer, bring fire to earth when they fall from heaven. Another who does so is the Etruscan blacksmith god, Sethlans, whose name may ultimately be connected with that of Saturn, who, since his downfall, sleeps on a sea-girt isle—that is, in the waters. But which waters are these? We must remember for a start that the Flood came onto the earth from both the waters above and those below. A Hebrew commentary on Genesis says that the waters above came out of the Pleiades, the group of stars that heralds the rains, the hole there eventually being plugged by two stars borrowed from the Great Bear, which nightly pursues the Pleiades to get them back. As for the underwaters, these were sealed off by the cubical stone or Ark, whose resting place is always considered to be the center of the world and therefore marks its axis. The waters are therefore those divided by the firmament of Heaven, whose apparent motion rules the season. At the end of every year and of every age, the axis of this movement is realigned and a new fire kindled.

This is the axis seen as a firestick. But it may also be seen as a mill, with which God grinds slow but exceeding small. We have seen that the word *Chronos*, time, comes from a root meaning "to grind" or "to erode," as does the Sanskrit *pramantha,* with the result that Cronos is sometimes personified as a miller. So too was Gargantua, who was given a golden mill by King Arthur—and one prophecy about Arthur himself is that he will make a new mill when he returns to his kingship. Gargantua is connected with many mills in his adventures—for example, he set four mills a-going with a single fart. And Gargantua's antecedents can be traced back to the Celtic god Mullo, whom the Romans identified with Mars but whose attributes relate more especially to the sun.

There is a biblical hero who worked in a mill—Samson, the light of whose eyes was put out and who brought the temple down upon the heads of the Philistines by heaving at its twin pillars, and so presumably brought one sun age to an end. The Finnish *Kalevala* is an epic concerned with the fabrication and ruin of a mill with a many-colored cover, which eventually falls into the sea. According to Danish legend, Hamlet too had such a mill, which now grinds out salt and whose action can still be seen wherever there is a whirlpool or maelstrom, such as the ones off Iceland, the Faroes, or Norway. Now we know that in Egypt the fate of certain discreditable personages was to have the lower pintle of a door set in their eye socket, which served the dual purpose of punishing them and giving the door a guardian spirit. Various dark stories from Scandinavia show that mills were similarly set up on the bodies of human victims. The fact that Cronos sleeps in the cave at the bottom of the universe after his fall from its top therefore suggests that his fate is to be the lower pivot on which the earth now turns. The same idea can be seen in Dante's *Divine Comedy*, where Satan is curiously said to fall from the south pole of the universe into the earth where he is now lodged. Dante says that the land that previously occupied the Southern Hemisphere fled before Satan to the northern one, and the ocean waters flooded in to take their place. The fall of Satan threw up a great mountain, the Mount of Purgatory with the Garden of Eden at its summit. Satan, as the lord of Tartarus is the heavenly blacksmith dwelling in the volcanic entrails of the earth, which a medieval astronomical text called the Dead Dragon. If there is any personage on which the axis of the world is set, it must surely be he, the nether millstone itself.

These scattered pieces of mythology show well enough how we may take Satan, or Saturn, to be Lord of this world, while the Lord himself rules from beyond the timeless heavens. But this leads to two problems: how the Timeless can give rise to Time, and how time-bound souls may find their way to their eternal homes. The second question seems easy enough to answer: they escape at the winter solstice with the rebirth of the sun, or at the spring equinox at the festival of righteousness. As for the first question, we must remember that if Cronos is a type of the primal man, his dismembered parts are to be found scattered through the universe. For a start, since he castrated his father during the night-time with a sickle, we can conclude that he is the new moon, for there is no other sickle-shaped body visible in the sky to make this legend comprehensible. The moon is the Measurer, both by etymology and by observation—and so, for that matter, is the mind. Measurement is that which allows us to divide one thing from another and to make a ratio, or reason, from its consequences. But Cronos is also the planet Saturn, of which—or rather of whom, since the planets are gods—Proclus said that he continuously gives the measures of the whole creation to his son Zeus, the planet Jupiter.

In an ingeniously argued book called *Hamlet's Mill*, de Santillana and von Dechend have shown how the Mill is an image not only of the turning universe, and so of time, but of Saturn's position in it. Saturn is the outermost of the traditional seven heavenly bodies, the one nearest the sphere of the fixed stars, though he began as the king of Earth. This reversal reminds us of the logic of creation in which the cubical Center reaches out into the furthermost bounds of space. Saturn is in fact associated with the square and the cube, as can be seen from Kepler's diagram, in which he assigned a different Platonic solid to each of the five planets, and boxed one within the other.

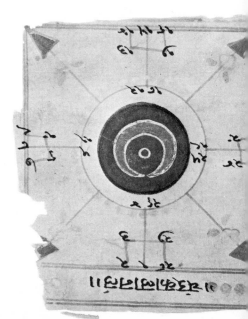

An 18th-century Indian moon calendar.

In addition, Saturn takes 30 years to travel around the zodiacal belt and arrive back at its starting place—its sidereal period—while it is in conjunction with Jupiter about every 20 years, and such a conjunction occurs in the same zodiacal sign every 60 years. Here apparently is the basis of the idea that Saturn gives the measures of the world to Zeus. He picks up the motion of the Primum Mobile and imparts it to the planetary ruler of the heavens in periods of 20 and 60 years (both of which have been considered as periods of rule—we may remember the 60-year cycle amongst the Dogon). The whole motion culminates every 24,000 years. In addition, the sidereal period of Saturn tallies nicely with the division of the circle into 360 degrees: 30 goes into 360 12 times, which is a numerological parallel to the number of zodiacal houses in each year. It is by just such overdeterminations of a given symbol that traditional systems find their consistency and justification.

But we have not done with Cronos yet. He is also to be found in the constellation of Orion, who wields that sickle-shaped sword called a falchion

Below, Kepler's scheme of the Great Conjunctions of Saturn and Jupiter that occur every 20 years. One angle of the Trigon so formed moves around the Zodiac in 2400 years. Right, Kepler's drawing of the polyhedra inscribed in the seven planetary spheres. The cube defines the outermost sphere of Saturn.

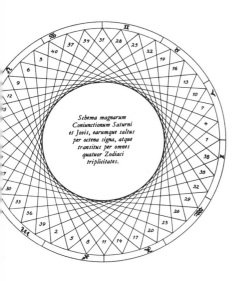

Schema magnarum Coniunctionum Saturni et Jovis, earumque saltus per octena signa, atque transitus per omnes quatuor Zodiaci triplicitates.

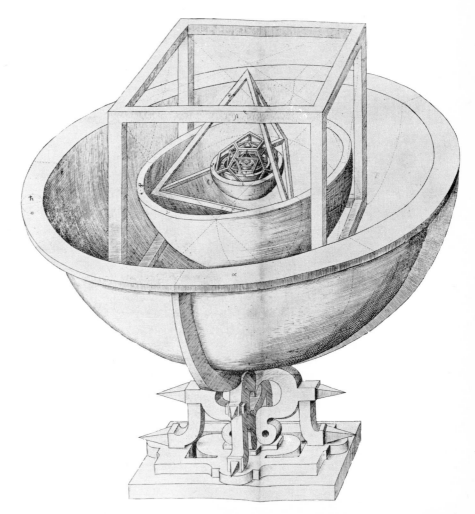

and which farmers call a billhook. Like all the constellations, Orion has been called by many names, though in his case they all bear a close family resemblance. For the Egyptians Orion was associated with Horus and the soul of Osiris; in the Hindu Brahmanas he is seen as Prajapati in the form of a stag; several nations in the Middle East refer to him as the Giant, or the hunter Nimrod mighty before the Lord; and he was Saturnus to the Romans.

There are, of course, stories that make sense of these various connotations. The Greek story was that Orion was a mighty hunter who cleared the island of Hyria of its wild beasts in order to win the hand of Merope, the king's daughter. But the king refused his suit, so he ravished the girl. As a punishment, the king had Orion's eyes put out—the same fate that Horus suffered at the hands of Set. Orion, on the advice of an oracle, traveled east, visited Lemnos, where Hephaistos has his smithy, and arrived at Delos, where he slept with Dawn and had his eyesight restored by Helios. Apollo—who is, of course, Helios—fearing that Orion would also ravish his sister Artemis and in the end prove to be a greater hunter than himself, tricked Artemis into shooting him with her sickle-moon bow. In the Hittite version of the story, she dropped this bow into the sea from chagrin when she found that she had killed Orion, and it became part of the constellation of Canis Major. The Hindus allude to the same story: they say that the Prajapati stag was killed

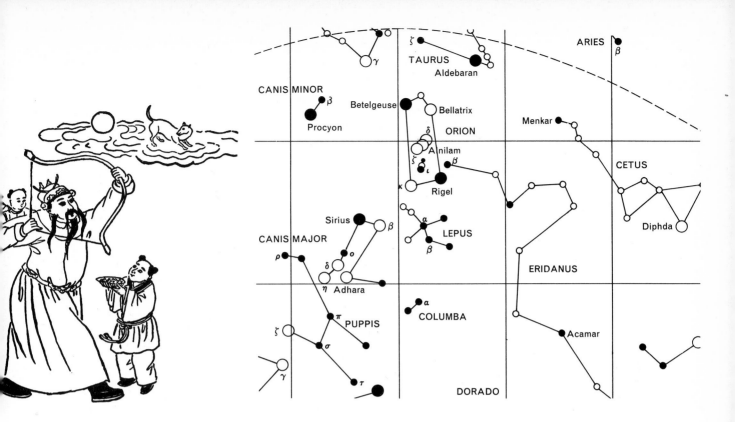

CANIS MINOR
CANIS MAJOR
ARIES
TAURUS
ORION
CETUS
LEPUS
ERIDANUS
COLUMBA
PUPPIS
DORADO

by a three-jointed arrow, now Orion's belt, the hunter being the star Sirius in Canis Major. Chinese star maps show a similar configuration.

The story now takes us to yet further constellations. Artemis applied to Aesculapius the Healer to restore Orion to life, and Aesculapius was in process of doing so when Zeus struck him dead for his daring, setting him and Orion in the skies. Aesculapius was the old name for Ophiuchus the Serpent-holder, the serpent being the tutelary spirit of medicine because it rejuvenates itself every year by sloughing its skin. Ophiuchus stands diametrically opposite to Orion in the heavens, just to the north of Scorpio. This is significant, because in a variant of the myth Orion is said to have been killed by a scorpion bite—a reminder of the scorpion sent by Set to kill Horus in the heat of summer, and of the Scorpion men who attacked Gilgamesh on his epic journey to the Well of the Universe where grew the plant of immortality. So if Scorpio puts Orion to death, Aesculapius is there to restore him to life. All this makes sense when we consider the course of the night sky throughout the year. Orion's rising at sunset heralds the approach of the winter storms, a few weeks after the Pleiades, containing the star Merope, have appeared. But when Scorpio rises at dusk, Orion has set below the western horizon, and though he reappears at dawn, the sun's rays blot him from our sight.

Above left, drawing the bow at Sirius, the jackal star, as was done by the mythical emperors of China. Above, star map showing how the stars of Canis Major form the bow of the Chinese and Babylonian asterisms.

A Greco-Phoenician jasper scarab of the fifth century B.C. showing Isis-Hathor as a winged scorpion.

Orion is the most impressive constellation in the middle heavens, being both bright and easily figured by the imagination. He also has the distinction of being upon the celestial equator and touching the Milky Way with one shoulder, while his left foot, the star Rigel, is the source of the river constellation Eridanus which winds far down into the Southern Hemisphere. When we remember that Achilles, like other heroes, was fatally wounded in his heel, we may suspect that Scorpio attacked Orion at Rigel, just as Sirius shot an arrow through his middle.

Now we know that the Egyptians placed the soul of Osiris in Orion, and that the vastly complex funerary rites of Egypt were aimed at immortalizing the soul of a dead pharaoh and giving him the status of Osiris. We know, too, that Osiris is the Nile, whose floods occur at the heliacal rising of Sirius. So we can properly assume that the astronomical figures we have mentioned are both time-keepers and representatives of this human and seasonal drama. Rigel is not only the left foot of Orion, and therefore sinister, but was, in the ancient Middle East, called the Whirlpool, which we have seen to be connected with the fall into the sea of the World Mill. It is into this whirlpool that Orion falls or, in another figure of speech, that his life flows when his heel is attacked by Scorpio. He then makes his way as the river Eridanus to the Saturnian realm at the bottom of the universe, whose first station is Achernar, the River's End. In the same latitude we find the star Canopus, which the Egyptians called the plumb line of the heavens and which is now the steering oar of the constellation Argo. Argo's prow is invisible, but it points in the opposite direction to that of the apparent motion of the sun: so if Orion is to be reborn every year, Argo is the obvious vehicle to carry him back to the east.

So far, so good. But according to the Egyptians the scorpion does his deadly work in August, though Scorpio now rises in October. Here we have to do with that important astronomical technicality, the precession of the equinoxes. The equinoxes occur every spring and autumn, when the days and nights are of equal length. The solstices, of course, occur in between these dates. Basically it is not difficult to know when these dates arrive. A stick set upright in the ground, and observed every day to see what happens to its shadow, is sufficient for rough purposes. More complicated instruments are needed to find the exact moment. The Inca of Peru, for instance, built two groups of eight towers to the east and west of Cuzco to observe the approach and moment of the solstices, and erected two pillars on an east-west axis in the courtyard of the temple to date the equinoxes. Equally, Stonehenge has long been thought to be a vast sundial, though it is only recently that Gerald Hawkins has put its various alignments through a computer and found that it serves to mark the solsticial and equinoctial stations for both the sun and the moon, besides having a device by which the probability of an eclipse of either luminary can be predicted.

It is by the observation of the solstices and equinoxes that man has arrived at the notion of fixing direction according to the four major points of the compass, which give to the number four a sacred significance that might otherwise be lacking. The use of an observatory indeed shows one of the ambiguities of time: it is measured in spatial terms, applied first to the temple precinct itself and to the night sky, where the four stations of the sun are marked by what are called the equinoctial and solsticial colures—the great circles that mark the advent of the sun at each of these stations and also pass through both of the Poles. The authors of *Hamlet's Mill* argue convincingly that the idea that the earth is flat and four-cornered comes from fixing the course of the sun through its four stations in the skies and imagining a plane that cuts through the earth to the stars marking these stations. This is the plane that is now called the ecliptic. The frame of the earth is thus celestial, and the earth itself has been domesticated, as it were, by the influence of the cosmic order. Interestingly enough, this square has been set in the heavens as the Great Square of Pegasus, Pegasus being the Horse who in the Vedas is the Prime Ancestor. The square was called by the Babylonians 1-iku, which was their standard field measure and the base on which a temple should be founded. When, at evening, Orion rises over the horizon, the Great Square will be seen standing overhead, ready to imprint its form on the earth.

Temples such as Stonehenge can be used to observe the solstices and equinoxes because they provide a foresight and a backsight to aim along: whenever the sun comes between these two sights, that marks the time of

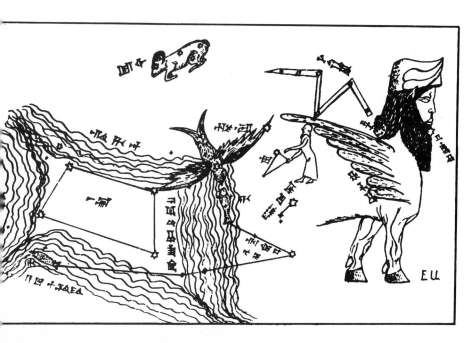

A reconstruction of Babylonian asterisms. Taurus and Triangulum, originally a plow, are to the right. Aries is above. To the left is 1-iku, the Great Square of Pegasus, enclosed by the rivers of Paradise, or the constellation of Pisces.

solstice or equinox. But observation over the years shows that the four stations of the sun are not in constant correspondence with the back cloth provided by the stars. As a result, the constellation of Aries now rises at the time when Taurus rose two thousand years ago and the age of Aries has been superseded by the age of Pisces, which will soon come to an end and give place to the age of Aquarius.

The reasons for this are complex. For a start, the axis of the earth is tilted at an angle of 23 degrees and 20 minutes from the vertical, which in turn is calculated in terms of the plane of the earth's orbit around the sun. The earth itself is not a perfect sphere, and the existence of the moon circling around it constantly alters its center of gravity. As the earth is a gyroscope, these irregularities make it wobble—not only does it revolve about its axis, but the axis itself revolves about an invisible center. Today, this axis points nearly directly toward the Pole Star, but in 13,000 years it will be pointing somewhere in the direction of Vega in the constellation Lyra. It will have traveled there via stars in Cepheus and Cygnus, and will return to its present inclination in about 26,000 years by way of Hercules, Draco, and stars in Ursa Minor. This last measure of time may well be the same as that which Saturn is said to have given to Zeus—the approximation is close enough to satisfy the contemplation of such a vast cyclical period.

To work out this kind of information astronomers have made use of two systems of coordinates, the one based on the earth's axis and the other on the plane of the ecliptic. Plato used these two systems when he came, in the *Timaeus*, to describe the creation of the world and that moving image of eternity that gives the body of the world its soul, or daimon. He saw them as being composed of a mixture of these two enigmatic entities, the Same and the Other, divided and compounded into that ratio of 243 to 256 which also gives the interval between notes of music. This mixture was formed by god into two outer circles with the same pole but set at an angle from each other. The outer one embraced the sphere of the fixed stars and its motion was that of the Same. The inner was subdivided into seven unequal circles to house the orbits of the sun, moon, and five planets, and its motion was that of the Other. It is by this conjunction of two different species of motion that there began "that never-ceasing and rational life enduring throughout all time. The body of heaven is visible, but the soul is invisible and partakes of reason and harmony."

These two conjoined circles refer to the celestial equator and the ecliptic, while the two places at which they cross each other mark the equinoctial colures. The traditional play of correspondences between various levels makes it necessary that man should copy the original Logos that formed the world's soul whenever he gives a new city or a new era a soul by founding it according to ritual prescription. The act is performed not only at the right place and according to the right directions of space, but at the right time, which God has ordained should come round every year.

But Plato did not take the precession of the equinoxes into his account of the creation, and without this it is obvious that a most unhappy state of affairs comes about every 2000 years or so, when observation of the equinoxes shows that the path of the ecliptic intersects the celestial equator at a different place. The stars no longer rise at their right times, the World Mill is thrown into confusion, the pillars of the temple are broken down, and a new mythology must be created in order to explain how the new order was formed out of the old one. That the Polynesians indeed called Chaos the debris of the old world order tells us something most important both about Time and about Chaos. It also puts in a quite different light the cataclysmic theories of Horbiger, Bellamy and Velikovsky, all of whom take the myths of the Deluge and of rains of fire at the end of a world age in a material way.

Cataclysms there surely have been: yet order is as much an effect of mind as of matter. If we then stick to the order of myth, an interesting problem presents itself: what was the original time of creation? Or rather, what date can we assign to the first systematization of the calendar and the figures of the constellations? Some have proposed a date reaching back to the time when Vega was the Pole Star. This is not in itself absurd, for Paleolithic man seems to have made lunar calendars, and when agriculture began, some ten thousand years ago, pre-existent astronomical knowledge must have been used to time the operations of clearing the ground and planting. But

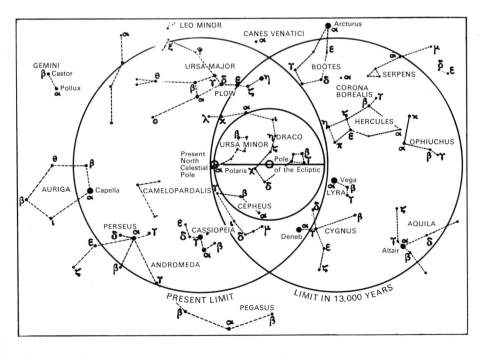

The northern circumpolar stars, seen from the latitude of Paris. The inner circle marks the trajectory of the celestial North Pole during a complete precession; the pole of the ecliptic is situated in one of Draco's coils.

the main features of the system as we know it from antiquity seem to date rather from about 5000 B.C. At this time the sun rose between Taurus and Gemini at the spring equinox, apparently in the middle of the Milky Way and just above the head of Orion. The Milky Way is the Stream of Ocean *par excellence*, and it is the first astronomical feature to be called Eridanus, which comes from a Babylonian word meaning the Confluence. Moreover it is in the Milky Way that, according to both Pythagorean and Polynesian tradition, the souls of the dead dwelt when they were not giving motion to their bodies on earth. The original Doors of the sun, therefore, are likely to have been the moments when the sun was in the Milky Way, which here crossed the celestial equator and marked its intersection with the ecliptic. At such moments, the souls of the dead could cross the intangible barrier between sky and earth, which were reconnected after their original separation. That, according to one Greek myth, the Milky Way was made when Rhea removed Zeus from her breast to hide him from Cronos is a parable telling us of the separation of the upper and lower firmaments. That Cronos fell in three distinct forms—as himself, as a phallus, and as a stone—tells us something of the reconnection of these realms.

Other names for the Milky Way also let us into the secret. The Assyrians called it the Course of the Sun, and in both Old and New Worlds it is sometimes called the Path of Ashes or the Path of Seeds—in Egypt, the seeds dropped by Isis when fleeing from the fiery demon Typhon. The Typhon story has antecendents in the Middle East, where the great serpent (another old name for the Milky Way) overcame the Storm-god but was defeated in a tempest. The Greeks have it that the serpent was the largest monster ever known. He was eventually defeated by Zeus, who threw mountains at him until one of them, Mount Etna, hit the mark and submerged him for ever: a fitting and cataclysmic end for a Cronian figure. As for the Ash Path, the Greeks tell of Phaethon, who drove his father's sun-chariot so erratically that he burned the earth when he came too low and the stars when he went too high, eventually toppling over and drowning in the great river Eridanus. The chariot is now the constellation of Auriga, which stands over Orion's head and that part of the Milky Way between Taurus and Gemini where, 5000 years ago, the sun rose at the spring equinox. It is here that originally the Way between heaven and earth was opened, and it is Orion, who is also Osiris, Prajapati, and Saturn, who both opens and shows the way to succeeding generations.

The various myths about Cronos and his counterparts thus tell us in figurative language something quite technical and abstract about Chronos. The fact that Cronos eats his own children and is none other than that hermaphroditic animal whose waste provides its own food—to use Plato's image of the world in its first state—tells us also that time is measured by the reincarnation of souls and the recurrence of specific events; and, even if it is a river in which people drown, it also provides constant refreshment for generations to come. As Plato said, the recurrence of time is reasonable, at least on the astronomical level: the fixed stars and the bodies of the solar system have a way of coinciding after certain periods, which can be counted in fours, sevens, twelves, twenties, thirties, sixties and so on, according to need. Considered in this way, the problem of time is not whether it had a beginning or will have an end, but how to make its periods harmonize into cycles of increasing length, like a nest of Chinese boxes.

Since time is measured by the movement of heavenly bodies whose periods of rotation are quite dissimilar, there will never be a moment when all the periods coincide exactly, and the chord that will resolve the grand harmony of time can never be heard. The attempt to formulate its character, however, has often been attempted, for example in the Hindu concept of the Four Ages. The first of these ages, the Krita yuga, is the Golden Age, which lasts for 1,728,000 years; then follows the Treta yuga of 1,296,000 years, the Dvapara yuga of 864,000 years, and finally the age we live in, the Kali yuga of 432,000 years, a period of which the others are simple multiples. These four ages total 4,320,000 years and are known collectively as a *kalpa* or "Great Age." But in cosmic time, this is a mere nothing. There are a thousand kalpas in a single day of Brahma, who lives for 108 years made up of 360 days. Only at the end of this time does he cease to exist and, with the entire universe and all its gods, fall back into the nothing from which all came.

This computation is not as absurd as it may seem, for all its stupefying consequences. One of its functions, for instance, is to account—by means of an involved calculation—for the precession of the equinoxes. Nor are the Hindu ages absurd when compared to the latest scientific estimates of the age of the solar system, which date its formation some 5,000 million years ago, a period but a fraction longer than one of Brahma's days. Like the Hindus, geologists also think in terms of four main ages of the earth, which progressively decrease in length as they approach our own times; they and the paleontologists date the start of the Cambrian period, when life began to evolve on a large scale, some 600 million years ago, which amounts to 140 kalpas or about $3\frac{1}{2}$ Brahman hours. As for the oldest stars in our galaxy, these are thought to be but some 3 Brahman days old; and we do not yet know whether the galaxy as a whole will last for a week or a month of Brahma's time. But the time of Brahma may safely be left to Brahma, for he has a universe of galaxies to play with, which seems to be expanding in all directions of space, and for which 108 of his years may well be needed before its limit, whatever it is, is reached.

Meanwhile the life of the universe renews itself according to the laws of cause and effect, of Karma and Natural Selection. In his *Voyage of the Beagle* Darwin has a fine passage in which he puts life into its geological setting. He is talking of a torrential river that rolled large stones along its course, which roared and rattled as they went. Says he: "It was like thinking on time, where the minute that now glides past is irrecoverable. So was it with these stones: the ocean is their eternity, and each note of that wild music told of one more step towards their destiny."

"It is not possible for the mind to comprehend," he then continued, "except by a slow process, any effect which is produced by a cause repeated so often, that the multiplier itself conveys an idea not more definite than the savage implies when he points to the hairs of his head. As often as I have seen beds of mud, sand, and shingle, accumulated to the thickness of many thousand feet, I have felt inclined to exclaim that causes, such as the present rivers and the present beaches, could never have ground down and produced such masses. But, on the other hand, when listening to the rattling noise of these torrents, and calling to mind that whole races of animals have passed away from the face of the earth, and that during this whole period . . . these stones have gone rattling onwards in their course, I have thought to myself, can any mountains, any continent, withstand such waste?"

But if life is to be thought of as a process of dying, it is also to be lived at each moment; and in each of these moments time is to be found entire. Being entire, even in its parts it lets us share in the mystery of the timeless. Such was the conclusion of Jalal al-Din Rumi, poet, mystic, and saint of Islam, who wrote so that his fellow men might see with their imaginations what he knew by experience:

> What worlds mysterious roll within the vast,
> The all-encircling ocean of the mind!
> Cup-like thereon our forms are floating fast,
> Only to sink and fill and leave behind
> No spray of bubbles from the sea upcast.
>
> The Spirit thou canst not see, it comes so nigh.
> Drink of this Presence! Be thou not a jar
> Laden with water and its lip stone-dry;
> Nor as a horseman blindly borne afar
> Who never sees his horse beneath his thigh.

*Indian miniature painting of the gods
and demons churning the Ocean of Milk.
The churning pole flowers as a lotus, on
which Vishnu sits as Supreme Being.*

8 The War of Alliance

Off the coast of New Guinea lies the island of Malekula. There, as in many other societies, it is a custom for the men to eat apart from their womenfolk. They obey the custom without question and usually without knowing why they do so. When the anthropologist John Layard was working among them he asked many times why they followed this custom, only to be answered: "Because it is the custom," which he did not find much of an explanation. Nor would he have got dissimilar answers had he asked why they obeyed the incest tabu, or practiced their particular rules of marriage. These also are customs, which is only to say that those who follow them do so because their forebears did, right back to the ancestral custom-giver.

Such an explanation, though something of a tautology, has right on its side. A custom is given to be observed because without it there is no society: it is something necessary, and where custom is king there is no arguing. The origin myths of custom are quite unhistorical and give no apparent reason for a custom being just so. What they state is that once upon a time an ancestor, a benefactor, or a god gave the custom to man, who knew nothing better than to make it his own. Where the custom-giver got the idea, and what he intended by it, are matters mythology ignores, or rather finds pointless. For a custom and its giver are not two things but the same: the god reveals himself through his custom, and the custom is followed to actualize the god.

Questions of human origin are always mysterious. We do not know how, when, or why the incest tabu was inaugurated, or language came to be spoken, fire to be made by rubbing sticks together, clay to be baked into pots, or seed to be sown. The traditions say that all such seminal inventions were either given to man or stolen by him, and many customs surrounding their use make it clear that the original owner is still incarnated in them and punishes those who forget the fact. There are always moments in history, however, when the fact is forgotten with impunity, and men ask themselves why on earth a custom is obeyed, what it is all about, and how

Balinese dancers wearing the mask of Rangda, the Mother as Witch.

it began. Take, for instance, the theories concerning the incest tabu. Thirty years ago Lord Raglan made a list of the main reasons put forward to justify the prohibition of incestuous marriages, and although others have been added in the meantime they fall into much the same categories. The various theories (omitting the names of their main supporters) are as follows:

Because such marriages are sterile

Because the children of such marriages are weak in mind and body

Because there is an instinct to forbid such marriages

Because such marriages are unnatural

Because such marriages would tend to take place between persons of disproportionate age

As a relic of a once universal practice of marriage by capture

Because relationship would be confused

Because respect for a father precludes marriage with his wife

Because marriage within the family would be without love

Because such marriages would lead to excessive love within the family

Because such marriages lead to family quarrels of various kinds

From a growing regard for the domestic proprieties

To promote chastity by compelling people to seek mates at a distance

As a penance for a primeval patricide

Because such marriages became a royal prerogative

For magical, religious, or superstitious reasons.

These explanations may be divided into those that focus on the cause of the tabu, and those that describe its effect. There are three varieties of each: the first is a matter of instinct; the second, of social history; the third, of the supernatural. Some of them describe the advantages conferred by the tabu, others the calamities that are thought to follow the breaking of it; and some are plainly tautologous, trying to explain the matter by describing it. In other words, these explanations settle on one of the three aspects of time—past, present, or future—and hope to understand a totality through one of its parts.

This is always a useful exercise, especially if the different forms of causality are distinguished. Some of them—such as efficient and secondary, material and occasional causes—can be thought about without difficulty. The formal cause, the essence or idea of a thing, enters into the realm of metaphysics. The first and final causes pass into the mystery of things and are matters of faith rather than proof. Scholastic systems the world over have tried to bring these different causes into an intelligible pattern, with varying results. The aim is to frame a plain fact in a mystery, and to reveal the mystery in the plain facts it produces—a difficult matter, which requires great skill in the manipulation of symbols. The practice of symbolic thought is a custom just as much as the incest tabu, being both instinctive and conscious. It points to the mystery of consciousness, which reveals itself to man the more clearly the more he is in a position to use it, and which is as much a gift as the invention of the bow and arrow or the revelation of what fire does to clay.

The place for a revelation is a mystery. Here we can return to Malekula and to Layard's inquiries into the custom of the sexes eating separately. He was at last rewarded for his persistence by an old man who had obviously thought deeply about custom: "We practice the pig sacrifice," he said, "and that makes us strong enough not to have to eat with our women." What better explanation could one ask for? Inverting the usual sequence of cause and effect, it introduces a motive that gives meaning to both of them: the meaning is to be found in the mystery of the pig sacrifice, in which the different varieties of cause are subsumed. All the major preoccupations of the Malekulans are to be found in the pig sacrifice. It spells out the structure of society and the exchanges that keep it going. It brings honor in this world and immortality in the next, into which the sacrificers are reborn. The birth in this context is that of the soul, the spirit, the self, call it what you will. The mystery is an initiation into a secret, which is, to put it crudely, that though men are dependent upon women for the generation of bodies, women need men to give those bodies real life. Like all masculine initiations, this forces the novice to sever his connections with women if he is to keep his self-respect. At the same time the physical act of generation, which the mystery half denies, is used as the model for the birth of the individual into a new awareness. This paradox is one reason why traditions so often say that the rites men practice were stolen from women, who originated them. The theft marks the end of the Golden Age when the earth was a mother, and the beginning of its successor, in which fathers rise to the skies with their sons. They do so by braving death, whom they figure as a devouring ogress: they breed up pigs (a favorite animal of peoples who worship the goddess) and offer them to the Great Mother as substitutes for themselves, to escape being eaten when they die. So they practice the pig sacrifice in order not to be eaten, and this indeed makes them strong enough not to eat with the representatives of she who devours what she gives birth to.

This well-knit complexity makes it hard for us to tell which came first, the chicken of the pig sacrifice or the egg of the eating tabu. Which is cause, and which effect? The mystery avoids the issue by allowing ends and means to reveal each other, and to show that they are related as negative to positive. Where the existence of one thing depends on that of another, the conclusion

is that both issue from the same polarizing stress. This stress is what anthropologists and psychologists alike have named the incest tabu. It has to do with the formalities of sexual intercourse, of eating, and of all the functions that set one group apart from another and relate them through their different duties and prerogatives. It is also at work in all intellectual constructions that name and order the world. But it is by no means unique to mankind. Animals undergo the same stress when nature requires them to act in concert, and to enable them to live together they have evolved various codes that are a nice compromise between cooperation and rivalry. The codes show themselves in what Sir Julian Huxley first called *ritualized behavior*, in which patterns of dominance and submission meet each other halfway and form a bond either between a mating pair or between individuals of a flock or herd. This is the beginning of a society in which an understanding is made as to what kind of behavior is permissible and what is not, and though the basic mechanism is instinctual its effects are often consciously manipulated. For in a gregarious species every individual must learn its place in society from experience, which is determined by its own efforts. What is more, the individual may bring about a social innovation that becomes traditional—for example, different groups of the same species of baboon, though all living in much the same environment, have found different things good to eat.

Above, a pig feast at a bride-price ceremony in New Guinea.

A Celtic bronze boar found in France.

A modern Indian ikon of Kali, goddess of Time and Destruction, treading on Shiva.

These traditions are rudimentary, because animals have no language in the strict sense of the word. Language extends society because it has to be learned; the function is innate, but only with practice does it produce the Word. With language, man can stage a play within the play, re-creating past events and planning future ones. Words point succinctly to what cannot be seen, and grammar becomes the model around which experience is organized and by which it is transmitted. The French anthropologist Lévi-Strauss has revolutionized anthropology by focusing on this issue, which allows him to treat social life in terms of linguistics. His volumes entitled *Mythologiques* demonstrate how language defines the relations between people within and without the family, between the five senses and what they perceive, between plants and animals, between noise and silence, between things dead and living, edible and inedible, and between many other matters. For speech is a medium of exchange, and as such it defines the properties of things and reveals how these things can become human property to be exchanged in their turn.

It was Marcel Mauss who first described these exchanges in terms of the gift, and showed how the anatomy of a society can be laid bare by discovering its rules of exchange and tracing the course taken by the things given and taken. Lévi-Strauss's first great work on kinship did just this. It showed how the rules concerning marriage in any society could be understood when seen as ways in which women were exchanged by men, and how a biological property became a social one. Social relations are first described according to the rules of this exchange. People are classed as being father, mother, uncle, aunt, brother, and sister, marriageable and nonmarriageable cousins, and so on. In some situations the terms are extended beyond the immediate family, so that "father" applies to the father's brother also; or a term may do double duty, so that the mother's brother is also father-in-law. The social family is always larger than the biological one, the formal reason being that the incest tabu makes it necessary for members of different families to intermarry and to call each other by terms expressing a relationship. The village, the horde, the tribe, the nation, all are first experienced in terms of the family, that system of procreative exchanges that makes a difference between its parts in order to make them useful. The system works only when a man denies himself the enjoyment of his own property, in order to be rewarded by the enjoyment of another's.

This mutual sacrifice is the mystery of the incest tabu, and on it the foundations of human society are laid. In every religion a sacrificer is he who gives a token of himself to God in order to receive back the fullness of existence: *Do ut des,* "I give that you may give." The mystery reveals that life is worth living when it is paid for, because only then is it given value. The dread surrounding incest shows that this value is something supernatural, above mere nature, and that the harder the bargain, the more the reward. On the sexual level, a man's reward for giving his sister to another man is that man's sister, or, if he is in no position to pay the debt, his gratitude in the form of payment in kind or by service. It is the same with God, whenever he is worshiped in the commerce of love:

Kanh have I bought. The price he asked, I gave.
Some cry, "'Tis great," and others jeer, "'Tis small"—
I gave in full, weighed to the utmost grain,
My love, my life, my soul, my all.

So sang Mírá Báí in praise of the great mystical union that Coventry Patmore also celebrated as the "double and reciprocal consciousness of love; that marvelous state in which each of two persons in distinct bodies perceives sensibly all that the other feels in regard to his or her self, although their feelings are of the most opposite characteristics; and this so completely, each discerning and enjoying the distinct desire and felicity of the other, that you might say that in each was the fullness of both sexes."

Traditional society has no place for bachelors and spinsters, unless they are married to a god. To be married is to be complete: it is the reward of initiation by which a man becomes reborn. "Therefore as long as he does not find a wife," says the *Satapatha Brahmana,* "so long he is not complete." Because of the incest tabu, what is completed is not only a man's selfhood but those parts of a society with a vested interest in the union, one of them acting the part of God the giver and the other of man the receiver. The contract between them is also a sacrament and as such its efficacy extends through society and into nature. Thus it is that the Hindu groom tells his bride, "I am the Sky, you are the Earth"; that the tribal Nagaras of Gujerat give the groom and bride the divine titles of Shiva and Parvati, god and goddess; and that in Babylonia the king impersonated the god of heaven by bedding his queen, the personation of earth, on top of the ziggurat, the image of the world, and so married society to nature. To paraphrase the old Malekulan: marriage is of the gods, and that makes us strong enough to be human.

Who are the gods here? In ancient Greece hospitality was given to the stranger because he might be a god in disguise. This is to say that whatever is strange must be propitiated, either to avert calamity or to attract blessings, and among many tribal peoples hospitality goes so far that the host comforts his guest not only with food but also with the company of his wife. The custom makes for neighborliness and, in countries where survival is difficult,

is also a mutual insurance scheme against disaster. (In a more aggressive vein, Sa'adi advised: "If thou sinkest in a calamity, be not helpless. Strip thy foes of their skins and thy friends of their fur coats.") The major difference between the rules of hospitality and of marriage is that the first regulate a temporary state of affairs, the second a permanent one. In between are the rules that decree the manner in which two mutually suspicious groups approach each other. Lévi-Strauss witnessed such an encounter between two groups of Nambikwara Indians, who had seen each other's campfires for several days before the men staged a meeting, the women and children scattering in the bush. Both leaders delivered a harangue, one of them bellicose and airing his griefs, the other peaceable and protesting his good intentions. Then the two groups camped together, each group putting on its own songs and dances and frequently provoking squabbles with the other through the use of stylized sexual gestures. At dawn, when things had quietened down, came the inspection of reconciliation. The adversaries roughly handled each other's ornaments, murmuring as they did so: "Give, give, look, look, that's nice." Then they exchanged their ornaments and their weapons, without bartering and with no expressions of satisfaction or gratitude. The Parintinin Indians welcome a visitor in much the same way, shooting arrows over his head and shouting war cries. Then the chief puts his hand on the visitor's shoulder in the same way that a warrior takes an enemy prisoner, and after an angry harangue offers him hospitality.

All these encounters are alliances in the making. Abbeville said of the Tupinamba that, "Those who are not related eat each other up," and of the Tupi that they found great difficulty in creating permanent relationships between groups. They did so only through the exchanges of war and peace, of cannibalism, hospitality, and present-giving. Gifts are used even now by

Left, a Kwakiutl Indian potlatch figure of a chief holding a "copper," the most valuable article used in ceremonial exchanges. Top, a totem pole with three frogs, erected by a Northwest American Indian chief as an insult to a rival potlatch chief—frogs were a symbol of prostitution.

the Brazilian Indian Service to pacify hostile tribes: they are left on the paths, and the pacifiers venture into the villages only when the gifts have been taken and something put in their place. Some pacifiers have been robbed of all their possessions in the course of their duty, because a refusal to give evokes murderous anger among such peoples. For them, goods are to be shared out equally to all who want them; the only exceptions are ritual objects belonging to a cult. The Tupinamba used gifts to create a special relation of friendship. Early European explorers found this much to their advantage, but only if they were as liberal as their hosts. The Tupinamba gave them concubines, which raised problems. After a time, the French governor forbade his followers to accept these women, which caused the Tupinamba to doubt the fidelity and friendship of the French. What was worse, the French never gave Frenchwomen in return in order to seal the alliance. The British in India who took native women found themselves in a similar difficulty when the memsahibs came out from the mother country and disapproved of such goings-on: as a result the British became a caste outside Indian society and could form alliances only on the administrative and mercantile levels. The color bar has always proved an uncertain instrument with which to rule an empire.

Marriage is the alliance gift, as feudal kings in Europe well knew. But alliances must be renewed by every generation, and they have lasting effect only when all members of the two societies labor under the obligation. It is very probable that many of the societies organized on dualistic lines, members of one half marrying those of the other and giving each other mutual services, originated in this way. In Fiji these halves, or exogamous societies, are called the Two Sides and are said to face or wait on each other. It is a disgrace for one side to be outdone in eating or drinking, in war, or in giving presents. It loses not only honor, but political power as well, for it is always better to give than to receive: the giver is one-up and the receiver is in his debt. Thus an exchange of gifts has all the marks of a vendetta, the participants trying to humiliate each other with wealth and splendor.

This is the game of Beggar-my-neighbor in reverse. Many a Plains Indian has gained honor in exchange for giving feasts and presents, only to find that his ascendancy over his fellows ends when he is bankrupt. Similarly, many a South American chief is noted for his poverty and industry; he has to work all the time if he is to become indispensable. But the more settled and wealthy the tribe, the more the chief can maintain his honor. He attaches men to himself by giving them his daughters, and others who want to be in his good books provide him with women. He creates a polygamous household at the center of an extended family, and so has a work-force at his

A deerskin robe, probably that of Powhatan, father of Pocahontas, given to John Smith when he was Powhatan's prisoner.

213

disposal to accumulate the goods he is expected to give away. If the chiefship becomes hereditary, kingship is not far in the offing. The king is the chief of chiefs, the head of the great family: the chiefs are his officers and retainers, each with a political and ritual function to perform, and each chief has his officers, who are members of his family. In Fiji, where society was organized on these lines, the court was coextensive with the people and the only specialists were those whose traditional prerogative it was to make ceremonial objects for the royal cult, whose priests they were.

Such a social system operates within a system of checks and counterchecks, because all men aspire to honor and lordship, even though few achieve them. Self-interest breeds factions, which can become allied by marriages and other exchanges, and destroyed by such political acts as intrigue, treachery, and murder. But a faction must take care not to be too successful, for if it destroys its enemies completely, rivalry breaks out in its own ranks. The best politician is he who has learned the art of making enemies where it suits him, or—in Abraham Lincoln's words—to produce an effect and then to combat the effect so produced.

Besides such considerations, enemies are needed to feed a man's sense of honor. Isaac Babel tells the story of how he, a bespectacled and intellectual Jew, joined the Cossacks during the Russian Revolution, first as a transport officer and later in a cavalry regiment. The regiment had no spare horses, and Babel was without a mount until the Cossack Tikhomolov disgraced himself by killing two prisoners out of hand, and was sent away. Babel was given his horse, which under his ignorant handling developed sores, swollen fetlocks, and a tortured expression. Eventually the Cossack returned to the regiment and claimed his animal. "So it's like that?" said he, eyeing the beast as though thunderstruck: "I'm not making it up with you." Babel went to complain to Baulin, the Squadron Commander.

"'You've allotted me an enemy,' I said to him. 'And how was I to blame?' The Squadron Commander raised his head.

"'I see you,' he said. 'I see the whole of you. You're trying to live without enemies. That's all you think about, not having enemies.'

"'Make peace with him,' mumbled Bizyukov, turning away.

"A spot of fire was printed on Baulin's forehead. His cheek twitched.

"'You know what comes of this?' he said, not controlling his breath properly. 'Boredom comes of it. Clear off, damn your eyes!'"

Cossacks have enemies, and that makes them strong enough not to be bored. It was the same with the Tupi, who fed on danger in order to acquire position, to keep their womenfolk in order, and to be intoxicated with fame and notions of immortality. We can see something of these notions in the Tupi word for revenge, *ayepi,* which means literally "to be inside oneself." The meaning is the same as that of the Chilean word *ensimismado,* though this refers rather to a sulk. It refers to a state of self-absorption, and a brooding over self-esteem. Among the Tupi, this brooding set a man above his fellows, and so had to be paid for. The executioner went into seclusion for a long period in order to expiate his deed, and his fellows took advantage of his absence by carrying off all his possessions. In this manner the exchanges that make up the game of honor were brought to a temporary conclusion, the hero of the affair having paid off his obligations and also acquired merit.

Heroes of honor are solar figures, who put rivalry into order by sacralizing power. The wars prosecuted by the Tupi in the name of revenge thus often gave rise to widespread alliances, headed by men who had proved their honor many times. But these federations were not stable, having no cosmological order to support them. Here we can make an informative comparison with the Aztecs, who did have such an order. They, like the Tupi, believed that "those who go to heaven are those killed in wars, and prisoners who have died in their enemies' power." Both peoples tied their prisoners with a rope that was thought of both as a snake and an umbilical cord, the prisoner's death being equated with his rebirth. The Tupi opposed jaguar and falcon, the one standing for the victim, the other for the executioner. The Aztecs developed this symbolism by confronting the victim with four warriors belonging to the Eagle and Jaguar orders. And there are other similarities that suggest a link between these two cultures, though one of them was barbarous, and the other lived in cities.

The cities were originally those of the Toltecs, much of whose religion, art, and technology the Aztecs usurped. The Aztec mission, as declared by their war god Huitzilopochtli, was war: "I have to watch over and join issue with all manner of nations, and that not kindly." Significantly, Huitzilopochtli became the divine leader of the Aztecs only after he had persuaded them to overthrow his sister Malinalxochitl, a witch who governed man and beast by magic. Having defeated the feminine principle, the Aztecs were then free to practice their equivalent of the Malekulan pig sacrifice, war. They advanced implacably, spurred on by their god's prophecy: "The four corners of the world shall ye conquer, win, and subject to yourselves . . . it shall cost you sweat, work, and pure blood."

The Tupi did as much, but with the difference that they set no store by the cardinal points, and if they held the number four as being sacred no chronicler recorded the fact. It seems unlikely that they did: they followed the seasons, not the solstices and equinoxes. These were known only to the high cultures of Middle and South America, and the knowledge in its geometric

Mexican stone head of Malinalxochitl, bearing on her cheeks the hieroglyphs for gold and on the stump of her neck those for union and sacrifice.

and symbolic form spread among their immediate neighbors: the Aztecs may well have been ruled by the number four before they conquered the Toltecs. In any case the Toltecs gave them all the fruits of this knowledge, which had been growing over the centuries—a grandiose apparatus of cities, temples, a priestly religion, astronomical time-keeping, hieroglyphic writing, irrigation, and a developed agriculture. All these things the Aztecs adapted to their own ends, with horrifying consequences.

According to Laurette Sejourné, in *Burning Water,* that brilliant account of Aztec religion, their fault was to take over-literally a religion of sacrifice. For a start it was a religion of agriculture and settled life, whereas the Aztecs were hunters and nomads. It was also a religion of war, but that was something the Aztecs took more seriously than did those they conquered. The result was as if the Nazis had become Christians and used their concentration camps in the service of the Church Militant, whose theology has often been made to condone violence even though (or perhaps because) it advocates love.

The central myth of Middle America concerns a feathered serpent called Kukulkan by the Maya and Quetzalcoatl by the Toltecs. Quetzalcoatl was of an irritating purity, and his antagonist Tezcatlipoca took it upon himself to engineer his Fall. He did so by giving Quetzalcoatl a mirror in which he saw—can we say created?—his body. "Then Quetzalcoatl saw himself: he was very frightened and said 'If my vassals were to see me, they might run away.'" He fell into the temptation of getting drunk on pulque, slept with a lovely maiden, and so lost his purity. In despair he stayed four nights in a stone box he had had made for himself (we can remember how Osiris was made mortal by Set tempting him to lie in a sumptuous coffin where he might find honor in his death), and then, putting on his regalia, he set fire to himself and disappeared into the West. Eight days later he reappeared in the East, as the great star Quetzalcoatl.

The great star is the planet Venus, which, having set as the evening star, passes below the earth and reappears some days later as the morning star, the sun's herald. This passage is purgatorial; through it Quetzalcoatl expiates his fault, regains his lost purity, and rejoins his throne in the sun's birthplace. This was also the fate of the sacrificial victim, whom death purified so that he could join the sun and accompany it on its journey to the zenith.

The sun itself was also born of a sacrifice, in which a scabby man threw himself into a fire and rose freed of his polluted body. This is the fifth sun, according to the Aztecs. The four previous ones harmonized with the elements and the points of the compass; the fifth centered these around itself

The war god of the Zuni Indians of New Mexico, carved on a lightning-struck tree.

and assumed a regular circulation. It had naturally to be maintained in its position by sacrifice, and it was fed at the proper intervals with human hearts. As mentioned in Chapter 7, the timing of these intervals was connected with both the solar and the Venusian year, and with their conjunction, when Venus had completed five revolutions to the sun's eight. The sun was fed human hearts because it was a great cannibal, and the heart is the organ of penitence that must be purified if the soul is to eat immortality like the sun.

The Dogon say that death first infected this world when certain young men imitated a funeral without having a corpse to bury. The Aztecs show just how true this curious explanation is. The sun rises and sets without needing any help from mankind, and it is only a fancy to hold that Venus has to die as the evening star in order to become reborn as the morning

Top, back and front view of an Aztec jadeite carving of Xolotl, the twin of Quetzalcoatl, representing the planet Venus. He bears the sun on his back, and the front view shows him as death. Right, an Aztec stone arrow—a votive offering to the god of war.

Above, the Aztec hieroglyph for "burning water", to be imagined red as blood on the right and dense blue on the left.

Above, a 19th-century German drawing (after an Indian original) of the Union of Irreconcilables, fire and water.

star. But, what a fancy it is! Taken literally it has enormous consequences, both good and bad. Among the bad ones is the creation of a guilty conscience. The Tupi certainly suffered from that, and it was largely because they were constantly plagued by evil spirits that they were at first so easily, and so superficially, converted to Christianity, whose priests they thought to be great exorcists. That Montezuma, too, suffered from a guilty conscience, can be seen from his reception of Cortes. He took Cortes to be the reincarnation of Quetzalcoatl, whose religion of self-sacrifice he and his predecessors had transformed into its opposite. The Aztecs flocked to be converted after the conquest, and begged the priests to impose harsh penances on them for their misdeeds. They had performed similar expiations before the conquest and, considering the number of victims they killed annually, and all in the name of a cosmic funeral without a corpse, well might they do so.

It is of course man who is the dying god, and it is his corpse he is most concerned with: his debts, his failures, and his resentments. To repent of one's evil is to remember the misery of these things, and to punish them in one's own person. Taken properly, misery can be penitential. Simone Weil wrote: "Misery is a marvel of the divine technique. It is a simple and ingenious device by which that immensity of blind force, brutal and cold, can enter into the soul of a finite creature. The infinite distance separating God from his creature reassembles itself all entire in one point to pierce the soul in its center." The Aztecs believed this so well that they organized misery on a grand scale, to mortify both themselves and their enemies. They pierced their tongues, ear lobes, and genitals with thorns; they fasted and made sacrifices; they pierced their enemies' breasts to extract their hearts and make them blossom as a burning water; they waged the Blossoming War, whose knights were members of the Eagle and Jaguar orders. Wherever there were opposites there was a conflict, and conflict was the center around which movement could circulate. The geometrical sign for this generative battle was the quincunx, the emblem of Quetzalcoatl, who, as the union of bird and serpent, is the very blossom of the war. At its center is the human victim roped to the stone of sacrifice and attacked by four warriors, the four suns around the fifth.

It is easy to see in this social and cosmological drama how rivalry and an alternation between extremes can regulate a cyclical movement, as if by a pendulum. There can be no doubt that the drama also had political reference, and that the central fifth was in some way personated by the emperor who governed the four quarters of the world. How he came to do so escapes us for lack of knowledge. But a quite similar process in ancient China is well documented, and is fully dealt with in Marcel Granet's *La Civilisation Chinoise,* a superb work of anthropological history.

Chinese society was originally organized in moieties, the members of one moiety marrying those of the other, burying their dead, giving them service, rivaling them in the exchange of gifts. Those of moiety A called those of B by terms expressing a marriage relation, so that a man would call a whole class of men "mother's brother," even though most of them were not his biological uncles. Since he had to marry the daughter of one of these men, it was as though he had to marry his cross cousin, and as a result there was but one term used to name both mother's brother and father-in-law. Among the Iatmul, who followed the same customs, the nephew son-in-law was given his name by his uncle, and his body was claimed by his uncle's clan when he died. He became the priest of his uncle's cult, making the cult objects, personating the cult ancestor, and being fed with the sacrifice made to the ancestor. In return he presided over his uncle's funeral, eating scrapings from the ancestral bones and thus expiating the death. This was part of a lengthy series of exchanges ultimately based on the marriage transaction, in which he paid both for his wife and for the secrets of his uncle's cult. But between father and son there was no such relation. They were ashamed of each other, because they were affiliated to opposite moieties by marriage and by religion.

It was much the same for the ancient Chinese, among whom a man married his mother's brother's daughter and presided over his uncle's funeral, drinking the broth made from his corpse to inherit his virtue. This form of moiety organization, based on inheritance through the mother's line, creates a zigzag of inheritance and makes an opposition between alternate generations as well as between the two moieties. It also involves the chiefship, which is transmitted from uncle to nephew. The transmission is effected by either banishing or sacrificing the uncle's son after the funeral ceremonies are accomplished; the nephew's son is in turn banished when the nephew's reign is over. In this way both moieties share the chiefship, whose original function was to serve the tribal cult.

The cult starts with an ancestress or queen mother, who comes to represent the Yin principle. She is at first more important than her many sons, each of whom is the founder of a race of nobles; his deeds include clearing the land of scrub, digging irrigation ditches, inventing pottery and metalworking, and harmonizing the seasons. The chief personates the founder by being master of the calendar and by arranging for couplings to take place at the holy places at the equinoxes, when the forces of Yin and Yang are equal. He himself couples with his queen at every full moon, and thus ensures the collaboration of man and nature. It is a marriage of heaven and earth, of Yang and Yin, of the growing and the dead seasons.

Although the Yang and Yin forces are complementary, the moment when one turns into another is held to be one of conflict. This is especially true of the turn of the year, when the Yang is struggling to free itself from the passivity of the Yin's winter and to start a new agricultural season. At this time the people have stored the harvest and are living in their villages, safely sheltered from the deadness of nature. A new form of social life is now possible. The village becomes what the Australian Aborigines call a Big Place, in which all the members of a tribe or group are gathered. There is food in plenty, and the ancestral cults are celebrated at the moment when the spirit of life needs to be rekindled. In addition the earth has to be propitiated against the sacrilege of breaking it open and making it bear crops. Agricultural peoples take the risk, but only by first making a blood sacrifice to the Great Mother. The death of a human being pays for the crops, his soul being bound up in their growth and having to be dismissed at harvest time so that the people can eat the Great Mother's produce without fear of retribution. The dismissal appears to have been as bloody a matter as the invoking of the power of growth, and it is the rites concerned with both that turn the sacrilege of agriculture into a sacred performance. Because agriculture also requires settlement, these sacred performances are coextensive with the foundation and maintenance of settlements, and with the possession of land.

Opposite, an Indian miniature showing a prince receiving his weight in gold during an exchange of gifts. Overleaf, an Indian manuscript painting of the War of the Kinsmen. The Kauravas, on the right, are ranged against the Pandavas, who are led by Krishna and Arjuna in the chariot.

What we know from ancient Chinese texts suggests that the moieties had the duty and privilege of personating the Yang and the Yin The winter ceremonials were the time when their rivalry flowered in games, contests, duels, and feasts, each side putting on dramatic performances to outshine the other. There were also fraternities, each with its own cult. Perhaps the most important was that of the blacksmiths, whose mystery it was to transform stone into metal by the use of fire. These Vulcans occupy a special position among founding heroes because their sacrilege is great, and the rites they must use to expiate it make smithwork a powerfully sacred art. What is more, it is the smith who produces two nefarious instruments: those used by farmers to cut open the Great Mother's breast, and those used by men to kill one another. Weapons of war were held to be so potent for ill that they were not allowed near sacred places at sacred times, and when not in use they were kept by the lord of the village so that they should not blight the crops. By this means the lord was able to regulate warfare and keep it under ritual control, so much so that the earliest feudal capitals were laid out as military camps, divided into four quarters with the ritual complex at the center. Each quarter was under a military chief, and they in turn were under the chiefs of the Left and Right. In the center was the feudal lord as chief of all.

The sacredness of agriculture and war undoubtedly did much to make the male principle predominate over the female. Who was to personate which in the combats of winter ceremonial must also have been a matter of the keenest rivalry, and the various ritualized combats were the means by which the decision was reached. The two rival chiefs, each flanked by his lieutenants of the Right and the Left, confronted each other, and the losers were put to death. Because of the moiety organization, we must infer that the rivalry could be seen as one between in-laws. Certainly fathers and sons belonged to opposite sides, so that matters of succession were also at stake.

The earliest rule of succession was for the nephew-priest or minister to succeed his uncle-king, which he did by propitiating the ghost and eating his flesh cooked into a broth. In this way he gained the virtues of both heaven and earth. How long the king's rule lasted is not known. The texts make it clear that to avert his own end he used substitutes at the winter ceremonial, and that he could resign in favor of his nephew, whose reign was ideally 30 years, which is also the period of Saturn's synodic revolution. During these 30 years the king prepared himself for immortality, and at his death the nephew or minister acceded to the kingship by the rite called *jang,* which means both banishment and the ceding of power. It seems that the nephew-minister ceded power to the king's son and then regained it by

A Chinese lacquer panel bearing the eight trigrams around the T'ai Chi, and the tiger, emblem of the fall and metal.

Opposite, Krishna sporting with the milkmaids—detail from an Indian wallpainting.

225

sacrificing him. He thus banished the fatality of the death and at the same time provided the dead king with a necessary attendant in the other world.

The winter ceremonial was the occasion when agricultural and funeral practices could be symbolically combined. The drums were sounded continually to stir the latent thunder of the creative principle; the people danced to stir it into movement, and drank themselves into a stupor to imitate the sun's fall into oblivion and to tempt it out of its useless purity. The end of the year was set apart by six days of special and terrible celebrations, beginning with a duel between rival chiefs, who played a kind of chess to decide which one would become the representative of heaven and which of earth. The winner, the representative of earth, presided over the six-day ritual, during which animals of each of the six domestic species were sacrificed. On the seventh day the human representative of heaven was killed in order to open the New Year. His blood was poured into a wineskin shaped like an owl, the Yin emblem, and called by the name of Chaos. The wineskin full of blood was suspended from the top of a tall tower, tree, or pole, and the sacrificer shot it with seven arrows, curved to represent lightning, and was duly baptized by the blood as it spouted forth. By this act he made Chaos give birth to the sun, for the sun is the face of heaven and every face has seven openings (so also does every heart, according to Chinese symbolism). At the same time he took to himself the power of heaven that the game had ceded to his dead rival, and so joined the virtues of the Yang and the Yin in his own person.

The feast ended with a period of naked sexual licence, which marked the overturning of the old order. There are indications that the old queen was sacrificed at this moment, and her flesh eaten at a communal meal, which would mark a most definite victory of the male principle. As for the victorious king, he secluded himself for a time in an underground chamber, as the sun is hidden in the Abyss, and then climbed the tower or tree on which the Chaos victim hung, to mark his installation. There he achieved the heaven power, which was also celebrated by a rite called *fong,* at which a human sacrifice was made on the top of a mountain, the place marked by a cairn and a standing stone. Iatmul shamans talked of sexual intercourse in terms of "setting up a standing stone," and the image is doubtless true for the Chinese also: the king has embedded the Yang power firmly in the earth, and he takes his wife from the earth moiety to prove the point.

All this puts factionalism into a very formal context, which also stresses the masculine element. The contests that decided who should be the sky representative must also have become formal, and the order fixed once and for all. Many of the rites of kingship were those performed by the smith fraternity, the one mystery most dominated by male action; as for kingship, that is but fatherhood writ large. However the change came, come it did, and with it the reversal of the old rules of succession. It was now the nephew-minister who was banished or sacrificed at the king's death, and his eldest son who drank the broth of the dead man's flesh and so claimed the title. He still had to marry the daughter of his mother's brother to claim the virtue of earth, but the new arrangement allowed him to keep it together with that of the heaven.

But the old system of alternation remained ritually. Ever since the time when they belonged to opposite cults, father and son have seldom been at ease in Chinese society. They are social adversaries, so much so that the son used to be fostered by his mother's family and presented to his father only on certain occasions in order to be adopted into the father's line. The relation was that of lord and vassal, which subsisted until recently under the term of filial piety, a mixture of several conflicting impulses. Its ultimate aim is for a son to become worthy of carrying on the father's line, which he can do only by preparing his parents for the moment at which they become ancestors, when he may take over their worship and the titles they have held. But father and son are as separate in death as they are in life, and their ancestral tablets are fixed on opposite sides of the ancestors' shrine.

Some have more ancestors than others. The lord has most: his line stretches back to the founding hero, from whom he gains his prerogative of being called Lord of Vassals and Chief of Kin. (This last phrase defines

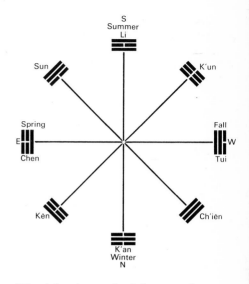

The eight trigrams in their seasonal arrangement. K'an, the Abyss, marks the winter, and Kên, the Mountain, precedes Chen, Thunder, which inaugurates spring.

Chinese inscriptions from bronze vessels of the Shang dynasty. At left, a man with his grandson, who is shaped like a frog, offers the smell of meat (held in his hand, bottom) to the ancestor (top). Center, an offering made to the ancestor, who shows his acceptance by leaving his footprints in the sanctuary. Right, the eyes of the ancestor regard the hide of a sacrificed victim behind the sanctuary doors. Underneath is an offering of meat.

our word *king,* both socially and etymologically.) His vassals are those living in his city, and members of the same social family. But families are always growing, splitting, and settling elsewhere; those who found new households then become the founding ancestors for their descendants. In this way a hierarchy of ancestors is established, the chief going back to the beginning, his vassals to the ancestor who split off from the main line. When the chief becomes a feudal lord he is able to assign a particular number of ancestors to each degree of nobility, and this fixes them in the hierarchy.

The hierarchy was also established by the sacrifice. The feudal lord was the expiator of the necessary sacrilege of agriculture and war, and the continuator of the foundation worship. Both good and evil were offered to him to be desacralized and made economic, and as a result he became the focus of the economy and the redistributor of its wealth. This is always the duty of kings. It is written in the Hindu book of Manu, "As the sun for eight months draws up water with his beams, so let the king draw up taxes, for that is the function of the sun. . . . As Indra (the king of the gods) rains down for the four rainy months, so let the king rain down favours on his kingdom." The common man among the Chinese offered his goods to the family head, the dignitary to his lord, the lord to the Son of Heaven, and the Son of Heaven to heaven itself. Or rather, he ceded the virtue of these goods to heaven, which is the act of expiation, and offered them back to his vassals. It was he who first ate of the sacrifice; his vassals ate what he left; what they left was offered to those next in the hierarchy; and so down the scale to the many whose work provided the offerings in the first place.

Again, it is the same in India: "The noble is an eater, the farmer food." But we must remember that the castes are born of the sacrifice, and that its virtues accrue to all men. The protocol of redistribution is jealously observed, because it is through it that a man gains honor. The lord gains honor by ceding honor to heaven, his vassals gain it by ceding tribute to him, the only way of affirming their rank. The lord's power to redistribute goods because of the sacrifice allows him to use the same power for political ends. Vassals are those who depend on a lord for food, which is the reason that feasts are offered to enemies in order to make them feel dependent. Women were also a handy weapon with which to envassal others: several lords are on record as having used their harems to satisfy the appetites of their guests, who thus became their vassals or, to use the Roman term, their clients. As for the feudal lord, he was not only the middleman in this complicated organization of exchange, from which he greatly profited, but also the one who could transcend it. He was at the center of many different rivalries and oppositions, and occupied the position of the fifth sun among the Aztecs, the cannibal lord who ate his subjects in order to give them back riches, honor, and the fertile consequences of movement.

All this is ritual behavior with a vengeance, which is one reason why people endure it. It is a game of honor in which life is at stake. He who tried to take all the honor to himself, and the power with it, soon found that he had made more enemies than he could manage. The game was the extension of the vendetta, played with a scrupulous knowledge of the rules and of the consequences of that overreaching the Greeks called *hybris*.

The principal rule of all feudal societies is not to lose face, and to avoid forcing your enemy to lose face. For this reason, feudal wars are full of strange courtesies, mutual compliments, and rules of honor. A lord fights a righteous war only in order to punish the committer of crimes. The loser can appeal to the victor's sense of honor by admitting his fault, and so keep his life and his possessions. A general does not attack an enemy who is at a disadvantage; he fights only those of equal rank, and thinks himself dishonored if he kills more than three of them. Nor will he try to gain an outright victory, for he can expiate that only by losing his own life at the hands of his lord, whom otherwise he would have to overthrow. As that Machiavellian Hindu book of politics, the *Arthasastra,* advises, a general or a minister should make himself indispensable to his king by keeping the king's enemies more or less intact. The king knows this well, and makes political alliances only with those who have the same enemies as himself. Once the enemy is defeated the ally has no reason to keep the alliance going, lest he be defeated in his turn. This logic gave rise to the first Indian war

game, formalized as a board with concentric circles and called the *mandala*. The king is at the center of the board, and any shift on the periphery alters the polarity at the center. All the arts of treachery, intrigue, and murder are called in to maintain a proper balance, and they are ultimately justified by the sacred courtesies of honor.

We could call these personal tabus, that is, a man's claim to his dignity and the control of his possessions. The word *tabu,* which comes from Polynesia, indicates this. It signified a power to sequester goods, land, or honor from other people, and it had force because the political reality went hand in hand with the religious one. Many Plains Indians had similar tabus. In one tribe, for instance, a powerful man had the tabu that he had to shift his tepee if he heard others driving tent pegs into the ground, which can be construed as a way of stopping his neighbors from making that kind of noise. A man can possess only that which ritual usage sanctions: other things may be stolen more or less with impunity, but anything with supernatural virtue can be transferred to another only by means of a rite ceding the virtue in an appropriate way, or by claiming it with ingenious quibbles drawn from mythology and backed by force.

This virtue is inherent in the owner as much as the object. In feudal society it makes for a scrupulousness of deportment, punctilio, dress, oratory, courtship, eating, warfare, and whatever is a matter of honor. In all things the proper etiquette is a mark of homage to the lord, and the clothes worn by the noble show the virtue of his soul. The word *virtue* expresses the essential characteristic of a person, a creature, or a thing as it is manifested in its appearance and activity. Thus the Urubu Indians describe a chief as being *porang* when he is dressed in his insignia, the word meaning "beautiful" in the moral as well as the physical sense. When *porang,* the chief is showing the virtue of manliness in the splendor of his appearance. Women also have their virtue, and for both sexes this virtue has much to do with sexuality, so that they draw attention to the organs in which their virtue is concentrated by decorating them. This seductive boast is at the same time a prophylactic against shame. One result is that human beings become ashamed of nakedness, in which they can take no pride. Beautification attracts other tabus and shames to itself; to repeat the Dogon aphorism, "to be naked is to be speechless." As for being speechless, that means having nothing to boast about.

In archaic societies, as in ours, beauty and boasting go very much together. Beauty gives value to desire and is also the sign of wealth—or, perhaps, of that wealthy self-possession that can be used to gain interest by challenging others to do better in exchanges. No wealth, no beauty; no beauty, no

A 15th-century Flemish shield, decorated in praise of the chivalry of courtship, shows a knight kneeling before his lady.

A Taoist scroll painting of two Chinese warriors, traditionally armed.

pride; no pride, no virtue. And if there is no virtue in things, there is no life, and nothing by which it can be generated.

It is the king's function to gather all such virtue in himself. He does so politically by accumulating vassals; ritually by accumulating ceremonies; spiritually (if that is the right word) by accumulating the merits of decorum; and first and foremost by accumulating the virtues of heaven and earth. He becomes like the blameless king of the *Odyssey*, "who, in the fear of god ruling over men many and stalwart, upholds the right: the black earth bears wheat and barley, the trees are laden with fruit, the flocks bear young without fail, the sea provides fish, by reason of good government, and the people prosper under him." If the king is maimed and impotent, as in the Graal legends, so that he cannot satisfy his queen the earth, or if he is without virtue, the land becomes waste. So the king, as the embodiment of health, wealth, and fertility, of rain and sunshine, of the largesse of mercy and the rigor of justice, becomes the proper scapegoat when these virtues are not present upon earth. Having collected the virtues of the world within himself, he is self-collected in a way no other man can be. He is the image of the self, and as such is bound by the rites and myths of the creation.

Left, the Vision of the Holy Grail, with Galahad in the Siege Perilous—from a 15th-century French manuscript.

Opposite, a Chinese bronze ritual vessel of the Shang period in the form of a tiger protecting a man.

A Chinese bronze model, dating from the second century B.C., of a horse-drawn carriage with driver and attendant.

Hocart, in his fine book on kingship, remarked that men like to have a king because the obligations he puts them under allow them to shine in his service. The king is the great shiner, the sun, and is therefore bound by etiquette even more than are his vassals. As the lord of measure he must at all times hold himself erect, whether sitting correctly upon the ritual mat, which must be correctly placed, or walking with the correct step of half a foot; he may listen to only a certain kind of music, may eat only the correct seasonal foods prepared in the correct way. He is dressed in the correct vestments, with jade tablets tinkling at his belt. At his appearance his vassals still the tinkling of their own jade tablets, and, by setting their eyes no higher than his chin, save themselves both from irreverence and from being blinded by the splendor of his countenance. None may speak to him directly, not even in the third person, but only to his counsellors, who put the argument into such a form that the king indicates his will in an indirect manner. He is enclosed by formalities of all kinds, being constantly under the eye of heaven, and his vassals form a barrier between him and the outside world in such a way that although he reigns, he can never govern. His ministers do that for him, for that is their prerogative.

The feudal states of China were a confederation. The fought each other not to annex territory but in the courtly pursuit of the vendetta. But it was a different matter with the barbarians encircling them, who were numerous and powerful enough to force the confederation to act as a whole, under the leadership of the strongest state. The lord of this state was called the Son of Heaven and he—or his general—was the war chief of the alliance. The title is significant. Heaven is common to all, unlike the founding heroes of noble lines, who are identified with particular territories. Moreover, Heaven was the god of oaths and of allegiance, and had to be propitiated with human flesh. The ritual practice of cannibalism ensured the succession among the Chinese, and the rules of feudal life made it impossible for one lord to eat another. This would have been tantamount to an annexation of the rival feudality, and would have brought many vexations in its train. But barbarians were fair game. Properly speaking they were not human beings, for they spoke different languages, had no recognizable manners, and were not related by the same cult practices. In their wars against the barbarians the Chinese ate their enemies and annexed their territories with a good conscience. The priest of this ritual was the Son of Heaven, who ceded the honor of the victory to Heaven by way of expiation, and by so doing established the Great Peace that was to extend over the whole empire.

The establishment of empire was the death of feudalism. Feudal states were transformed into provinces, officials took the place of the nobility,

A Chinese bronze ritual food vessel, of the Shang dynasty, decorated with the faces of victims of ritual sacrifice.

conquered peoples were moved from one land to another, and armies were no longer composed of vassals and their retainers, but of adventurers and brigands who cared nothing for the old chivalry of warfare. Law replaced custom. The merchant class became the natural ally of the emperor because it was now possible for him to accumulate wealth in the name of universal government, and to redistribute it by a quite different logic.

But in spite of this the old forms never died, although feudal lords had their particular cults discontinued and local custom was undermined wherever it had political reference. For the emperor had still to lay claim to his empire in person, by accumulating the priesthood of local cults, annexing their power, and going on a sacred triumph around his dominions. In India such a ruler was known as a Cakravartin or Wheel King, one who extended his reign to the four quarters by letting a horse, accompanied by an army, roam where it would. Wherever the horse went unchallenged, there the Wheel King's rule went too. The first emperor of the Chinese Han dynasty, a forceful but illiterate warrior, made a similar claim: "I have conquered the empire on horseback, and on horseback I propose to hold it." Yet he too had to obey the dictates of kingship: within two years his administration, in the hands of soldiers as unused to administration as he was himself, was in such confusion that he was forced to bring in ritual experts of the old school to help him to govern. They insisted that he should be installed in the traditional manner. His architect-minister built a splendid audience hall in which the nobility, the generals, and the officials took up their proper stations; the army stood in its place, ranked under its distinguishing standards; there was the traditional banquet, and all hierarchical matters were scrupulously observed. At the end the emperor exclaimed: "Now I know what it means to be an emperor!"

His words are perhaps ambiguous, for another translation has him say, with a sigh, "I now only know the exalted status of the Ruler of Man," a remark that confesses his bondage to the ritualistic values the new breed of warriors despised. It was for his dynasty that the color yellow and the number five were chosen to be the marks of the new order. He also reformed the calendar, for every ruler must mark out the seasons in order to make his sway effective, and a calendar house, or Ming Tang, was erected for him. It had four rooms (one for each season) and 12 windows (one for each month), and in this ancient image of the political cosmos he performed the appropriate rites, going from room to room and window to window according to the season. So powerful was the influence of this rite that it continued, marvelously elaborated, to the present century. For, as Granet said, an empire has no other foundation than the virtue proper to a dynasty, and this virtue is void if the empire is not well governed, prosperous, at peace with itself, and in harmony with heaven and earth.

There are many forms of kingship. Some are rulers who cannot sacrifice; some are sacrificers who do not rule; others, with difficulty, are both priest and king, for example the Mitra Varuna of the Hindus and the Melchizedek of the Hebrews. But, whoever gains the primacy, priest and king belong together because both are expected to transcend the rivalries of exchange and to create the great peace that is the property of heaven. It is a peace that is not of this world, because it deserts the world so often, and it is also one that is founded upon the waging of a sacred war. The theme is that of the *Bhagavad-Gita*, that majestic summary of Hinduism that is the centerpiece of the epic *Mahabharata*. The epic describes a war between kinsmen, a vendetta that began with a dice-match in proper feudal style. The warrior Arjuna has Krishna as his charioteer, but when he sees the ranks of his enemies, among whom are many of his kinsmen, he is overcome with sorrow and a sense of crime.

Is he indeed so greedy for greatness, he asks, that he must kill his kinsmen? Rather let his enemies take him:

> I shall not struggle,
> I shall not strike them.
> Now let them kill me,
> That will be better.

Krishna rebukes him for cowardice, ignorance, and a fatal lack of discrimination; he preaches the doctrine of the Atman or Self that can neither slay nor be slain, explains the nature of illusion, and tells him to fight and have no fear. He who knows the mystery of action knows also how to renounce the fruits of his action, and by giving up all things he achieves the unfailing serenity of the Self.

> He who regards
> With an eye that is equal
> Friends and comrades,
> The foe and the kinsman,
> The vile, the wicked,
> The men who judge him,
> And those who belong
> To neither faction:
> He is the greatest.

The sun shines alike on the just and the unjust. Such is the great peace issuing from the great sacrifice, at which priest and king officiate: a terrible matter in which all causes are married to an endless conclusion.

9 The Healing Madness

The Yanoama Indians of the Amazon basin are much given to feuds, killings, and matters of honor. The older men and women often lecture the warriors on their insensate passion for putting themselves and others to the test, but to small effect. To live peacefully gains no fame and few adherents, and an ambitious soul strives after both.

Some years ago one of their chiefs, called Fusiwe, who had gained the just reputation of being a strong man in a feud, became so impatient for his own honor that he killed several of his own supporters who had displeased him. Neither friend nor foe dared attack him openly, but one day he was invited to bury the hatchet at a great festival in a neighboring village. He accepted, arrived on the appointed day, and was shot to death by his hosts.

The story is curious, not for the commonplace treachery involved, but because Fusiwe had been told that the invitation was a trick and that an ambush had been planned. He declared that this was very likely, and added that, because life for an orphan child would be intolerable, he would take his much-loved son with him to share his end. The son was killed without difficulty, but Fusiwe was another matter. Not that he defended himself, but he stood silent and implacable until he had been shot with as many arrows as a porcupine has quills.

He then fell with a terrifying groan, and so great was the fear instilled into his enemies by his feat of endurance that they scarcely dared to drag the body out of the village. Fusiwe no doubt knew this would be the case, and that by this suicide at one remove he would haunt their imaginations for many a year. It is the same trick of one-upmanship that Chinese feudatories sometimes played on lords who had overstepped the mark, and by which they diminished them of honor and service in the correct ritual manner. But Fusiwe must have had other reasons for his decision. Perhaps he was tired of slaughter and guilty of too much success; perhaps he knew that he had exhausted the goodwill of his friends; perhaps the dare was too great for his sense of honor to forgo.

A 15th-century Turkish manuscript illumination showing two shamans dancing or fighting.

Perhaps, lastly, he knew that the way of a warrior comes to an end only when he dies willingly in the land of his enemies, a passion through which his soul would be instantly translated to the other world. As we have seen among the ancient Chinese, this is a way of ceding power to your adversary in order to appropriate its benefits later; it exercises *hybris*, and lays the spirit of Nemesis at rest. In any case, Fusiwe removed himself from the scene of his actions, and in so doing appropriated the strength his enemies had used to kill him. In a sense, he received absolution.

This quest for finality can be compared with R. L. Stevenson's fable called "Faith, Half-Faith, and No Faith At All." It deals with a priest, a virtuous person, and a rover with his axe, all going on the same journey. The priest and the virtuous person believe justice shall prevail in the name of Odin, the one because this is in the nature of things, the other because Odin can do no less for mankind. The rover says nothing. After witnessing a couple of unnatural omens, which the priest and the virtuous person agreed need not be taken seriously:

". . . at length one came running, and told them all was lost; that the powers of darkness had besieged the Heavenly Mansions, that Odin was to die, and evil triumph.

" 'I have been grossly deceived,' said the virtuous person.

" 'All is lost now,' said the priest.

" 'I wonder if it is too late to make it up with the devil?' said the virtuous person.

" 'Oh, I hope not,' said the priest. 'And at any rate, we can but try. But what are you doing with your axe?' says he to the rover.

" 'I am off to die with Odin,' said the rover."

The myth Stevenson refers to here is that of Ragnarok. Odin's "Heavenly Mansion" was called Valhalla, the Hall of the Fallen, and his retainers were those killed with weapons upon earth. They did everlasting battle with each other in the afterworld by day, and were brought back to life and feasted by night. The ultimate purpose of the assemblage was to support Odin during Ragnarok, the Day of the Wolf, when he and all his followers would be defeated and the world come to an end.

Inasmuch as the world comes to an end for all those who die, there seems little point in comparing a Fusiwe with a rover and his axe. However, the belief in Ragnarok is known among the Guarani tribes of South America, where it is a Blue Celestial Jaguar rather than a wolf who will devour the world. The myth may refer in part to the ending of one zodiacal age and the beginning of another, but a suspicion remains that Fusiwe did not believe that he was dying in a hopeless cause and that only extinction awaited him.

The god Odin, on a stone slab from the Isle of Man. An eagle perches on his shoulder and his leg is in the mouth of the Fenris Wolf.

Nor, for that matter, did most rovers with their axes, because they could look forward to Valhalla.

For who is Odin? His name is connected with the Scandinavian word *othr,* "poetry," and the Latin *vates,* "a prophet," "a poet," "an inspired singer." The quality of this inspiration is shown by the related Old English word *wood*, meaning "mad," and is paralleled by *giddy*, originally "to be possessed by a god." The root of the name may also mean "wind" and "storm," and, because gods of storm are commonly those of war, it is no surprise to find that Odin is also a war-god. In short Odin is the god of inspired frenzy and glorious deeds, and his followers become one with him in the Wild Hunt of which he is the leader.

The rover died with Odin, not for him, which means that he and Odin are of the same spirit. Odin thus represents the wisdom of self-sacrifice. In the *Lay of the High One* he speaks of himself in these terms:

> I trow that I hung
> on the windy tree
>   swung there nights all of nine;
> gashed with a blade
> bloodied for Odin,
>   myself an offering to myself
> knotted to that tree
> no man knows
>   whither the root of it runs.
>
> None gave me bread
> none gave me drink,
>   down to the depths I peered
> to snatch up runes
> with a roaring screech
>   and fall in a dizzied faint!
> Well-being I won
> and wisdom too,
>   I grew and joyed in my growth;
> from a word to a word
> I was led to a word,
>   from a deed to another deed.

The tree on which Odin hung is of course Yggdrasil, the Horse of Ygg, the World Tree, which shows him to be yet another incarnation of the god who creates the world by dismembering himself. Those who do the same find in themselves the wisdom of being Odin—a wisdom that is high,

lonely, and not to be found in the cycles of time. And although Odin has passed away in name, his successor has not disdained to exemplify the same basic truths. He too died upon a tree, promises well-being, wisdom, and joy to those who become one with him, and in the Book of Revelation is threatened by a Ragnarok, although this defeat is to be followed by the Day of the Lamb.

The differences between the religion of Odin and that of the Christ are of course numerous. To take but one, Christianity is messianic, which means that justice will after all prevail and that the salvation of the world lies in its ending. In the Gospels, it is plainly said that salvation would come during the lifetime of the disciples, after the Son of God had taken the Kingdom of Heaven by violence. Hope springs eternal; although the promise was not fulfilled, neither was it forgotten, and it has undergone many a modification in the hands of priests and virtuous persons, who have their own reasons for avoiding finality.

Christianity is not the only messianic religion. The Tupi tribes, to whom the behavior of a Fusiwe would have been quite understandable, were messianic in their own fashion. Their Benefactor, Maira, was also the victim of a ritual death. Like many virtuous persons, the Tupi spent their lives in emulating the deeds of his persecutors while dressing themselves up in his image. By the rules of the game they often had to endure the fate they were dealing out to others, whereupon they believed that they would be translated from this world to the next in a proud and unforgiving glory. All things exist only by virtue of a lively opposition, however, and the principal Tupi virtue of being "hard" alternated with that of turning the other cheek. They were stirred up to this unlikely state of affairs by their prophets, as the early chroniclers called them, and set off to find the Land without Evils in a spirit of penitent abnegation. They did penance, suffered hardship, and performed the proper rites, without the promise of this earthly Paradise ever materializing. Those who were alive after acting out this pre-Columbian version of the American Dream then reverted to their old ways of earning a livelihood, and again revenged themselves on whatever disappointed their ambitions or stood in the way of their ideals.

The Tupi never learned the moral of this failure, being ready to embark on such an expedition whenever a new prophet arose and they had grounds to be persuaded by his preaching. We must remember that the myths charge the Tupi with ingratitude for having killed their Benefactor, and on the face of it his murder does appear unnatural. But if he was anything like their prophets, who did all they could to appear like him, his end is understandable. He was killed to avenge the loss of a powerful illusion.

The Four Horsemen of the
Apocalypse—*woodcut (1465) by
Albrecht Dürer.*

William Blake's illustration to his poem "Milton" of the inspired poet, or vates, *with a star at his foot.*

Although there is no doubt that the advent of Europeans on the coast of Brazil stimulated many of these ill-fated journeys, the myth of the Land without Evils must have been at work long before. As we have seen, the habit of revenge brings with it a desire to do penance, and the failure of penance to achieve its messianic ends turns man back to the habit of revenge. The Tupi and the Aztecs are excellent examples of this swing between two extremes, and so for that matter is Christianity, with its persecution of heretics on the one hand and its institutions for self-mortification on the other. Illusion is a powerful intoxicant, and it can produce a most disagreeable hangover.

There is no doubt that man has a fatality for getting drunk, both literally and metaphorically. He can get drunk with glory, power, ideas, lusts, and religious certitudes as easily as he can with alcohol. He enjoys putting himself into a passion for the feeling of life it gives him. His spirit has been infected with sensuality, according to Genesis, ever since he ate that intoxicating fruit of the Tree of Knowledge, and he is now an addict.

However, as Blake said in his "Proverbs of Hell," "The road of excess leads to the palace of wisdom," for "If the fool would persist in his folly, he would become wise." Elsewhere he quotes a verse from Numbers: "Would to God that all the Lord's people were Prophets." Blake was indeed a *vates*, an inspired poet, a man of visions and mystical purpose, who believed that Christ had walked on England's mountains green, and there vowed to re-build Jerusalem.

He was a messianic prophet, in fact. Because he was born in an age that frowned upon Enthusiasm—literally, possession or inspiration by a god—and that knew nothing at first hand of what it means to snatch up runes "with a roaring screech," he was driven to write an Apology for his vocation, his *Marriage of Heaven and Hell*—a significant title—in which the "Proverbs of Hell" are to be found. It is an attack upon those he calls Angels (the priest and the virtuous person of Stevenson's fable) whose vanity is to think themselves wise because of their systematic reasoning. Angels divide mind from body, call reason good and energy evil, and hold that hell is for those who follow their energies. Blake announced the following contraries to be true:

"1. Man has no Body distinct from his Soul; for that call'd Body is a portion of Soul discerned by the five senses, the chief inlets of Soul in this age.

2. Energy is the only life, and is from the Body; and Reason is the bound or outward circumference of Energy.

3. Energy is Eternal Delight."

And two sections later, in one of his "Memorable Fancies," he writes: "As I was walking amongst the fires of hell, delighted with the enjoyments of Genius, which to Angels look like torment and insanity. . . ."

Let us remember that genius is an inborn faculty presiding over a man's life, or the particular spirit of a place or thing; that in ancient times it was the generative spirit housed in the brain, the spinal cord, and the genitals; and that the genius of a man was thought to turn into a serpent at his death. That it is to be enjoyed in hell, according to Blake, identifies it with Lucifer the Light-bearer, whose Fall, according to Dante, created Mount Purgatory with the Garden of Eden at its top; and that hell is a place of fire tells us that genius is Promethean and does blacksmith's work.

All these allusions are borne out when we come to consider the prophets or *shamans*, as they are usually called, of tribal peoples. But first we must return to Odin and the fact that he was the god of poets and warriors alike. The same is true of the Tupi tribes, of whom only the shamans and warriors went to heaven after their deaths, because only these two kinds of men truly make themselves one with the spirit that animates their lives.

"Life may be death, death life—who knows?" remarked Euripides. The answer lies with those who claim to have tasted both, or who have at least put themselves into such a state that out of the difference they find wisdom. The state is a form of intoxication in which a man loses his head, or that part of it that Angels employ to reason systematically. This figure of speech is found in several of the myths concerning Dionysus, the god of intoxication. He is credited with two principal victims, Orpheus and Pentheus. Both were torn to pieces by the god's women devotees, Orpheus because he worshiped Apollo and neglected to honor Dionysus, and Pentheus because he actively opposed the cult of frenzy. Both had their heads torn off, and that of Orpheus went floating down a river to the sea, singing as it went, and was finally taken to a cave where it gave oracles. However, it is likely that Orpheus was himself a form of Dionysus, being credited with the invention of his mysteries; that he became the victim of the god he worshiped puts him on a level with Odin offering himself to himself. That his head gave oracles is as much as to say that Orpheus also snatched up runes from the depth when his frenzy had dismembered him. The story has been interpreted to mean that Orpheus was either a shaman or some kind of sacred king undergoing his necessary sacrifice. Whatever the truth of the matter, it reflects shamanic usage closely enough for our purposes. We must consider what this tearing apart signifies, for shamans regularly report that at the outset of their careers they have been dismembered and afterwards put together again.

This cannot be done literally. Nor can it be done symbolically, if by that we mean that the action is a mere representation. Nor is it a fantasy, for the tearing apart is truly felt to be a tearing apart. It is more like a nightmare during which the dreamer is racked with pain and terror, although a nightmare is usually something one awakes from alarmed and not much the wiser. In this nightmare the shaman does awake, not in this world but among the fires of hell. He is excruciated through death, and yet lives to tell the tale.

"Death is a fearful thing," says Claudio in *Measure for Measure*. And his sister replies, "And shamed life a hateful." In a nightmare all these matters combine and become monstrously visible. The appalling drama proceeds relentlessly while the heart pounds, the body breaks out in a cold sweat, the breath sticks in the throat, and the dreamer is paralyzed in all the joints of his imagination. Many things can bring on a nightmare: indigestion, hangovers, suffocation by a blanket, feverish sickness, and of course a bad conscience. All of them poison sleep and torment the body as well as the mind.

Yet some fevers have their recompense. The naturalist A. E. Wallace suffered a bout of malaria while traveling through the jungles of Southeast Asia, and among the vivid images that took his mind was the solution to a biological problem he had long been concerned with. He communicated his discovery to Darwin, who, unknown to him, had been secretly amassing evidence in support of the same theory for 20 years. The result was a joint paper to the Royal Society, in which they proposed the working of natural selection as the principal agent of evolution.

Likewise Keats wrote his best poetry while suffering from the combined attacks of tuberculosis, a hopeless love affair, and grief for his dead brother; Mallarmé his short stories while suffering from syphilis: and Strindberg his plays while slowly dying from a stomach cancer. Now, although it is obvious that there is no point in a dolt contracting syphilis in order to become a master of prose, yet a mental or physical illness in a man who has already developed his talents may have curious and marvelous effects upon his art before it becomes fatal. For if to pursue one's normal course of action is, as Dr. Johnson said, to drive on the system of life, then it follows that, when that system is being made to gallop, one's pursuits will be correspondingly animated.

The same is true of a shaman: a nightmare without discipline leads nowhere. But what is the cause of this nightmare that transforms him into a visionary, and why is the visionary experience rare and hard to come by?

"Certainly Adam in Paradise had not more sweet and curious apprehensions of the world, than I when I was a child," wrote Traherne. "All

A Tlingit Indian wooden figure from Alaska representing a shaman as a skeleton singing the death song.

appeared new, and strange at first, inexpressibly rare and delightful and beautiful. I was a little stranger, which at my entrance into the world was saluted and surrounded with innumerable joys. My knowledge was Divine . . . .

"The corn was orient and immortal wheat, which never should be reaped, nor was ever sown. I thought it had stood from everlasting to everlasting. The dust and stones of the street were as precious as gold: the gates were at first the end of the world. The green trees when I saw them first through one of the gates transported and ravished me, their sweetness and unusual beauty made my heart to leap, and almost mad with ecstasy . . . . Boys and girls tumbling in the street were moving jewels, I knew not that they were born or should die; But all things abided eternally as they were in their proper stations. Eternity was manifest in the Light of the Day, and something infinite behind everything appeared: which talked with my expectation and moved my desire . . . . So that with much ado I was corrupted, and made to learn the dirty devices of this world. Which I now unlearn, and become . . . a little child again that I may enter into the Kingdom of God."

There are many things to corrupt the divine exuberance of a child, and psychoanalysts of various persuasions have cataloged so many of the dirty devices to which children are subjected that the heart sinks. Each one of them is a cause of complaint, and every complaint destroys spontaneity and creates what Traherne called "churlish proprieties," and divisions, and bounds—everything, that is, that marks off the sacred from the profane.

And at the heart of the complaint is the fact that consciousness, though given to a child, yet takes time to develop. The human infant is born with a minimum of automatic responses, remains helpless for longer than the young of any other animal, and learns the use of its body and the meaning of its experience only after much practice. These two activities are of course closely related. In Piaget's terminology, one can assimilate experience only by accommodating oneself to the objects one perceives. The child can articulate meaning only when his musculature and his senses are brought together by an intention. But in a world full of contradictory intentions it is no wonder that children seldom articulate their functions into a harmonious whole, or that they develop complaints in the place of understanding. Moreover, the worlds of the imagination and of action are poles apart. To translate the one into the other is a laborious and uncompletable art.

As we have seen, many traditions lay the blame for this state of affairs upon God himself. The Hindu tradition, as summarized by Coomaraswamy, shows a more courteous understanding of what is involved. "The Progenitor whose emanated children are as it were sleeping and inanimate stones, reflects 'Let me enter into them, to awaken them': but so long as he is one, he cannot, and therefore divides himself into the powers of perception and consumption, extending these powers from his hidden lair in the 'cave' of the heart through the doors of the senses to their objects, thinking 'Let me eat of these objects': in this way 'our' bodies are set up in possession of consciousness, he being their mover. And since the Several Gods or measures of fire into which he is thus divided are 'our' energies and powers, it is the same to say that 'the Gods entered into man, they made the mortal their house.' His possible [capable of suffering and experience] nature has now become 'ours'; and from this predicament he cannot easily recollect or rebuild himself, whole and complete."

The predicament becomes worse when, as is usual, the Progenitor becomes identified with the objects he desires to eat. This act, which makes his dismemberment mortal, is known to psychoanalysts as *projection*. The rebuilding of the Progenitor is accomplished ritually by the sacrificer setting out these identifications and then separating the Several Gods from the objects that condition them. The Several Gods are then freed, as are the objects to which they imparted their nature. The rebuilding of the Progenitor thus starts with the destruction of the forms his emanations had desired for themselves, while the death of the victim relates the sacrificer to the god.

All such rites are but the acting-out and demonstration of what should happen within the sacrificer as well as without. The sacrificer is then called a Comprehensor, and only a Comprehensor can truly put the dismembered deity together. Thus the *Sankhayana Aranyaka* declares: "If one sacrifices, knowing not this interior burnt-offering, it is as if he pushed aside the brands and made oblation in the ashes." Other texts add that the powers of the Comprehensor's soul build up this fire even when he is sleeping.

In the Fire Sacrifice, man repeats all that the gods once did, but in the reverse direction. Earth and heaven are rejoined, after they have been sundered by the act of creation. The same process must be gone through when making the interior burnt-offering. The articulations between mind, body, and the objects of experience must all be broken, and this process liberates the passions that emerge from the activity of the Several Gods or measures of Fire.

It is of course these passions, however conditioned, and with all their singularities, that are the causes of the shamanistic nightmare. There have been many attempts to diagnose them in psychiatric terms. Shamans have been accused of suffering from hysteria, epilepsy, schizophrenia, apoplexy, neurosis, homosexuality, and a great deal of sado-masochism. Certainly the symptoms of the initial shamanic disorder are ominous enough. Among

248

the Bororo of Brazil the shaman-to-be is in a continual tremble, and stinks of carrion; among the Araucanians of Chile, he is subject to fainting fits, a weak heart, and bad digestion. In Siberia he is haunted by evil spirits, gashes himself with knives like Odin, and sweats blood. Among the Selknam of Tierra del Fuego he sings in his sleep. Elsewhere he can do nothing but sleep day and night for weeks on end. Among the Tungus of Manchuria he is taken by a wild spirit and disappears into the hills. There, like a follower of Dionysus, he kills animals with his teeth and eats them raw, and eventually returns dirty, torn, and savage, mumbling incoherent words. Among neighboring tribes he is afflicted with spasms, falls into trances, howls, dances, and collapses in epileptoid seizures.

To diagnose is one thing; to cure, another. Many people go mad, and their madness does take recognizable forms. Few of them, however, become shamans. It is therefore significant that in societies where shamans exist, those who are mad and those suffering from the onset of a shamanistic frenzy are sharply distinguished. Certainly, they have much in common, but the shaman is marked by a feature conspicuously absent in others, the

Dancing maenads—three ecstatic followers of Dionysus shown on a Roman bas-relief.

power to transform his disabilities into an asset. Not only does he see visions, but he knows how to apply them; moreover he becomes endowed with a vigor, endurance, and application that far outstrip those of other men, let alone those of the mentally sick.

In some societies this power is known to be hereditary, and so it can be recognized easily enough when it appears. In others it is a vocation, or calling by the spirits: and for those who know how spirits call, and what brooding must take place before an answer is made, this also must be not too difficult a matter to diagnose. In either case, however, the initial crisis is painful, dangerous, and something to be treated with care, for the call is that of the Progenitor saying: "Let me enter into my child, to awaken him."

It is also an attack, which puts it into the class of illness, war, and sorcery— of everything, in fact, that the patient feels is directed against him. It makes no difference here whether the attack is real or only imagined. In either case something intentional is experienced, and this implies the activity of a person, a spirit, a demon, a soul, or a conscience.

Shamanism is an art that deals with all such intentions, and the shaman is a kind of Hermes, a director of souls. Souls are everywhere to be found in traditional societies, for men kill animals to eat, and other men in war, and these souls must be laid to rest. Sexual matters are full of soul and death too, as well as of birth; sacrifice and expiation deal with the transference of soul, identity, and responsibility; plants have soul, and so do the weather and the stars. The world is thus full of souls, some of them seeking bodies to occupy, others being dispossessed of their habitations and seeking retribution, or at least a monument. In the play of correspondence between man, his society, and the external world, the idea of a soul performs the function of creating, transforming, and destroying relationships.

Deeds have their souls as well; this fact led the Chinese to expiate their victories as well as their defeats, and is inherent in ideas of honor, immortality, and a glorious death—all of which enter into the activity of a shaman, and into the disorders that attack him at the beginning of his vocation.

The attack sometimes comes in what seems to us a plain accident. An Eskimo was hunting walrus with some friends when a walrus came out of the sea, grasped him in its flippers, and dived back into the water. There, deep down, it gored him with its tusks. The man at last managed to struggle free, with a broken collarbone and a perforated lung. An igloo was at once built for him a little distance away and there he was shut up, still wearing his wet clothes and without food, drink, or fire, for three days. During this time the village shaman purified the man's wife and mother of the various tabus they had broken. At the end of the three days the man had not only

A fourth-century B.C. vase painting from Naples depicting a maenad being carried off by an excited satyr.

Opposite, *the spirits of an Eskimo shaman as drawn by the shaman himself.*

Left, *satanic monsters attacking St. Antony in* The Temptation of St. Antony *by 16th-century German painter Matthias Grünewald.*

recovered but had become a shaman. His first spirit helper was the walrus that had failed to kill him.

Another Eskimo shaman has said: "All wisdom is only found far from men, in the great solitude, and it can be acquired only through suffering. Privations and suffering are the only things that can open a man's mind to that which is hidden." This going, or being driven, into the great wilderness is a commonplace among those who are being called by the spirits. Plains Indians, for instance, would choose some dangerous place such as a track used by bears, or a high cliff, and there await their vision of the Great Spirit. The solitude, the real danger from wild animals, and the nature of the Vision Quest itself, all combined to put their minds into the highest apprehension. In addition they fasted, slept little, and continually sang prayers to the Spirit, thus preparing themselves for its irruption.

Psychologists have lately subjected volunteers to a period of seclusion in a dark room, filling their ears with "white noise" such as the hum of an air-conditioner, and sheathing their hands so that they cannot easily touch anything; they have also submerged them, with a breathing apparatus, in a dark tank of water heated to blood temperature. Deprived of sensory stimulation and all idea of time, the volunteers soon become oppressed by their isolation, feel an uneasiness often amounting to panic, and may eventually see the most vivid hallucinations. Being undirected, such hallucinations arrive at no definite conclusion. But the effect is significant, and wherever shamanism practices seclusion in any of its forms we can expect visions, for the mind is greedy for stimulation and when nothing comes from without, it will create from within.

But shamanism adds to isolation both danger and a belief in a form of reality other than this one. The combination powerfully concentrates the mind in one place, and stretches it thin in another. The attack is then most likely to succeed, and the images produced by it are most likely to be given meaning. Novices therefore go to the place of danger in order to invite, or dare, the attack, whether this place be the wilderness, the tomb of a powerful shaman, or the haunt of the Australian Rainbow Serpent or some other spirit. This is known as the incubation of the visionary function, after the practice followed in temples to Aesculapius, where patients slept in order to discover in a dream the nature of their complaints.

Incubation is sometimes stimulated by physical pain, which further irritates the nervous system, besides being a simulation of the attack itself. "Madmen are all sensual in the lower stages of the distemper. They are eager for gratifications to soothe their minds, and divert their attention from the misery which they suffer, but when they grow very ill, pleasure is too weak for them, and they seek for pain." So said Dr. Johnson, who, as a sufferer from melancholia, scrofula, and minor obsessions, no doubt recognized in himself the truth of this observation.

Solitude, danger, expectation, and pain are all intensives, and their effect is to swing a man from one extreme to another. What happens then is that the attacker—be it human, animal, spirit, or disease—is turned into a helper, because it has been suffered, overcome, and made obedient. Spirit helpers are transfigurations of complaints, which is why their advice is so useful when shamans come to deal with the complaints of others. The road of excess leads to the palace of wisdom through this doorway, the spirit helper being the doorkeeper and the key to the whole matter.

There is a lampoon on metaphysical argumentation which runs: "What is Matter? Never mind. What is Mind? No matter." Here we must take

matter as that which can be embodied, mind as that which can be disembodied. The shamanistic attack empties the body of that which for convenience we call soul, and fills the mind with its spiritual counterpart. In the process the foundations of a man's existence are profoundly shaken, because all his habits are dismembered in order to be articulated in another sense. We have seen how closely symbolic structures are patterned on those of the body, and in shamanism we must take this similarity at face value, but in the reverse direction. Everything that was symbolic now acquires an immediate and intimate application.

For instance, another Eskimo shaman reported that when his spirit came to him it was as though the roof of his house was suddenly lifted. Then he saw through the house itself, across the world, and into the far reaches of the sky. This supernal power of vision was produced by a light shining from within him, flooding his being, and proceeding outward wherever he might direct it. The same experience comes to the Nuba of Africa when they shamanize. Their heads become opened, they say, and there is the light. This experience therefore puts together three aspects of the house and the light: first, the house as the world, its roof being the sky, and its light the sun; second, the house in which man lives, its light being the hearth-fire; third, the body of man, whose roof is the skull, and whose light is in the mind.

We are here at a point where the different aspects of symbolism must be thought of simultaneously, and where there is no longer a real distinction to be experienced between them. To see through the house is to see through the world, and also to see through the body. This is sometimes known as X-ray vision, and in various parts of the world it has produced fascinating

Left, an Eskimo soapstone carving of a spirit fish. Above, a shaman's wooden rattle, in the form of a sea monster, from British Columbia.

pictures in which animals are drawn with their internal organs plainly visible. To see thus is to use the inner light, which, according to Plato, is active in the ordinary process of vision. Its rays meet those coming from the outer light, and in mingling with them create the images of what we look at. (In modern optics this mingling of two lights is said to create an interference pattern, and some neurophysiologists are now trying to understand the formation of mental imagery on just this analogy.) In shamanism, of course, the exterior light is purposefully shunned or ignored, and things are seen in their spiritual aspects alone—that is, by what animates them.

If the roof is to be understood as the head of the shaman, the other structural members of the house will refer to the rest of the body and the skeleton in particular, which is now envisioned from within. The skeleton is of course a figure of death, the word coming from the Greek *skeleton soma*, the dried body, or that which is left after corruption has done its work. But bones are also thought of as though they were seeds, because it is from them that the body will be resurrected on Judgment Day. It is for quite

"*Putrefactio*," *from Mylius's* Philosophia reformata *(1622). The skeleton stands on a black sun, with the volatile spirit of darkness perched on its right hand.*

similar reasons that many hunting peoples honor the bones of the animals they kill, in order to ensure plentiful supply of game. In addition some peoples, such as the Dogon, use the main bones to signify a man's relatives. This convention we also find in Siberia, where the shaman, after he has been dismembered, is given as many spirits as there are bones left over when he is reconstituted. These spirits are often those of his relatives, who must die if he is to become a shaman.

These ideas can be found in the famous vision of Ezekiel:

"The hand of the Lord was upon me, and carried me out in the spirit of the Lord, and set me down in the midst of the valley which was full of bones.

"And caused me to pass by them round about: and behold, there were very many in the open valley; and, lo, they were very dry.

"And he said unto me, Son of man, can these bones live? And I answered, O Lord God, thou knowest.

"Again he said unto me, Prophesy upon these bones, and say unto them, O ye dry bones, hear the word of the Lord.

"Thus saith the Lord God unto these bones; Behold, I will cause breath to enter into you, and ye shall live.

"And I will lay sinews upon you, and will bring up flesh upon you, and cover you with skin, and put breath in you, and ye shall live; and ye shall know that I am the Lord.

"So I prophesied as I was commanded: and as I prophesied, there was a noise, and behold a shaking, and the bones came together, bone to his bone . . . .

"Then he said unto me, Son of man, these bones are the whole house of Israel . . . ."

An 18th-century shaman's coat from Siberia. The embroidery on the robe represents the spine and ribs, and the arm bones are similarly depicted on the sleeves.

Of all the bones, those of the spinal column are the most important. They represent the ridgepole or the central house-post, and as such are equated with the World Tree. Throughout Siberia it is held that shamans are hatched in nests lodged on the branches of this tree—a great shaman takes three years to come out of the shell, a mere conjurer only one. The eagle, bird of the sun, perches at the summit. To interiorize the light of this sun, the shaman must climb the tree, branch by branch, heaven by heaven, bone by bone. It is a journey during which he meets various personages and adventures, and which he recounts to his audience in great detail. He impersonates all the characters of this other world, and acts out his own laborious efforts. Often he goes by horseback, the horse symbolized by horsestaves; when the horse tires he mounts a gander, on which he wings his airy way to the heavenly throne where he makes his requests.

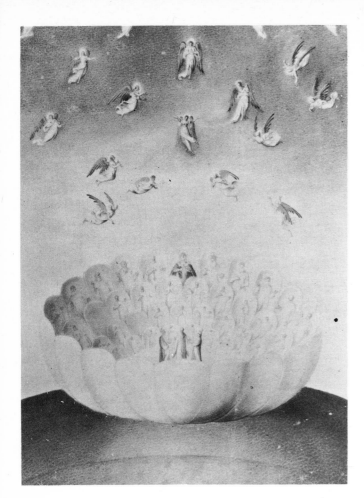

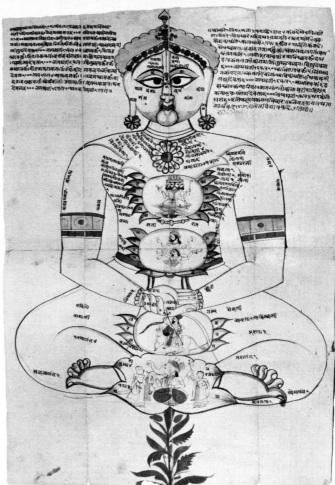

The identity of tree and backbone is well known in the theory of Yoga, which pictures the snake as the ascending force. This dweller in the entrails of the earth is the Kundalini, a female principle, and when it is awakened from its cave in the place where the genitals are attached to the spine, it uncoils and climbs up the backbone, passing through the several centers of energy experienced in the belly, the chest, the throat, and the eyes. It finally breaks through the roof of the skull and flowers as the thousand-petaled lotus of radiant enlightenment. This traditional account shows clearly how the fall into generation is reversed. The sexual power is repolarized and made to animate the tree of the backbone, which then serves as fuel for the inner light, here termed "the Jewel in the Lotus."

The light is therefore crystalline—a Philosopher's Stone made by dissolving one form of matter and coagulating it into another. Its jewel-like character must be of ancient origin and archetypal significance, because we find it around the world. Australian shamans, for instance, find rock crystals

Far left, a manuscript illumination to Dante's Divine Comedy, *showing Dante and Beatrice in the Heavenly Rose.*

Left, a Tantric diagram of the Kundalini. Right, a Huichol Indian painting of a shaman about to fetch the starry soul of a dead colleague from the top of the Tree of Ascent.

in the pools where the Rainbow Serpent lives; it comes at them with fiery eyes, entrances them, and fills their bodies with splinters of its light. These shamans are often initiated by older practitioners, who help to dramatize the attack and who afterward draw out the crystals from their bodies by sleight of hand. Teacher and novice are then ready to mount the serpent itself, which they do as if climbing a rope, and on its back ascend into the sky where they make rain, consult the spirits, and visit the firmament. It is from the firmament that they ultimately get their power, for it is crystalline—a tradition also known to us in the Book of Revelation, which states that the throne of God is above the sky and made of crystal. With these tokens of the heavens that exist above the roof of man, shamans acquire the power of that higher world.

The traditions found in myth and rite thus cohere with the shamanic experience. The parallels could be extended in great detail. For instance, shamans have not only spirit helpers, but spirit wives, whom they meet on their ascent. This puts them on a level with the king who must sleep with his queen on a platform set high on a treetop, or in a temple at the summit of a ziggurat. The cosmic meaning is that both king and shaman wed the powers of heaven and earth by virtue of their offices, and so re-establish the unity the creation had divided. One symbol for this coupling is the rainbow, the apotheosis of the serpent-soul, which makes a bridge from the solid to the insubstantial. The rainbow-bridge often figures in shamanic experience and in the adventures of the soul after death. It can be trodden only by spirits, and is therefore also described as a sword-edge. Underneath it, can be seen the bones of all those who failed to keep their balance and fell back into the

weight of their bodies. Like the pope, the shaman is thus a pontiff, a bridger of the opposites.

Among the opposites is the sexual one of male and female. In many Siberian tribes the shaman must practice sexual abstinence during his novitiate and before his performances. The reason is plain: the Progenitor dismembers himself out of desire, and it is only by raising desire to a higher level that he is rebuilt. Desire obeys the incest tabu upon earth, but the shaman's marriage to his spirit bride transcends the tabu—he becomes the androgyne that can enjoy a mutuality of pleasure in its own person.

We know from Dante the danger of this state. In the first circle of hell he meets Paolo and Francesca, so sweetly locked in an embrace that their hearts and minds are closed to all but each other. It is perhaps to escape such a predicament that Siberian shamans refuse the meal prepared for them by their spirit wives. But the union is in any case difficult to maintain, and the shaman's desire for power always tends to disrupt it. Thus in the old songs of Chinese shamans, translated by Waley, we find the spirit addressed in erotic terms; but it is fickle, and does not always come down in "a blaze of brightness unending," to give the shaman power.

> In our union was no faithfulness, only grief has lasted;
> She did not keep her tryst; told me that she was not free.

Or, from the song of a woman shaman:

> You love me, I know it; despite all doubts that rise,
> His chariot thunders, the air is dark with rain,
> The monkeys twitter; again they cry all night.
> The wind soughs and soughs, the trees rustle;
> My love of my Lord has brought me only sorrow.

This erotic element is found both in shamanism and in the slightly different practices of possession cults such as voodoo, principally in the seizures undergone by the devotees. These seizures are sometimes orgasmic, and are often barely distinguishable from hysterical fits. Hysteria, as we know, has a large sexual component. In addition, both shamans and possession priests may liberally indulge their sexual appetites, sometimes with both sexes. Siberian shamans in particular have as their duty the arousal of sexual passion in women at certain seasons. These facts are understandable if the shaman is sexually disordered in the first place, and they are finally justified by the fertile nature of the Progenitor, which the shaman and his kind assume.

But all opposites are as fertile in their own way as those embodied in sexuality, and reproduced after their kind. The mind also has its generative apparatus, spawning images that give life to objective facts. Here, too, the shaman has his predicament, because his powers can benefit mankind only

Shiva and his Sakti, or the hermaphroditic union of masculine Time and feminine Space—stone carving on an Indian temple.

261

if he turns the spirit into matter after having transcended his own matter by the spirit. We have seen how he does this with rock crystals, taken to be the solid fragments of the insubstantial sky. A strict application of the laws of correspondence between man and the universe, however, suggests that they are also to be thought of as remnants of the house-roof that is broken through during the shamanic ascent—they have to do with pains in the head.

Such an interpretation is confirmed by the Cuneo of South America, who say that the spirits implant crystals in the eyes and brain of the novice, where they gnaw at him painfully until he sees the light. Crystals are plainly spirit helpers in mineral form, since they are what attacks a man. In the treatment of ordinary illness, shamans extract from the bodies of their patients the crystals that are the embodiment of the disease, and also other hard, sharp objects that make blood flow, such as thorns, arrow heads, claws, teeth, beetles, ants, wasps, and mosquitoes. These are the equivalent of the recent Western obsession with germs, the seeds of a disease, and it is not surprising that the crystal also has a proper germ form in the shape of maggots and small tumorous pieces of meat.

Such cures as are effected by this technique are classic examples of suggestion and stagecraft, and tribal peoples have no monopoly of them. The Danish playwright Holberg described the technique in 1722. One of his characters recalls the case of a man "who thought his head was full of flies. He could not rid himself of the delusion, until a most clever doctor cured him in the following manner. He covered his patient's whole head with a plaster in which he had embedded masses of dead flies. After a while he removed the plaster and showed the flies to the patient, who naturally believed that they had been drawn from his own head and therefore concluded that he was cured."

Hypnosis and faith healing are variants of the same theme. So is the use of a placebo, an inactive substance given to a patient as though it had a real pharmacological effect, and producing such an effect in many instances. The technique works because the mind is ever open to sensory impressions and so becomes pregnant with meaning. There is no great mystery about the meaning of meaning: meaning directs the attention to a certain path through a pattern of associations, and it is therefore part and parcel of intention. All society is based on the mutual perception of intention, whether it be active or reactive, conscious or unconscious; every intention activates the mind and infects it with meaning.

Intentions are also physical, because they prepare the body for action. Although action requires a social context in which to play itself out, we must remember that the body is itself a scene for action and that internal

A 19th-century figure from the Nicobar Islands, carved from wood and used to frighten off devils of disease.

sensations can be made to act out all manner of private fantasies. The art of the shaman is to connect this inner drama with the outer one, and he does so within a kind of amphitheatre. "An amphitheatre consists of two theatres," said Donne at the beginning of a sermon. "Our text hath two parts in which all men may sit and see themselves acted." What is more, they are unavoidably acted upon by what they see in such a situation, whence the purgative function of drama.

The art is that of illusion. All shamans impersonate the forces they experience; they are excellent ventriloquists, and can imitate the cries of birds and animals. They pantomime their ascent to the heavens and their search for the spirits that are responsible for illness and well-being. They are expert conjurers and can produce powerful stage effects—such as shaking the huts in which they hold their séances as if by an unseen agency, and making footsteps sound around the walls. By such means they fascinate their audience into a willing suspension of disbelief, and turn private fantasies into common property.

Their stagecraft sometimes includes the use of masks, puppets, trees with ropes stretched between them to represent the world axis and the heavens, even a turning platform on which novices are seated in order to become giddy and fall prey to the spirits. Although such tricks and props encourage charlatans, they are at bottom devices necessary for the staging of the transformation scene, at which time the inner and outer stages are experienced as one. The shaman is in any case a transformer. Among the Bororo of Brazil he changes himself into a tapir to ensure good hunting for his villagers. Elsewhere he becomes a tiger, jaguar, wolf, dog, or bull, according to his power and the nature of his spirit helper. We are hardly in a position to describe what reality is experienced by means of such transformations. All we can say is that they are to be thought of as mysteries, and that mysteries are to be shown and not explained. Whatever is mysterious finds its natural home in the theatre, and what is played out is, of course, the myth.

We know the power of the theatre from St. Augustine, who fulminated against it. In *The City of God* he reminds the Romans that dramatic spectacles were established by their gods, in order to counter the plague. But, "if you still retain some glimmers of intelligence to prefer the soul to the body, choose which are worthy of your adorations; for the evil spirits, foreseeing that the contagion would cease physically, seized with joy this opportunity of introducing a much more dangerous disease, since it attacks not bodies, but morals. . . ." The passage is quoted by Antonin Artaud, who coined the phrase "the Theatre of Cruelty" to denote all that a play is and should be. He drew far-reaching parallels between the plague and the theatre, such as the infectiousness of both, the feverish intoxications they produce, which reveal the sleeping disorders of the body social and individual, and their similar crises or catastrophes, which either kill or cure. "Like the plague," he wrote, "the theatre is made for the emptying out of the abscesses."

The cruelty of theatre was also noted by Geoffrey Gorer in his study of the Marquis de Sade. De Sade, though he was obsessed with the theatre throughout his life, was a bad playwright. Unable to dramatize his fantasies, and finding no public to applaud his private world, he turned sadist, his audience being reduced to himself and his victim. Had he been able to turn shaman, he might have done better, enjoying a power that he could safely attribute to the spirits that helped or possessed him.

There is no doubt that sado-masochism plays a large part in many shamans' lives. For instance they suffer the attacks of the spirit in a hysterical mode. Having annexed its power, they can direct it against others and do sorcery, just as they can use it to help their fellows. Few resist the temptations of abusing the power that comes into them.

Shamans have many privileges. They acquire more women and more possessions than their fellow men, although in some tribes they are regularly made to disgorge their wealth. What is more, their spiritual ascents give them a foretaste of immortality and a sure passport to the other world. In South America, many shamans prepare their abodes there by annexing the souls of those they magically kill, who form the retinue that will attend them for eternity. Those who have power will always be suspected of using it for their own ends, and powerful shamans do not bother to diguise the fact. On the contrary, they often boast of it, by accepting responsibility for the deaths of their neighbors whether they have acted against them or not. They continue these provocations until their fellow men rise up in indignation and put them to death, which they embrace like Fusiwe, knowing that by this they are initiated into immortality.

A psychiatrist confronted by such a case might, with some reason, diagnose it as paranoia. This can be crudely defined as a form of insanity characterized by fixed delusions, especially those of grandeur, pride, and persecution. This is almost a definition of that part of human life which is concerned with rivalry, competition, and power, and with all institutions that require obedience to a creed and a set of rules. The sense of conviction that paranoids enjoy, indeed, makes them natural leaders of men, and it is only those who fail to obtain a following who are accused of the infirmity.

Shamans are certainly filled with ideas of grandeur, pride, and persecution. Persecution, indeed, is something of a necessity for them. Not only does shaman fight shaman when tribes are at war, but he must be gifted with a nose for a fishy smell whenever he makes a diagnosis. For the causes of disorders among mankind must often be ascribed to men themselves. People fall ill not only with diseases but because of breaches of social order, of tabu, and of goodwill. Many of the activities going under the name of shamanism have to do with witch-hunting, with the fixing of blame for one man's distress upon the shoulders of another, and with the eventual shifting of that blame into the void by various kinds of expiation. Like voodoo priests in Haiti, many shamans are knowledgeable in the private lives of their parishioners, and may even use an efficient band of informants to keep them up-to-date. But undoubtedly they also have a well-developed intuition. Their inner light can be made to illuminate a kind of psychic crystal ball in which the machinations of time are made visible. "If we could obtain a magic glass," wrote Bacon, "we might view all the enmities and all the hostile designs that are at work against us." All human beings have such a magic glass built into their consciousness, but only a few develop it to any extent. It was the same magic glass that gave Tezcatlipoca his name in Mexico; it means Smoking Mirror, and it must have been in this mirror that Quetzalcoatl saw his own reflection, lost his purity, and became mortal.

Tezcatlipoca had but one foot, the other having been bitten off by an alligator. The mirror took the place of the missing foot. This is a strange figure, and it recalls others in the Old World, such as Vulcan and Lucifer, both of whom were lame. All three have been taken by various students to represent the polar axis of the world, the World Tree, the one-legged being of the earth—and so in part they may be, but a further explanation is in order. All three figures are embodiments of cunning knowledge and magical practices. Lucifer is the very type of rebellious ambition, and he and Vulcan walk unscathed through the fires of hell. These two, also, broke their legs when they attempted to scale the battlements of heaven, which means that they attempted to seize the very throne of the Inner Light but brought back only a powerful fragment of it—just one star, in Lucifer's case. Now, Siberian tribes recount that their first shaman, the greatest who ever was, attempted to take God's throne for himself, but was repulsed. The Caribs of South America tell the same story. Since those times, shamans can reach heaven only while in trance or ecstasy, and their powers have been greatly diminished. As for Vulcan, in Siberia the shaman is called the elder brother to the blacksmith, who makes his costume—an extremely heavy costume of iron, made to look like a skeleton.

Tezcatlipoca, Lucifer, and Vulcan, then, are shamanic figures. Their one sound leg is indeed the pole of the world—the pole they ascend in their ecstasy to reach the light by whose rays all things can be seen. Siberian

shamans display the same pole by placing a birch tree, sometimes upside-down, through the smoke hole of their tents. In Australia it is the serpent, the tempter itself. Shamans mount this backbone of the world and of themselves to find out the causes of things, and to free the souls of the living from the prisons of the other world.

All ambition is directed upward, and of all ambitions the hope of immortality is perhaps the strongest. The shaman is an immortal because already in this life he can leave his body and reassume it. Like Orion, he goes continually toward the East, and has his image pricked out in stars. But Orion stands at the head of the Eridanus River, which, far from mounting, drops down into the Southern Hemisphere and the land of departed gods. Gilgamesh took this trail also, looking for the herb of immortality.

There are Siberian shamans who, like Orpheus, descend into the underworld looking for lost souls. These "black" shamans—they are connected with sorcery and death—are opposed to the "white" ones, who besides their other functions have to do with an ancestor cult. Some scholars have suggested that black shamans were originally women, and although the question is still in doubt, it reminds one of the traditional scheme that associates woman with the earth and its entrails, man with the sky and the great light: the one being body to the other's head. All this makes good shamanic sense, but it raises a problem about the nature of immortality.

Men are great purveyors of death, both as hunters and warriors. Although shamans court death in order to be made perfect, they nonetheless go hunting for souls in order to keep death at bay, and do everything they can to stimulate the fertility of women and of the land. It is the old opposition between the ever-lasting round of Physis and the immutable nature of the center, the summit, and the crystalline light. Of these two, which is the truly immortal? A Fusiwe and his shamanic counterpart seek their eternal abode in Heaven, and are thus trying to escape from change; they hope to become fixed, like stars, and to shine forever. But Gilgamesh, Orpheus, and the black shamans descend instead of mounting, and seek rejuvenation rather than immortality, the Tree of Life rather than the Tree of Knowledge.

We have remarked how man uses his passions to intoxicate himself, how illnesses can serve the same purpose, and how theatrical suggestion can stimulate and direct the energies thus stirred up. So, of course, can singing, dancing, drumming, and all forms of rhythm, the traditional standbys of enthusiasm that set body and mind a-going together. In South America we find shamans also using tobacco, which they smoke in quantities while also gulping in great lungfuls of air, thus combining the powerful effect of nicotine with the equally powerful one of hyperventilation. Either of these, taken alone, can produce giddiness, nausea, and trance.

But this is nothing compared to the use of the hallucinogenic drugs that are found in plants the world over. The Conquistadors reported the use of several such plants in Mexico, including the cactus peyote, the creeper oloiuqui, and certain fungi. They were told that many people ate these plants during Montezuma's coronation and afterward recounted the visions they had seen. Peyote is still in use by the Native American Church. Its spread dates from the time that the Plains Indians were being killed by the whites and driven off their lands. During this period various other messianic movements arose among the Indians, as a way of dealing with the destruction of their lives and traditions, such as the ghost dance and the hand-clapping game. But all these movements have now died away.

Peyote remains, because its effects do not spring from resentment or temporary passions. It is taken as a sacrament that, although filled with

A ritual stone mushroom from Guatemala.

symbolic meaning, yet contains an active pharmacological agent, and is used to cure various kinds of sickness, to teach wisdom, and to illuminate the mind. Its taste is bitter and nauseating enough to cause vomiting in some, and the course of its action strangely parallels that of the shamanistic crisis. The eater goes through an initial disorder, sees visions, passes through "the crucifixion hour", reaches a place of peace and healing, and returns to his ordinary life convinced of a spiritual reality lying behind all appearances.

It is now well known that such drugs, especially mescalin and lysergic acid, can produce visions of marvelous beauty—of great palaces, landscapes, statuesque figures, and of brilliantly colored jewels, each lit by an inner light. Those who are accustomed to think in terms of the spirit, see the spirit, and may be gifted with some of its powers. Here is the account of a Winnebago Indian who has eaten peyote:

"The one called Earthmaker is a spirit and that is what I felt and saw. All of us sitting there, we had all together one spirit or soul, at least, that is what I learned. I instantly became the spirit and I was their spirit or soul. Whatever they thought of, I knew. I did not have to speak to them and get an answer to know what their thoughts were. Then I thought of a certain place, far away, and immediately I was my thought. . . .

"Then someone spoke to me. I did not answer, for I thought they were just fooling, and that they were all like myself, and that it was unnecessary for me to talk to them. So . . . I only answered with a smile."

In Siberia, powerful visions are produced by the fungus *Amanita muscaria*. Some tribesmen use it as though it were alcohol, for pleasure, but it always has a religious side to it, and the shamans of certain tribes take it to enhance their own disciplined capacities. Mircea Eliade, the great authority on shamanism, has decried this use and declared that it is a degeneration of the original technique of ecstasy, which he sees as powered by psychological methods alone. But this conclusion now seems one-sided. R. G. Wasson has recently suggested that this fungus is none other than the soma of the Vedas, and this implies that the tradition of Indian spiritual life began with artificially induced visions.

The authors of the Vedas came into India from the north, where the tradition of eating the *Amanita* fungus is still known. It does not, however, grow on Indian soil, and after a time the Brahmins had to prescribe a number of substitutes for the original plant, whose identity was by then lost. But none of these plants has the effects imputed to soma, which is called a divine plant, a giver of visions and of immortality. (The Sanskrit word *amrita,* often applied to it, like the Greek *ambrosia,* means "deathless.") As a result, soma was at last taken to be a figure of speech: "Though men

The Earthly Paradise of Tlaloc, god of rain and patron of visionaries—a reconstructed wall painting from Tepantitla, Mexico, first to sixth century.

268

fancy, when they crush the plant that they are drinking of very Soma, of him the Brahmins understand by 'Soma' none tastes who dwells on Earth."

On the face of it, *Amanita* may well be the soma that dwells on Earth, and as such must have been regularly tasted. In any case, a plant of like properties was certainly worshiped in Vedic times, and there is no doubt that hallucinogens open the doors of heaven and hell in an unmistakable fashion. The plant being lost, the Indians perfected other techniques to gain the same end; but when it was still in use, it and the shamanistic ecstasy may well have gone hand in hand.

Perhaps, then, the plant that Gilgamesh sought at the ends of the earth was one of the various kinds of soma; so, too, may have been the forbidden

Dreaming of Immortality in a Thatched Cottage—*a 16th-century Chinese hand scroll, probably by Chou Ch'en.*

fruit in the Garden of Eden. All things sacred fall under tabus, and that which is sacred to one people is often despised by another. This is especially true of hallucinogenic plants, whose effects often disgust the uninitiated observer. And, although there must be many reasons for their declining importance in religious matters—one being scarcity—their sacredness cannot be in doubt, or their intoxicating powers.

The prophet, the warrior, the shaman, the yogi, the drinker of soma—all in their different fashions make an assault upon the sacred to taste the nectar of the gods, the deathless drink. Some die to get it, others pass through a frenzy like that of death, and yet others take an illuminating poison and know bliss. What, then, is it to be immortal?

10 The Image and the Light

If Adam had eaten of the Tree of Life before Eve had succumbed to the wiles of the serpent, we should all be immortal—though, perhaps, not wise to the fact. There was no commandment to stop him doing so; rather, an encouragement that he should. For did not the Lord tell him that he might eat of all the trees in the garden, except of the Tree of the Knowledge of Good and Evil?

We have dealt with the meaning of the Fall already, but we need to refer to it and a number of other topics again to show how our long argument is made to come to an end. Adam is, of course, the name for the collective man or ancestor, created by God in his own image—a word that in Hebrew also means "shadow" or "reflection." The Hindu account of the creation does not distinguish between God and Adam, for the original self is both; and it is by coupling with the reflection of its desire that it makes a mare for its stallion, a cow for its bull, a woman for its man. This is referred to in Genesis when the Lord brings to Adam all the beasts of the field, that he might name them and find a helpmeet among them. Tradition has it that Adam was 500 years old at the time, and still without a soul. Only when the rib was taken from his side could he see his reflection in the woman made from it, who proved to be his helpmeet and as a soul to him.

The creature that tempts Eve to bring this act of self-reflection into the world is another figure for the collective man—the serpent. Its function in Genesis is to transform the act of creation into one of generation. Its temptation is baited with the promise that Eve's eyes shall be opened as its own are—for it has no lids to close over them—and that she and Adam, whose reflection she is, will become as gods, knowing good and evil. The serpent is thus also a figure for the Tree of Knowledge—its wisdom when joined with the gentleness of doves is commended by the Christ—and as such it stands for desire and for a reflection of the Tree of Life.

It is thus that the Progenitor extends his powers through the doors of the senses to their objects, the reflections of his desire. This perhaps

The enlightened Buddha, victorious over the forces of conflict—from a second-century frieze at Gandhara, India.

explains why Adam did not eat of the Tree of Life, which is the desire rather than its reflection. Eating of the Tree of Knowledge, Adam ate his reflection with the object; but this, far from reuniting with him, conceived his likeness in a third nature. This new self, which can be understood either as a child or a thought, also has desires and objects it wishes to eat, and its existence forces its parents apart so that it may have room to move. In such a way does a concept stand between desire and gratification. The intervening space, which the Norse called Mithgarth or Middle Earth, is the cradle of consciousness, where thoughts are embodied in a society, and the collective man is separated into his individual parts.

This interpretation of the story can be found in Hinduism, where the child of concept is born free from the conjugation of mind and voice. As the moon reflects the light of the sun, so the mind is commonly thought to mirror a light peculiar to itself. As for the voice, this is the creative principle uttering the word into the mind, which then conceives the names of things and their relations.

There is nothing in the Old Testament to suggest that the act of reflection is in itself evil, or that either the sexual or the intellectual ways of conceiving merit death. On the contrary, it was God who enjoined Adam to name the creation, and Abraham to be fruitful and multiply; to eat of the Tree of Knowledge can mean neither of these acts. In the New Testament, too, St. John's use of the term *logos* to mean both word and light implies that there is something to be heard and seen, and that the creation reflects God's utterance. So we can understand the nature of the Tree of Knowledge better if we think of it not as a simple reflection of the Tree of Life, but as a double one, in which the sexual and intellectual functions can be mistaken for each other. The result is a chimera, that creature of ambivalent gender with the head of a beast or a man and the body and tail of a snake.

In *The States and Empire of the Sun*, Cyrano de Bergerac tells how, when Adam and Eve ate the fatal apple, God punished the snake by placing it in Adam's body, where it formed his entrails. Its head nevertheless protruded at the base of his belly, always ready to bite a woman and make her swell with its poison for nine months. This is a raw but telling description of the chimera's nature, for the snake is a cold-blooded creature, and it may be called wise for its cool head as well as its ever-open eyes. The chimera, however, has a hot head and its symbolically phallic body is cold. This reminds one that in medieval times witches reported that Satan's penis was icy cold, and of the old story about a girl seduced by a monk, who persuaded her that it was her religious duty to put his devil into her hell. What can this mean but that Satan is cold and hell is the place where he is warmed up?

A page from the 10th-century Bedford Book of Hours showing Adam and Eve in the Garden, with the murder of Abel at the right and the death of Adam in the foreground.

The workings of both head and loins are sacred, which means that the province of the one should not be mistaken for that of the other. Yet they also correspond, so that one image can do duty for both, as we know from previous chapters and also from Freud. For Freud, too, was a student of the Tree of Knowledge, and inquired deeply into the effects of its fruit upon the apparently innocent eater. His conclusion is much the same as ours, namely that most of our mental productions are chimeras born from the unholy conjunction of physical and intellectual functions, the energy of the loins being the fuel for the machinery of the head.

This conjunction is the basis for each man's "I" or Ego. It is formed as the child learns its place in the world and how to control its limbs, its sphincters, and its desires. Each stage of training is marked by the repression of libido, whose original nature undergoes a reflection and comes out as a sublimation or intellectual habit. With sublimation goes the process known as upward displacement, which signifies the heating of the head by passion and the cooling of the loins by conscience; and, as Freud's follower Ferenczi remarked, this allows the phallus to be experienced as a representative of the entire ego.

This particular synecdoche, however, is the result of a more famous process, the Oedipus complex. Freud defined this—in men, at any rate—as "the wish to be the father of himself." In tribal societies this wish to be his own cause leads many a man to seek actively for death, so that he and his cause may be one, and Freud is no doubt partly correct in assuming that the Oedipus complex leads to the idea of the soul as an entity in itself, and of its immortality.

The Oedipus complex, which is one form taken by the chimera, is also another word for self-consciousness, and psychoanalysis is largely the study of this human disease. In a famous passage Freud called neurosis the caricature of religion, and elsewhere he did his best to show that religion was but a caricature of neurosis. In so far as religion has to deal with the problem of self-consciousness, he was right, and he was not above using an almost religious program to cure the disorder. This was to recollect verbally the pathways that lead from a present problem to its origin in childhood, and so dissociate desire from its repression, and conscience from consciousness. We need not go into the difficulties this method has experienced, except to remember that Freud doubted in his later years that it could do the job he required of it. The method itself, however, is based on the principle of sacrifice, by which you give up what you have in hopes of receiving what you wish for; and its axiom, that head and loins should be kept apart, is nothing strange to religious traditions.

Psychoanalysis, indeed, is in some ways a modern counterpart of initiation rites, during which a man is separated from his childhood and made to join the world of men. Those initiated are twice born: their first birth from women is superseded by their second birth from men, who thus affiliate themselves to a non-material and intellectual principle. By this means men are able to feel pride in themselves. We can remember the Tupi tribes, where the men kept themselves away from women in order to retain their vigor, sense of detachment, and wakefulness. The rule is that women destroy men's self-possession, whereas solitude and asceticism strengthen it.

The rule is also followed by shamans, who abstain from their physical appetites in order to detach themselves from the body, to ascend with the spirit, and to have their eyes opened by the inner light. But there are several drawbacks to the shamanistic vocation, all of which could be ascribed to an unresolved Oedipus complex, if that is thought worthwhile, although a more orthodox Jew than Freud would simply look upon them as the results of eating the fruit of the Tree of Knowledge in order to get intoxicated. Shamans are, for a start, believers in the immortality of their own spirit, which they expect to be served in the afterlife by the souls of those they have killed. They are addicted to power. Their vocation is such that if they do not continually practice it, it takes revenge by plaguing them with the illness out of which it was originally born. They manage to climb the tree to the light, but they do it in such a way that they fall down again on emerging from trance; after recuperating from their exertions, they are driven to climb again, and so on until death draws their souls from their bodies for the last time. These matters, together with the theatricality of shamanism, imply that shamans still suffer from that divided awareness known as self-consciousness, and that they build up a stock of selfhood to fuel their exploits.

The ban upon eating of the Tree of Knowledge, which in Genesis marks the time when mankind first comes across the notion of the sacred, is also a ban upon the fruits of self-consciousness. The ban works by separating the material from the immaterial principle, and the penalty for breaking it is death and sacrifice. This is the fate of every chimera, which must be periodically sacrificed. And here we may see in simple terms the relation between the sacred and the chimerical. The one divides, the other joins.

The division of the material from the immaterial principle takes concrete shape in the division between earth and sky, matter and mind, woman and man, object and subject, and all other symbolic opposites. The moment the fruit of self-consciousness is eaten, the eyes of these opposites are opened, and they know that they are divided and naked. Then, in the words of the

Bible, they sew fig leaves together and make themselves aprons. In other words, shame comes into the world, and is covered by an appearance.

What hides behind appearances is not only self-consciousness but mystery, and these two together provoke a man into thought. Science, our present method of gaining knowledge, has done much to dispel mystery, superstition, and also the sense of the sacred, though it has done so by increasing self-consciousness in curious ways. Its instrument is a two-edged blade that cuts nature into definable parts and so emphasizes the distinction between a subject and an object. This double edge is the systematic use of doubt, first propounded by Descartes in his famous *Cogito, ergo sum*, "I think, therefore I am," whose counterpart is *Dubito, ergo sum*, "I doubt, therefore I am." The axiom underlines all science, which can verify its theories only by attempting to falsify them. If the attempt fails, the theory is held to be correct, or at least workable—the appearances having been seen through and the mystery uncovered. It is only by such a method that, in the words of Paracelsus, "Ere the world comes to an end, many arts now ascribed to the devil must become revealed, and it will then be evident that most of these effects depend on natural causes."

To objectify knowledge by this method has had many obvious consequences. One of them, as Freud remarked, has been to deal some shrewd blows to man's narcissism and to destroy his house of symbolism. At the same time, any idea of a world-soul has disappeared with the rise of determinism, and universal necessity reigns once more.

Necessity, however, has shown itself to be pretty odd. So, for that matter, has scientific thought, which is slowly rediscovering the use of symbolic manipulations as, for instance, in its attempt to understand time. The very new, in fact, has a strange way of looking like the very old. Freud himself was caught in such an anachronism: "By the way," he wrote in a letter, "what have you to say to the suggestion that the whole of my brand-new theory of the primary origins of hysteria is already familiar and has been published a hundred times over, though several centuries ago? Do you remember my always saying that the medieval theory of possession, that held by the ecclesiastical court, was identical with our theory of a foreign body and the splitting of consciousness? But why did the devil who took possession of the poor victims invariably commit misconduct with them, and in such horrible ways? Why were the confessions extracted under torture so very like what my patients tell me under psychological treatment?"

The method of science, as John Gillies said in 1797, is to put nature to the torture instead of, like Aristotle, catching her in the fact. Religion also puts nature to the torture, in sacrifices; the results are different, but the impulse is curiously similar. For both, nature is but a grandiose appearance behind which can be glimpsed the workings of a deeper reality. Unfortunately for science, the job is never done: the workings of a deeper reality are only to be found in other appearances, and how to relate these Chinese boxes remains problematical. The metaphysics of science is like that of the chief diagnostician of the Medical Academy, in Thurber's story "The Last Clock," who was "familiar with so many areas that totality itself has become but a part of wholeness."

But totality is not an object, and cannot properly be investigated by rational thought. We can attempt to do so by making a part stand for the whole, and so personifying it, but this can lead only to partial understanding. Synecdoche, however, has various aspects. It is not only the taking of a part for the whole, of the container for the contained, but of the means for an end, and of a representation for the thing itself. But the reverse is also true: synecdoche is the taking of the whole for a part, contained for container, and end for means. In science, this means that the relation of the observer to the observed must be taken into account before any conclusion can be drawn, as Heisenberg posited with his well-known principle. In particle physics this implies that the method of observation, or of putting nature to the torture, has a bias and cannot do two opposite things at the same time. It can define the speed of an electron or its position, but not both together. The same is true for all thought based on the opposition of subject and object, those duplicated embellishments of reason: it is a question of jam yesterday and jam tomorrow, but never jam today.

This is indeed a chimerical situation, and as much a matter for comedy as for science, as Speed observed in *Two Gentlemen of Verona*:

Stone head of Mictlantecuhtli, a Mexican god of death.

> O jest unseen, inscrutable, invisible,
> As a nose on a man's face, or a weather-cock on a steeple!
> My master sues to her; and she hath taught her suitor,
> He being her pupil, to become her tutor.
> O excellent device! was there ever heard a better?
> That my master, being a scribe, to himself should write the letter?

The jest is much appreciated by Zen Buddhists, to whom it is known as mistaking the finger for the moon it points at. The following story makes the same point in another way: "Shan-tao was walking one day with his master in the mountains. The master, Shih-t'ou, saw the branches of a tree obstructing the path, and asked Shan-tao to clear them away. 'I did not bring a knife with me,' said Shan-tao. Shih-t'ou took out his own knife, and held it out blade foremost. 'Please give me the other end,' said Shan-tao. 'What do you want to do with the other end?' retorted Shih-t'ou."

It is always somewhat disheartening to have to explain a joke, but to do so may be useful in this case. This particular joke seems to be two in one: it implies that if the other end of the subject is object, the other end of something is nothing. We can understand this by means of a medieval diagram, which ingeniously fits together the two ways of affirmation and negation. The diagram is in the form of a triangle representing the three Persons of the Trinity, which are united at the center through the lines labeled "Est" and separated at the periphery by the sides of the triangle, which are labeled "Non Est." This means that for every act of affirmation there is a reciprocal one of negation, and that unity is possible only in multiplicity.

This is a truism. All the same, its philosophical expression can run into difficulties. The Greek Hyolozoists, for instance, found that they could account for the affirmations of movement only by postulating a void in which it could take place. Buddhism also makes use of the idea of the void, or Sunyata, as that emptiness in which thought may move without obstruction. In its development as Zen this emptiness becomes the topic of many subtle and logically impenetrable stories. For although we can talk about something that by nature is empty of meaning, this emptiness does not bear examination, nor can it be isolated. It it could, it would no longer be empty, and so would be a something rather than a nothing.

It would seem that nothing of any purpose can be said about nothing, yet many people have tried. Freud, interestingly enough, was one of them, for he was a convinced dualist and held that the somethings of psychology had to be balanced by an equivalent nothing. He called this the death instinct, or Thanatos, and he had this to say about it:

"So long as that instinct operates internally, as a death instinct, it remains silent; it only comes to our notice when it is diverted outwards as an instinct of destruction. It seems essential for the preservation of the individual that this diversion should occur; the muscular apparatus serves this purpose. When the super-ego is established, considerable amounts of the aggressive instinct are fixated to the interior of the ego and operate there self-destructively."

This passage has an obvious application to shamans, who are able to turn the death instinct into a weapon against various inimical forces. But the observation that the death instinct is silent, and that it is heard, as Freud mentions elsewhere, only when Eros (the life instinct) is speaking as well, is much to the point, and tells us that even though a principle may be immaterial, it cannot be ignored.

Freud's attempts to define the death instinct are interesting but too technical and complex to elaborate on here. However, certain of his conclusions are important. His first essay, for instance, described the death instinct as the release of tension, or the consummation of desire—a view that he later abandoned but that has much to be said for it. Later he treated the death instinct in the context of sadism, with the passage we have just quoted. This makes it as plainly invisible as the nose on a man's face. In another paper he alluded to its invisibility in what appears to be a quite unrelated context, the relation of consciousness to memory. His theory is that the processes underlying these two states are in some way incompatible with each other. We can paraphrase this by saying that while memory is obviously the result of conditioning, consciousness must remain unconditioned if it is to perceive anything. Finally, we must note his saying: "The word 'No' does not seem to appear in dreams."

It remains for us to add these remarks together. Consciousness and the death instinct seem to have certain remarkable similarities. Neither of them can be caught directly in the act, but only at one remove and in their products. Ideally, both are unconditioned in their essence, which makes sense of Freud's belief that the discharge of tension is the work of the death instinct, which deconditions the organism. His final remark makes waking consciousness the begetter of negation and separation, the "Non est" of death.

The word "no" in fact represents the articulation of the mental body. Without it there is nothing to sit in judgment on the constant affirmations desire longs for, and it is no accident that by it seven of the Ten Commandments are given their force. Nothing can be affirmed in science but that which has been tested by this word. The same is true in Hinduism, where the search for God is conducted under the guidance of two phrases: the affirmation *tat tvam asi,* "that art Thou," and the negation *neti, neti,* "not that, not that."

Here is how the argument is carried out in the *Chandogya Upanishad.* Svetaketu, a young Brahmin, returns to his father full of conceit because of having studied the Vedas. His father asks him if he has also sought for "that teaching whereby what has not been heard of becomes heard of, what has not been thought of becomes thought of, what has not been understood becomes understood." Svetaketu asks to be enlightened.

" 'So be it, my dear. Bring hither a fig.'

" 'Here it is, Sir.'

" 'Divide it.'

" 'It is divided, Sir.'

" 'What do you see there?'

" 'These rather fine seeds, Sir.'

" 'Of these, please, divide one.'

" 'It is divided, Sir.'

" 'What do you see?'

" 'Nothing at all, Sir.'

"Then he said to him: 'Verily, my dear, that finest essence which you do not perceive—verily, my dear, from that finest essence this great sacred fig thus arose. Believe me, my dear,' said he, 'that which is the finest essence—this whole world has as its self. That is Reality. That is Atman. That art Thou, Svetaketu'."

Only that which is not itself a thing can be the essence of a thing, its self and its soul—Meister Eckhardt would have said, its unity. Interpreting St. Paul's words, "One God of all who is above all and through all and in us all," he wrote:

"A master says, One is the denial of denials. Every creature makes innate denial; the one denies it is the other; an angel denies being any other creature. But God makes the denial of denials; he is one and denies all other, for there is nothing without God. All creatures are in God; they are his very Godhead, that is to say, the fullness. . . . By the fact of denying God something—and by denying God goodness I am not denying God—I say, by denying God something I conceive something about him, that he is not. Even this has to go. God is one, he is the negation of negations."

This double negative is significant: it is used also in Hinduism, where it is said that God is the death of deaths. We thus have a series from the dreaming state, where opposites may turn into each other, as Freud noted, to that of waking consciousness that uses the word "no" to discriminate and make for multitude, and finally to a state in which unity is discovered by doubling the negative upon itself. For this reason Eckhardt also said: "It is a question, what burns in hell? Doctors reply with one accord, 'self-will.' But I maintain *not* burns in hell."

Now a double negative is tricky to play with. It is not meant just to affirm what it denies, but to transcend both affirmation and negation and with them the subject-object relation. In Judaism, Christianity, and Islam this is the purpose of the second Commandment: "Thou shalt not make unto thee any graven image, or any likeness of any thing that is in heaven above, or that is in the earth beneath, or that is in the water under the earth." And this second Commandment is younger brother to the first, uttered in the Garden and broken almost as soon as heard. For the Lord is jealous for unity, and knowledge and graven images fragment it into innumerable reflections, each proclaiming its own selfhood.

These selves are all offspring of the chimera, which is, as it were, a double affirmation. We can understand the matter in this way: a graven image is the likeness of a thing, and the mind being able to see likeness only through the medium of its own workings, it is also the likeness of the mind. The double negative is needed to stop the mind believing that it too is a graven image, and to make it see that behind all likeness is a Likener, which, though it produces knowledge, is not itself an object of knowledge.

This Likener goes under many names: the Progenitor, the Ancestor, the Creator. We can also call it the Personifier. Though it is not an image, it is often called one by mystics and theologians, following two principal texts. The first, from Genesis, says that God created man in his own Image—male and female created he them. In the second, from the New Testament, the Christ announces "No man cometh unto the Father, but by me." (To avoid confusion we shall use a small i when talking of sensory images, and a capital when speaking of the Image in which God and man are alike.) To understand in what sense a Likener is also a likeness, let us take the 14th-century English mystic, Julian of Norwich, for our guide.

Lady Julian was an anchoress. When she was young she had desired three gifts of God—to have mind of his Passion; to have bodily sickness when she was 30; and to have three wounds. Her wishes were granted, though the last one only metaphorically, in her 30th year. It was a grievous sickness, and as her end seemed to approach, her curate set the cross before her face, saying: "I have brought thee the Image of thy Maker and Saviour: look thereon and comfort thee therewith." The sight of it unlocked the door of her soul. She looked, and as the Image took her sufferings upon itself, she was freed of her pains, although they returned the moment doubt entered her mind. The oscillation from sickness and doubt to health and faith continued throughout the course of her revelations, which mirrored both these states.

It seemed to her as she first looked that the upper part of her body began to die, and her breathing was stopped. When this spasm was over, it came to her mind to ask for a sight of the Passion, which she then saw manifested in the upper part of the Image. Blood flowed from below the crown of thorns and dried on the face, and the flesh of the face dried upon the skull. The pain of this drought she felt in herself also, until she realized that it was in this way that "our Lord Jesus was made naught for us," which allowed her to make herself naught for him. At once the Image took life in her eyes, and its smile in her mind revived her body.

She then entered into the meaning of the Passion by gazing into the wound in the side of the Image. It showed a fair, delectable place and his heart cloven in two, which she understood to figure the mystery of the Godhead. She then asked to be shown sin, which being atoned by the

An 18th-century Jain brass ikon of the Jina or Victor, the spirit liberated from matter. The spirit is represented as a cut-out space.

Passion was nowhere to be seen. She did, however, see its deadliness in the vision of a stinking body that lay upon the ground, and the life it would kill as a little child coming out of the body, "fully shapen and formed nimble and lively, whiter than lily, which sharply glided up into heaven." This ascent left her behind in her suffering body, which tormented her even in her sleep. For she woke from a nightmare of the Fiend gripping her throat, seeing a light smoke come in at the door with a great heat and a foul stench. The next day she had her last Showing, as she called her revelations, of the Lord Jesus, God and man, sitting in the worshipful city of the soul—a city so large that it was an endless world. The purpose of this vision came to her through his words: "Wit it now well that it was no raving thou sawest today: but take it and believe it, and keep thee therein, and comfort thee therewith, and trust thou thereto, and thou shalt not be overcome."

That the kingdom of God is within you is a truism few manage to confirm in themselves. The advice was needful also to the Lady Julian, for the kingdom of the devil was soon upon her again, and amid much heat and stench she heard "a bodily jangling, as if it had been two persons; and both, to my mind, jangled at one time as if they had holden a parliament with a great busyness; and all was soft muttering, so that I understood naught that they said." It was only after she had conquered this that she was whole, in her body as well as her soul.

Before we look at other matters raised by her revelations, it is well to point out how, in this almost shamanistic crisis, the Image served to detach her from her bodily sufferings and to release the energy imprisoned by her sins, "her vain affections and her vicious pride." Atoned in the Image, they still had to be atoned in her life, as her bodily janglings made plain. These taught her "that two contrary things should never be together in one place"— not that is, unless the Image is the place where body and mind come together.

According to theology, Christ is the Image uniting the natures of God and man and, by extension, that place in the devotee where the divine substance and his material sense-soul make the Image visible. It is here that, in Julian's words, "the token of sin is turned to worship"; and one great cause for worship is to understand that the matter of this transformation is also the place of it. She herself saw it in several guises, all of which can help our understanding too. The first time it was in the Lord showing her "a little thing, the quantity of a hazel nut, in the palm of my hand; and it was as round as a ball. I looked thereupon with the eye of my understanding, and thought; What may this be? And it was answered. It is all that is made."

The second time, she saw this all as "God in a Point, that is to say, in mine understanding—by which sight I saw that He is in all things." That her understanding could be in all things was made clear to her in the last Showing. "For I saw assuredly that our Substance is in God, and also I saw that in our sensualitie God is: for in the self-point that our Soul is made sensual, in the self-point is the City of God ordained to Him from without beginning; into which seat he cometh, and never shall remove it."

This self-point is the place of marriage, as we can infer from the vision of the child gliding sharply up to heaven, because it is only there that two contrary things may cease from jangling together and join into the image of a third, through which they love each other. And because love is productive in whatever form it takes, the inner marriage is also celebrated in outer forms. The love of Jesus for the Church, which Christians see in the Song of Songs, is paralleled by the love of saints for their fellow men, in Judaism by the love of one's neighbor through which Israel becomes the bride of the Lord, in Buddhism by the Boddhisattva's vow that he will not enter into Nirvana until all sentient beings are saved. In Lady Julian, it is simply Love. "Wouldst thou learn thy Lord's meaning in this thing? Learn it well: Love was His meaning. Who shewed it thee? Love. What shewed He thee? Love. Wherefore shewed it He? For Love. Hold thee therein and thou shalt learn and know more in the same. But thou shalt never learn therein other thing without end."

If there were no self-point in the individual, with love as its nature, every religious effort based on the principle of correspondence, of images, and of sacrifice, would be in vain. So, for that matter, would the study of the mind. It is interesting to note that Freud postulated just such a function in the preconscious, though he scarcely made use of his insight. In his scheme, the preconscious is a semi-voluntary mechanism in which the attention, the senses, the intellect, the memory, and the motor apparatus are all linked. Through it pass what he called the instincts, to translate the demands of the body into mental constructs; through it, too, pass the orderly actions that let these demands be satisfied. It seems a far cry from this to the self-point of Julian, presumably because Freud mistrusted what he called the black mud of occultism. When light shines into this darkness, however, it can be seen that self-point and preconscious are identical in function.

We must be struck on reading mystical works at the frequency with which spiritual operations are described in terms of light, a matter we shall go into more fully later. For the present we can recall how Meister Eckhardt, whose teachings were known to Julian, used the term *spark* for her *self-point*. This, "the so-called husband of the soul," is "none other than a spark of divine light, a ray, an imprint of divinity." Its relation to the "sensualitie" of Julian is described as follows: "The soul has a ghostly spot in her

where she has all things matter-free, just as the first cause harbours in itself all things with which it creates all things. The soul also has a light in her with which she creates all things. When this light and this spot coincide so that each is the seat of the other, then, only then, one is in full possession of one's mind. What more is there to tell?"

Hinduism has its own account of a coincident duality. It has an image of the two birds, one eating the fruit of the tree and the other watching. Buddhism has its own image:

> The two trees spring from one seed,
> And for that reason there is but one fruit.
> He who thinks of them thus indistinguishable,
> Is released from Nirvana and Samsara.

A similar logic animates Gnosticism, whose emphasis on knowledge rather than love allows for a detailed elaboration of the matter. The text quoted below begins: "These are the secret words which the Living Jesus spoke and Didymus Judas Thomas wrote." Judas is the name for one of the brothers of Jesus, and Didymus and Thomas both mean the same thing—"twin." (The Gnostics held that Thomas was twin to Jesus.) The name can also be read to mean "abyss," standing for the waters on whose surface God brooded his reflection at the start of the creation. In the Gospels, Thomas is also the doubter, who needs physical evidence for an immaterial fact. This symbolism is connected with Syria, the home of twin pillars and twin gods, which in turn was influenced by Indian practices. It is not an accident that Thomas is held to have evangelized the Indies.

The "secret words" enshrine the teaching of how to use dualism as a meditative exercise. One passage runs:

When you make the two one,
and when you make the inner as the outer and outer as the inner and the above as the below,
and when you make the male and the female into a single one, so that the male will not be male and female will not be female,
when you make eyes in the place of an eye,
and a hand in the place of a hand,
and a foot in the place of a foot,
and an image in the place of an image,
then shall you enter [the kingdom].

Here two apparently different processes are commented upon, though it is impossible for one to occur without the other. In the first half of the passage the prime opposites are made to coincide with each other, so that each is the seat of the other. In the second half this seat is distinguished from what sits in it: that is, images from the eyes that perceive them, and the place of the Image from what appears in it. Lady Julian would have said: the eyes of the body from the eye of the mind. But when these coincide, then the eye of God is opened in the soul, as we may learn from another of the "secret words," for which we can find an exact parallel in Eckhardt. In this passage sensory images are said to contain the light that is hidden in the Image of the Father, though this Image is in turn hidden by the light that streams from him.

This highly metaphysical remark is made somewhat easier to grasp in the Apocryphal Acts of Thomas, where the result of making the opposites coincide is figured as a Pearl and a Robe. The moment the devotee discovers the Pearl, which is hidden within him, his outer man is clothed in the Robe: "Suddenly I saw the garment made unto me as it had been in a mirror. And I saw myself wholly in myself, and I knew and saw myself through it, that we were divided asunder, being of one; and again were in one shape."

Exactly the same experience is recounted by Dante at the end of the *Purgatorio*, when he sees Beatrice and the Griffon standing face to face. The Griffon is called two-natured and is a figure for the Christ. Beatrice the blessed is Dante's lover, both as a woman and as a religious principle. In her eyes—"those emeralds whence Love first shot his arrows" at Dante—he sees those of the Griffon reflected like the sun in a mirror, "now with the one,

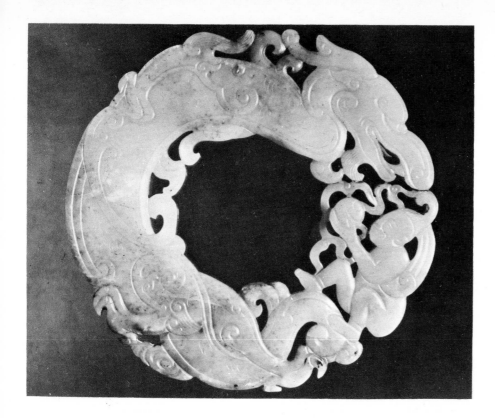

now with the other nature. Think, reader, if I wondered in myself when I saw the thing motionless in itself and transmuting in its image."

What all these descriptions amount to in practical terms is summed up by Eckhardt: "Loving thyself, thou lovest all men as thy self." At the same time, all the masters agree that the kind of control this entails is one of obedience and not of willfulness. We have seen how the mind can be thought of as a mirror, and the usual precepts for meditation insist that the mirror should be kept clean and constantly polished. Hui-neng, the sixth patriarch of Chinese Buddhism, contradicted this:

> There is no Bodhi tree
> Nor stand of mirror bright.
> Since all is void,
> Where can the dust alight?

The implications of this are told in the story of the king who gathered some beggars in his courtyard, and promised the first one to fall asleep a great treasure. Their efforts to lose consciousness merely kept them awake until the dawn, when the king brought the trial to an end. At this moment, of course, the beggars all dropped off into sleep. The situation brought about by the king is known as a double-bind, after Gregory Bateson's use of this term to explain the social genesis of schizophrenia. It catches you in a contradiction where every effort merely serves to entangle you further, and it is only when no means are used—the Chinese term is *wu-wei*, non-action—that the way out shows itself. Eckhardt says: "The kingdom of God is for none but the thoroughly dead," which has the same sense.

The idea that one must put oneself to the test and die, like Fusiwe, in order to reach heaven, is thus correct. But to make the great coincidence occur by an act of will is impossible, unless that will has become love, the function by which all opposites concur. Without it, the mind is always taking sides, and thus disrupts the balance. This leads to certain interesting results. Geometrically, we have seen how the four elements, or the four directions, only hang together around a center. By the means of these four, space is laid out, concepts are made clear, clan relations established, and time measured. The center, however, is not thought of as having dimension, and, although all turns around it, it does not itself turn. A man who stands at the center, therefore, is not involved in space, time, or social relations in the conventional way. As Evelyn Underhill remarked, duration is there transformed into succession so that only the present is experienced, continuously. As for space, the author of the medieval work *The Cloud of Unknowing* urges any who would follow the mystical way to be neither outside himself, nor yet above, nor behind, nor on one side, nor on the other. " 'Where then', sayest thou, 'shall I be? Nowhere, by thy tale!' Now

A 15th-century book illustration (from Bartholomaeus Anglicus, Le Propriétaire des Choses) *of the Christ as Anthropos, standing on the globe of the world and showing the four elements.*

truly thou sayest well; for there I would have thee. For why, nowhere bodily is everywhere ghostly."

This, as we can see, is the other half of the Gnostic picture, which suggests that one should be everywhere—everywhere ghostly, that is, so no real contradiction is involved. We cannot then locate love, or the self-point, in any place or any time, our allusion to Freud's preconscious notwithstanding. For it comes into existence between opposites, in the void between subject and object, matter and mind, wherever these may be experienced.

There are some things so opposed to human existence, however, that it seems no at-oning with them is possible. William James has this somber passage about them:

"The normal process of life contains moments as bad as any of those which insane melancholy is filled with, moments in which radical evil gets its innings and takes its solid turn. The lunatic's visions of horror are all drawn from the material of daily fact. Our civilisation is founded on the shambles, and every individual existence goes out in a lonely spasm of helpless agony. If you protest, my friend, wait till you arrive there yourself!" He continues with a Tennysonian view of nature red in tooth and claw and concludes: "It may indeed be that no religious reconciliation with the absolute totality of things is possible. Some evils, indeed, are ministerial to higher forms of good; but it may be that there are forms of evil so extreme as to enter into no good system whatsoever, and that, in respect to such evil, dumb submission or neglect to notice is the only practical resource."

In Christianity, as in Gnosticism, it is heretical to believe that Satan will ever be redeemed—perhaps partly because that would spell the end of God as goodness, although Eckhardt insisted that he who would really possess his mind must do away with such ideas as good and evil. Although it is pointless to argue on one side or the other, it is interesting to note certain practices that arise out of this implacable duality. In Judaism, for instance, we find the idea of the holy sin, which is to be committed in order to liberate the divine self that the forbidden act contains. Even the purity-loving Gnostics turned to this way at one moment: "Not otherwise can one be saved than by passing through every action. . . . At every sinful and infamous deed an angel is present, and he who commits it . . . addresses himself by his name and says, 'O thou angel, I use thy work! O thou Power of such and such, I perform thy deed!' And this is the perfect knowledge, unafraid to stray into such actions whose very names are unmentionable."

Performed with other rites, the forbidden action is also celebrated in Tantric yoga, which breaks the law concerning food, drink, and sexual intercourse in order to fulfil the law of transcendence. A class of ascetics

A yoni-lingam representing the union of the male and female principles.

devoted to Shiva pushed this to extremes by haunting cemeteries, eating from human skulls, and devouring human bodies, refuse, and excrement. The aim of this cult, whose members were called the Aghori—the name means, paradoxically, "the not-terrible"—was to destroy the natural instinct for pleasure, and to seek the joy of Shiva's creation in the disgust caused by its destructiveness.

All these attempts to break through the appearances of the material world are of course also efforts to destroy the tabus that distinguish it from the immaterial one. We have spent most of this book discussing how the distinction, experienced as the sacred, creates the human world of thought, emotion, and action, and the rites by which the dismembered progenitor is reassembled in symbolic form. We must now realize that the point of his reassembly is to make him disappear, leaving the laws of his form behind him. At the same time, it seems that the rites for his reassembly are at bottom the same as those for the making of a king. Shamans often go through the kingly state at their initiation, and in Judaism and Christianity the elect live in God's kingdom. The Sufis of Islam concur, although they affirm that the only king in the kingdom is the fellowship of those who serve him.

Opposite, 10th-century Chinese painting of Queen Maya, the mother of the Buddha. His conception is announced to her by a dream of a child riding on a white elephant.

*The workings of both head and loins are sacred, and one image
can do duty for both. Above, an 18th- or 19th-century Indian
painting of sexual intercourse. Opposite, a Tantric painting
(of about 1700, from Nepal) showing the sexual position
known by the name of "Mula bandha."*

A Tibetan painting of Maya giving birth to the Buddha. She has taken the posture of a yakshi *or dryad.*

We have reached the place where the Way of Affirmation turns into that of Negation, and there can hardly be a better story to illustrate the turn than that of Gautama Siddhartha. It shows, for a start, how those who would be enlightened must first aspire to be kings, at first perhaps over others, finally over themselves. (When Dante crossed into the Earthly Paradise, his guide Virgil said to him: "Your own will now is free, true and integral; it would be a fault not to act as it bids; I crown and mitre you over yourself.")

As an avatar, Gautama chooses to be born of Maha Maya, queen of King Suddhodana of the Sakya Clan in the Middle Country. His birth is announced by the vision of a white elephant, symbol of royalty, descending into her womb, from which it is predicted that Gautama will be either a Universal Monarch or a Buddha. Maha Maya is delivered while supporting herself from the branch of a tree, the child issuing from her side and thus making the birth a virgin one. The king, learning of the prediction, wishes that Gautama shall be a Universal Monarch and protects him from knowing anything about suffering, disease, death, and the true immortality. Gautama practices kingly arts, marries, and gets a child Rahula—literally, "obstacle"— but the gods foil the king's intention by appearing in the royal park as an old man, a sick man, a corpse, and a monk.

Overcome by the transiency of duration, Gautama leaves all behind and joins five ascetics who mortify their flesh in the effort to be enlightened. (Those five can stand for the five senses, which asceticism is always trying to subdue.) Finding this of no avail, he seats himself under a tree and vows he will not rise till he has gained enlightenment. He is assaulted by Mara, or death, evil, and desire, at whose approach the gods flee, leaving Gautama alone. But he remains unshaken and in the course of the night that follows he realizes the cycle of causal origination and becomes wholly awakened. He then sings his famous paean of victory:

> Seeking the builder of the house
> I have run my course in the vortex
> Of countless births, never escaping the hobble of death;
> Ill is repeated birth after birth!
> Householder, art seen!
> Never again shalt thou build me a house
> All thy rigging is broken,
> The peak of the roof is shattered;
> Its aggregations passed away.
> Mind has reached the destruction of cravings.

We see here many images we have already looked at, as is only proper if the doctrine of Physis is to find its consummation in the light. For instance,

Buddha in samadhi, from Cambodia.

not only is the Buddha associated with trees, but during his meditation he is sheltered by King Naga, the snake who spreads his seven hoods over Buddha's head; and soon after his enlightenment he pacifies a fire-dragon by taking on a dragon-form himself. But with the Buddha the house of Physis comes to an end, which is as much as to say that, like the Son of Man, he has nowhere to lay his head. Significantly, too, there is no mention of his ecstatic ascent up the tree, which would imply a descent back into the house of the senses, such as shamans must endure. And perhaps partly to show the Buddha's disentanglement from all prideful knowledge, a customary way of figuring him is with his eyes closed.

The cycle of causal origination realized by the Buddha states that individuality is not a lasting entity but an aggregate, a bundle of conditions brought together at birth and dissipated at death; that consciousness as usually experienced is also not a being but a passion, and that its desires are fundamentally ignorant, because there is nothing in the world that can truly be possessed. What there is in the world is just what it is, the suchness of things: they arise just as the Buddha does himself, as his title *Ththagata* (Thus-come) implies.

To the question, Whence do things arise? the answer is, From nowhere, from the void. This nowhere is also called *nirvana*, a word meaning a blowing out, as a candle flame in the wind. Metaphorically it means the quenching of passion and the end or perfection of the pneumatic soul and all its doings. The word is also used for the various stages in the training of a royal steed, which is made obedient to its rider and not to its own desires. This marks the last stage of domestication, which is represented by living in a house with a fire in the hearth: the house vanishes, the mind becomes the hearth for the internal burnt-offering, and the virility of consciousness is tamed.

Eckhardt sometimes uses the term *despiration* and sometimes *de-mentation* as his equivalent for nirvana. It means to lose the consciousness of being somebody, as the Buddha was nobody. When asked if he was a god, an ancestral soul, a fairy, or a human being he answered No each time, saying simply: "Take it that I am Buddha," which means, literally, awake. Not being anyone, he was for a long time not represented by anything but an empty throne bearing the mark of his footprints, to show that the Way-Maker was Thus-come and Thus-gone.

We can see that despiration is important from the practice of controlling the breath, which is of such importance in meditative techniques. It should, in the end, be completely unforced and imperceptible—the Chinese call this fetal breathing—and it undoubtedly shows the importance of breathing in the whole psychic economy, and the way in which passion and uncontrolled

*Japanese painting of the Pari-nirvana,
or final extinction, of the Buddha, with
all things mourning his death.*

breathing go together. We have not room to go into this matter, except to say that breathing, like Freud's preconscious, is a semi-voluntary function, and that its control is all part of the function of the self-point. The state of despiration, in any event, gives back to God what God first breathed into Adam, and in it man gives up the self-will that was the cause of Adam's fall.

But to be in the state of nirvana is not to fall into inanity. As the Hinayana form of Buddhism says, it means not to grasp after sense-pleasures, speculative views, rites and customs, and the theory of the self: not, that is, to be caught in the doctrine of Physis and its religious personifications. The Buddha by no means denied the existence of the Self—it is that which thus-comes—and although he proclaimed that all might know this Self, they could not do so if they thought they were selves.

Yet selves do exist in the Image of the Self, and the two certainly reflect each other's nature. The relation between them is beautifully illustrated by the modern discovery of the hologram. This is produced by photographing an object by the coherent light from a laser. Half the light illuminates the object, the other half is directed into the camera, where the coming together of direct and reflected light creates an interference pattern. The photographic negative then shows not an image of the object but the pattern of interference. To unscramble the interference, the pattern must be projected onto a screen with coherent light from the original source, and then the original image reappears.

There are two curiosities about this projected image and the hologram it comes from. The image is three-dimensional, and by moving one's head one can see what lies behind the object. As for the hologram, any piece of it contains a miniature of the pattern that makes up the whole, so that by illuminating just a corner of the hologram we can make the whole object appear on the screen.

The parallel to the coherent light of physics must be looked for in the clear light of Buddhism, which shines when no distinction is made between subject and object. The parallel to the hologram is found in the Tower of Illumination, the abode of the Buddha of the future. The relevant passages are to be found in the *Gandavyuha Sutra*, a Mahayana work that deals with the experience of the interpenetration, or what we might call total synecdoche.

"This is the abode of those who make one age enter into all ages, and all ages into one age," says the *Gandavyuha Sutra*, making the same remark about lands, things, beings, Buddhas, and instants. It is as wide and spacious as the sky, ornamented with innumerable marvels; and within this Tower there are innumerable other towers, each as wide and spacious as the sky

Sol in Leo: an image of the Interpenetration. An Indian manuscript illumination of a goddess on a lion formed of other animals and humans.

古寺天寒夜一宵
不嫌風凛雪盈盈
無暑鉢阿寺特些
取堂中木佛燒

Left, a Japanese Zen Buddhist painting of Tan-Hia burning the written word.

Opposite, Giovanni Bernini's statue in St. Peter's, Rome, of St. Teresa receiving the arrow from the angel.

and ornamented with innumerable marvels. Each is distinct in itself and yet collectively a part of all, so that he who enters the Tower becomes the Tower, and sees himself in all it contains.

The *Gandavyuha Sutra* then describes in detail the omniscience to be enjoyed in the Tower as the lives of all the Buddhas, past, present, and to come, are seen unfolding, and their every word heard issuing from the pores of their skin. What this means in terms of Physis we can learn from Jakob Boehme, who had a similar experience. "In one quarter of an hour I saw and knew more than if I had been many years together in a University. . . . I saw and knew the Being of Beings, the Byss and the Abyss, the eternal generation of the Trinity, the origin and descent of this world, and of all creatures through Divine Wisdom. I knew and saw in myself all the three worlds—(1) the Divine, Angelical, or Paradisiacal World; (2) the dark world, the origin of fire; and (3) the external, visible world as an outbreathing or expression of the internal and spiritual worlds." The outbreathing he describes thus: "The whole outward visible world, with all its being, is a 'signature' or figure of the inward and spiritual world, and everything has a character that fits an internal reality and process, and the internal is in the

external." It is then the self-point that is at the center of the doctrine of correspondence, and from which the signature of things can be read in one's own mind.

At this moment we should perhaps recall the Hassidic rabbi who thought to write a large book in which the nature of man should be exhaustively expounded. Then he considered the matter, and thought not. The world after all is a big place, and if everything in it is signed according to the inner reality of man, a book about man will be an encyclopedia of the universe, or maybe the universe itself. There is, too, a curious lust involved in explaining deep matters that might better be left hid, as the reader of this book may already have suspected. In visionaries, however, this lust becomes an afflatus, as we know from Eckhardt himself, who was inspired to write copiously on the subject of his experiences.

This surge of joy, which St. John of the Cross expressed in love-poems, can issue in Christianity from contemplating the wounds of the Christ. St. Francis experienced these in his stigmata; St. Teresa in a dart of love that reverberatingly pierced her; the Lady Julian by looking into the wound in the side of the Christ. The analogy in myth is to be found in the story of the Grail, and the wound in the generative parts of the Fisher King—the only difference being that it is when this wound is healed that the king's land becomes fertile once more, whereas in the return to the immaterial principle all riches stream out of the wound as soon as it is made.

But why should the Image of God be wounded? It can only be because the Image has to be built up in all men before it can be realized in its plenitude by any man; the enlightened are kings before they are Buddhas. Every Image obeys canonical laws, that of Buddhism as much as that of Christianity. It explains the relation of human functions, promotes the social forms that embody them, rules conduct, erects temples, and disciplines the faithful. This is the kingship of the Image, responsible for the health, wealth, and fertility of the land and its inhabitants. It is also its priesthood, because the Image dies if not served outwardly and inwardly, and the canon is the door through which the self-point can recognize the Self in others.

It is also the veil in the Holy of Holies, for no man can see God and live. The Living God of Judaism is as terrible in his works as Shiva dancing, for he declared that there was no evil in the city that he did not do. We must distinguish this God, to whom Satan is a mere messenger, from the God who stands opposed to Satan. Jung, who was no mean theologian and a seer in his own right, was inspired to write of this matter in "VII Sermones Ad Mortuos." The totality of things, evil as well as good, he calls by the old term the *pleroma,* God being the title for its effective fullness, the devil for its effective void. The being of the totality itself, unknowable by nature, he called by the Gnostic name Abraxas.

"Abraxas is effect. Nothing standeth opposed to it but the ineffective; hence its effective nature freely unfoldeth itself. The ineffective is not, therefore resisteth not. Abraxas standeth above the sun and above the devil. It is improbable reality, unreal reality."

He describes Abraxas also as force, duration, and change; as the begetter of life, which in turn is mother to good and evil; and as all contradiction, paradox, and power.

> It is abundance that seeketh union with emptiness.
> It is holy begetting.
> It is love and love's murder.
> It is the saint and his betrayer.
> It is the brightest light of the day and the darkest
>   night of madness.
> To look upon it, is blindness.
> To know it, is sickness.
> To worship it, is death.
> To fear it, is wisdom.
> To resist it not, is redemption.

A canonical form is as a veil covering this effectiveness. As Bergson said of consciousness, it acts as a filter through which certain parts of reality may pass, and not others. By its means biological and physical regularities are approximated into that ideal of society, the human kingdom. But the ideal becomes real only when images are seen through rather than merely looked at. This nailing down of images allows Eckhardt's spot and light to coincide, and effectiveness issues as life from the wounds they make in each other. Instead of living on a diet of apples, man can then enjoy what St. Augustine called "the food of the fully grown."

The act appears to be a destruction of the law, but is properly its *telos*—its *perfection,* or the end prophesied for its beginning. A man in whom the law is fulfilled need no longer be attached to it, as Virgil reminded Dante, and as the Buddha declared when he likened his teaching to a boat that could ferry pilgrims to the other shore, and which should be abandoned when it had served its turn.

The other shore—of what? Buddhism calls the river *Samsara,* or "the confluence." It signifies the world of appearances, and therefore that of effect, of blind chance, and of impersonal force. It is to be feared—which is wisdom. It is not to be resisted—which is redemption. And because it cannot be resisted, those who are redeemed find immortality in living a mortal life, on whose waters they walk because they no longer have need of a boat.

The mind of the Buddha, say Zen Buddhists, is in fact no different from that of an ordinary man, although his sense of identity has suffered a sea-change. To the question "What am I?" he can only answer, "That art Thou." This is the mystery of the sacred in a point. In it, as Coomaraswamy says, theology and autology—the science of the principle each man calls "I"—prove to be the same. "For," as he continues, in words which put our argument finally to rest, "as there are two in him who is both love and death, so there are, as all tradition affirms unanimously, two in us; although not two of him and two of us, nor even one of him and one of us, but only one of both."

Opposite, Charon ferrying a soul over the river, by Joachim Patinir.

Right, Japanese Zen Buddhist painting of Bodhidharma, after nine years of meditation, crossing the River of Existence on a reed.

Index

Credits

Key to picture position = (T) top, (C) center, (B) bottom, and combinations; for example (TL) top left, or (CR) center right.